Explaining
Organizational
Behavior

The Limits and Possibilities
of Theory and Research

Lawrence B. Mohr

✳✳✳✳✳✳✳✳✳✳✳✳✳✳✳✳✳✳✳✳✳✳

Explaining
Organizational
Behavior

Jossey-Bass Publishers

San Francisco • Washington • London • 1982

EXPLAINING ORGANIZATIONAL BEHAVIOR
The Limits and Possibilities of Theory and Research
Lawrence B. Mohr

Copyright © 1982 by: Jossey-Bass Inc., Publishers
433 California Street
San Francisco, California 94104
&
Jossey-Bass Limited
28 Banner Street
London EC1Y 8QE

Library of Congress Cataloging in Publication Data

Mohr, Lawrence B.
  Explaining organizational behavior.

  Includes bibliographical references and index.
  1. Organizational behavior.   I. Title.
HD58.7.M63   302.3'5   81-20747
ISBN 0-87589-514-X   AACR2

Manufactured in the United States of America

JACKET DESIGN BY WILLI BAUM

FIRST EDITION

Code 8203

The Jossey-Bass
Social and Behavioral Science Series

✳✳✳✳✳✳✳✳✳✳✳✳✳✳✳✳✳✳✳✳✳✳✳✳

Preface

A large investment of effort in social science research, including much of my own, has gone into the development of explanatory theory—that is, the development of stable explanations for why or how general, recurring social phenomena come about. This book analyzes that investment. It is motivated by the thought that social scientists want to consider from time to time just what they and their colleagues are doing and to step back a bit from the course of regular research activities to reflect on past and future choices. The book uses organization theory as the focal research field for the analysis, but much of the investigation applies equally to the systematic study of social behavior in all the other major disciplines, particularly management, political science, sociology, social psychology, and economics.

The first three chapters deal primarily with general ideas rather than particular research, conceptualizing some of the major

problems encountered in the pursuit of social theory. These formulations were not arrived at by a process of deduction from
philosophical principles but rather by reasoning from the aims and
results of research practice. The orientation of these chapters is
toward the philosophy of social science, but from the bottom up
rather than from the top down. The next three chapters illustrate
the abstract concepts in action in the discipline of organizational
behavior. The terms and issues will therefore be comfortable for
scholars and students in organization theory, but I have tried to
avoid an undesirably narrow focus both by including some basic
background information on the issues analyzed in depth and by
intermittent reference to literatures outside organization theory.
The final chapter is a summing up, emphasizing the conclusions I
believe one must draw about what is promising and what is not
so promising and about the role of explanatory theory in social
science.

I feel immensely grateful to a number of colleagues for their
inspiration, suggestions, reactions, and support. The book has ben-
efited immeasurably from these, and so have I. A goodly share of
the fundamental inspiration, as well as support of the most meaningful kind, came from Frances Reid. Ronald Brunner and George
Downs read the whole of the manuscript and provided running
commentary that has greatly strengthened both the individual
chapters and their integration. All or parts of earlier versions were
also read by Stanley Seashore, Michael Cohen, Thomas Anton,
J. D. Eveland, Leslie Eveland, John Strate, and my graduate pro-
seminar in organization theory of winter 1980. Each provided a
critique that led to what I considered great improvements. It would
have been difficult and painful indeed to write a book without this
kind of help.

The critique of the research literature on job satisfaction and
participative management was begun in partnership with Lorraine
Uhlaner. Much description and thought grew out of that collabora-
tion. I regret that circumstances prevented our continuing the research together and gratefully acknowledge Professor Uhlaner's
contribution.

The manuscript was patiently typed and retyped by Judy
Jackson, who provided much valuable consultation along the way,

and the references by Jeanne White. I thank them both, as well as the Institute of Public Policy Studies, the University of Michigan, for making their assistance available and for providing much additional support.

An earlier version of Chapter One was presented as a paper at the meetings of the American Political Science Association, 1978, under the title "The Frustration of Theory in Organizational Behavior." An earlier version of Chapter Two was submitted as a paper for a conference on the diffusion of innovations under the title "Process Theory and Variance Theory in Innovation Research." The conference was organized by the Center for the Interdisciplinary Study of Science and Technology at Northwestern University and supported by the National Science Foundation, Division of Policy Research and Analysis. I am grateful to the participants at both meetings for ideas that helped me produce the current versions of these papers. Chapters Three and Six took root while I was a visiting professor in the Department of Political Science at the University of California, Davis. I thank both students and faculty of the department for the stimulation and the opportunity and for reacting to my initial thoughts on these topics.

Lastly, moral support has been important. I thank Ronald and Marjorie Brunner for shoring up my spirits repeatedly when the going was difficult and Bill and Gloria Broder, David and Glenna Osnos, and Gunther and Susan Balz for providing the context that makes an effort of this kind meaningful.

Ann Arbor, Michigan   LAWRENCE B. MOHR
December 1981

Contents

Contents

The Author

Lawrence B. Mohr is professor in the Department of Political Science and research scientist in the Institute of Public Policy Studies, the University of Michigan. He received his A.B. degree from the University of Chicago in 1951, his M.P.A. from the University of Michigan in 1963, and his Ph.D. in political science from the University of Michigan in 1966. He has written previously on the subjects of organizational innovation, goals, structure, decision making, and democracy, as well as on methodological topics related to social science research.

To my children,
Carol and Eric Mohr

Explaining
Organizational
Behavior

The Limits and Possibilities
of Theory and Research

Introduction

The Nature of Theory

This book is about organization theory, as the title suggests, but it puts somewhat more than usual emphasis on theory. It is not concerned with organizational studies in general, no matter what their orientation, but with the process of cumulatively developing and testing theories about behavior in and of organizations. The effort will be to assess where the field stands in this process and why. In general, as one might guess, the field is not very far along, but it is not in any part the aim of the book to quarrel with particular hypotheses or berate the supposed inadequacies of individual works. I hope to be more constructive by singling out pitfalls in the theory-building process itself, illustrating how research runs afoul of them, and trying to point at least one way out of each troublesome situation. Unfortunately, I am not certain that the pitfalls are altogether avoidable in several current areas of inquiry.

Many philosophers and social thinkers propose that powerful empirical-scientific theories of organizational behavior or of any human social behavior are not possible (see, for example, the debate in Krimerman, 1969). Substantial additional numbers have not made up their minds but also harbor serious doubts. I do not believe that this issue will be settled solely by philosophical discussion. Rather, it will tend to be resolved for practical purposes either when social scientists succeed in producing strong, useful theory or when they essentially abandon the effort. At the moment, it almost begins to look as though the nays will have it: There are those who believe that many fields of social science are indeed seriously bogged down (see Cronbach, 1975). However, there is good reason to suspect that progress may have failed to occur because vulnerable strategies have been adopted in the pursuit of theory rather than because theory is intrinsically unattainable. In this light, it is necessary to analyze what practicing social scientists are actually doing and to compare it with the requirements for theory. That is essentially the purpose of this book, which uses as the basis of its analysis primarily one field, organizational behavior, rather than all of social science. It is written from the standpoint of the practitioner, not that of the philosopher.

My conclusion will be that the requirements for theory may well be attainable but that some rather drastic changes in theoretical goals and in research tactics will be necessary if the pursuit is to be truly productive.

Normative Theory

The concern here will be mainly with empirical theory rather than normative. Little of past interest will be omitted on this ground, however, since the normative trends that have been important in organizational studies are normative in a special sense. The works of Weber (1947), Taylor ([1911], 1967), the classical management theorists (Fayol, 1949, for example), the public administration theorists (Gulick and Urwick, 1937, for example), the human relations theorists (Likert, 1961, for example) and others contain much normative advice on how to organize properly. However, the instruction is not that organizations should behave in a certain manner derivable from the nature of God, human beings, or the healthy society, as in much pure normative philosophy; rather, the emphasis is on how an organization should behave in order to be effective and efficient. The advice is therefore based (sometimes explicitly, sometimes implicitly) on the *empirical* hypothesis that certain structures or behaviors will be functional, or efficacious, in performing a task. Hypotheses of this kind are subject to support or disproof through empirical evidence on the relation between the recommended behaviors and their outcomes, and it is not unfair to be skeptical of normative organizational theories in the absence of such evidence. The latter idea was an important basis of Simon's well-known critique of the "principles of management," which were so fashionable in the new discipline of administration through the first half of this century (Simon, 1976, pp. 20–36). What is apparently wanted from the normative perspective, then, is an empirical theory of organizational effectiveness.

One might well appeal to common sense instead of to research in these matters. For example, I include myself among the many who find the work of Henri Fayol (1949) to have substantial intuitive validity and broad applicability, not only for his own time but even today, some seventy years after the original publication of his book. This is in spite of the fact that Fayol's work is closely linked to the subsequently discredited "principles of management." Fayol rested his case primarily on good sense. He eschewed claims to "scientific" principles. To him, the "principles" were flexible. He was accordingly criticized by his followers who, in claiming to be scientific while never doing any systematic research, failed by far to measure up to his standard (Urwick, 1949, for example).

Still, intuitively appealing norms can be wrong, or, as Simon (1976) emphasized, are likely to be right only part of the time. One can have little quarrel with skillful and insightful normative appeals to common sense (there is indeed little else to guide management practice at this crude and feeble stage of theoretical development), but it is also appropriate to continue to challenge such appeals with research and analysis. Subsequent chapters will touch on two of the specific hypotheses on effectiveness currently discussed (human relations theory and structural consonance theory), and one chapter is devoted entirely to an analysis of the general issue of a theory of organizational effectiveness. To anticipate the conclusion, it is highly doubtful that it will be possible to develop such a theory in anything like the forms in which it has traditionally been sought.

Explanatory Theory

To this point in the discussion, the term *theory* has been used ambiguously. Because the concept of theory is at the core of the inquiry that follows, it is essential to have a definition before proceeding further. The definition to be offered is, I fear, arbitrary and rather inelegant. The arbitrariness needs no apology, because all definitions are essentially arbitrary and there has never been close agreement on what the term *theory* means. Some might perceive this lack of agreement to be an ultimate hindrance, but the important requirements are, after all, to be clear about what is being discussed, whatever its label, and to agree that it is worthy of consideration.

Inelegance is less common than arbitrariness in discussions of theory. In the present case, it is excused by the inelegance of the theories themselves that underlie the discussion. There is little point in making elaborate distinctions among terms like *law, theory,* and *symbolic generalization* when hardly anything to be discussed is a shining example of any of those concepts. One would expect to find useful, if not unanimous, definitions of the concept of theory by reading the works of the prominent philosophers of science. The truth is, however, that such discussions, though elegant, are not easily applicable to an analysis or an appraisal of current practice in organizational studies. What is done in the struggling new field of organizational research is hardly visualized by Nagel (1961) or Popper (1963) or Hempel and Oppenheim (1948). There is, in my opinion, little conception in the philosophical literature of the groping inductionism of much of behavioral science. I have found in personal discussion with physical scientists that in spite of their interest in nondeterministic models, the very nature of a correlation of .30 produces an anomic reaction that effectively terminates the conversation.

Even the philosophers of *social* science, with few exceptions, are of little assistance. As noted previously, this discipline tends to be preoccupied, in part, with the issue of the abstract possibility of a social science (Krimerman, 1969, pp. 1–138). The remainder of the subject matter, understandably enough, is rather eclectic, dealing separately with individual concepts such as rationality, functionalism, language, change, structure, and intention, as used in social science, or with the application of philosophical concepts such as causality, explanation, verification, and reduction. Philosophers of social science have not shown a preoccupation with offering reasonable working definitions of *theory* or *laws* and examining the progress made by the practitioners of research toward producing theories and laws.

We will take, here, the practitioner's view of what one is trying to accomplish. I will propose a rather inclusive definition of social theory in general and later (Chapter Two) become more precise with the suggestion of two subtypes.

By way of general definition, to say that social scientists are concerned with the development of theory is to say that they are concerned with the development of powerful explanatory generalizations about human behavior, where *powerful* signifies "highly accurate with respect to a large and well-defined scope of occurrence of an important behavior." It is extremely important to establish that the present treatment deals with the explanation of behavior that is conceptualized as being *recurrent,* not with unique events. The focus is not on how or why something happened but on how or why something happens. The explanation of a unique event, such as the outbreak of one war or the demise of one organization or the high morale of one work group, may follow from the application of one or more theories or may suggest theory, but it is not theory itself as the term is used here. The preceding definition, then, provides the technical referent of *theory* and *explanatory theory* for the remainder of the volume.

In truth, the subject matter of this book, to which the foregoing definition refers, would, in the philosophy of science, customarily be called "laws" rather than "theory." In philosophical writing, a theory generally contains and integrates laws; social scientists would probably designate the same category as "grand theory." It is problematic whether there are indeed theories in social science in the sense in which philosophers apply that term to natural science, but if there are, the candidates would include Marxian theory, Freudian theory, structuralist theory, and dissonance theory. In this book, I will almost never use the term *theory* in that integrative sense. Rather, the term will carry its much more usual sense among practicing social scientists—namely, to refer to relatively confined statements about what causes the recurrent behavior Y or how Z comes about. Social scientists have chosen *theory* rather than *laws* to designate this sort of subject matter in ordinary disciplinary communication, perhaps because it carries an edge of connotation of "unproved, tentative," whereas *laws*, by contrast, carries the connotation of "certain, invariable."

The inelegance of the definition lies partly in the ambiguity inherent in four of its terms: *highly, large, well-defined,* and *important.* Because of this ambiguity, theory becomes a dimension rather than a category, so that the more an explanatory generalization satisfies these criteria (the more important the behavior, the better defined the scope, and so on), the more it deserves the label *theory,* and nothing is clearly either in or out.[1] Inelegance is aggravated in that the four criteria are unweighted; one is unsure whether an increment of accuracy is more meritorious than an increment of importance, and so forth. Nevertheless, this definition will enable us to proceed and will be consulted repeatedly for guidance and consistency in the chapters that follow.

[1]This approach is not entirely without precedent. Compare the following: "This notion of 'degree of rationality' will be found also applicable to other kinds of scientific research and expectations, theoretical and otherwise." And in a footnote to that statement: "The whole tenor of the present analysis has been in the direction of making the line between 'science' and 'nonscience' a matter of degree rather than a sharp distinction in terms of some 'line of demarcation' " (Shapere, 1977, p. 542).

❊ 1 ❊

Obstacles to
Explanatory Theory

The analysis of several streams of organizational research suggests that as research is practiced, there is one major impediment to the realization of theory, with two underlying sources. The impediment operates in part by frustrating a given theoretical effort taken in isolation but in large measure as well by obstructing cumulativeness, so that theory within each separate stream of research has been inhibited by the absence of sets of related ideas, of pieces that might be fitted together to form the springboard for important, innovative departures. The idea of cumulativeness is emphasized in this chapter, but it will be quite apparent that the same forces that inhibit cumulativeness also function to limit the value of research efforts taken in isolation. They do so by depressing *potential* cumulativeness, the potential of ideas for the further development of their power—that is, for development toward the status of highly accurate and important generalizations about human behavior.

The major practical obstacle is not atomization—a failure of investigators to be interested in the same topics. Rather, it is a lack of reasonable and warranted *stability* in results (Downs and Mohr, 1976). We keep getting different answers to similar questions. Particularly, a variable that is a strong determinant of Y in one study will often fall flat in the next. A certain amount of instability is always to be expected. Indeed, it is one of the primary stimuli toward the continuing development of a science. I refer here, however, to rampant or hopeless instability.

Innovation research provides a good example because the results in that area are voluminous and have been well codified. In the appendix to their book on innovation, Rogers and Shoemaker (1971, pp. 350–376) review the fortunes of thirty-eight variables as possible determinants of innovation in an exhaustive catalogue of studies. The presentation is compelling and illuminating from the standpoint of movement toward a theory of innovation. For example, a positive relation between the social status of the potential adopter and earliness of adoption is supported in 275 studies (68 percent) and not supported in 127 others. Why is that? A relation between innovativeness and the size of the adopting unit is supported in 152 studies (67 percent) and not supported in 75 others; a positive association between innovation and the relative advantage of the new idea considered is supported in 29 studies (67 percent) but not in 14 others; a positive relation involving innovation and the compatibility of the new idea with existing activities is supported in 18 studies (67 percent) and not supported in 9 others; a relation between earliness of adoption and general attitude toward change is supported in 43 studies (75 percent) but not in 14 others; age is found to be positively related to innovation in 76 studies (33 percent), unrelated in 108 studies (48 percent), and negatively related in 44 others (19 percent). The list continues in this vein, unequivocally exemplifying instability. One can understand and accept these results. The world is complex; it is not surprising that sometimes older managers are the first to innovate and sometimes younger ones. What one cannot do is make any *theoretical* sense out of such a record. Moreover, it cannot be productive, at this point, to add either the 276th supporting study or the 128th nonsupporting study to the running tally on social status and innovation.

Analysis suggests that this sort of instability has two significant sources. One source is inconsistency in focus, a certain vagueness or confusion about the theoretical question actually being
addressed, so that at times what may seem like the same question or
phenomenon is in reality a different one. Different answers to
such questions are then experienced as a lack of stability. The second major contributor to instability is interaction. Both these
sources of instability can best be discussed in terms of the subtypes
that compose them. The relations are presented schematically in
Figure 1.

Chapter Two will distinguish between two important types
of theoretical orientation in social research, to be labeled variance
theory and process theory. It is necessary to anticipate that discussion to some extent in the present chapter by a brief characterization of the two terms. Variance theory, roughly, is the common sort
of hypothesis or model, such as a regression model, whose orientation is toward explaining the variance in some dependent variable.
Process theory presents a series of occurrences in a sequence over
time so as to explain how some phenomenon comes about. Diffusion models are often good examples of the latter.

The present chapter is organized mainly with variance-
theory research in mind, because that is by far the most frequent

Figure 1. Impediments to Theory

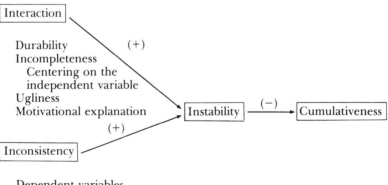

Dependent variables
Labeling tides
Process versus variance theory

type. True process-theory undertakings have unfortunately been considerably less popular to date. Nevertheless, the comments that follow are related for the most part to process theory as well, and this will be noted where it is especially pertinent.

I emphasize that the following discussion is not intended as a general treatise on the techniques of organizational research. In particular, the itemized caveats have emerged from analysis as impediments to explanatory theory. They are not necessarily undesirable in and of themselves; they are so only to the extent that the development of theory is a criterion of appraisal. Moreover, this chapter does not contain a theory of good theory; that orientation lies deep within the province of the philosophy of science. The approach taken to the concept of explanatory theory in the following pages emphasizes its control rather than either its complete explanation or its definition. Which general practices bear on the nonattainment of theoretical goals? The pitfalls to be discussed are proposed to stand to the frustration of explanatory theory very much as air pollution and cigarette smoking are proposed to stand to the incidence of lung cancer.

Sources of Inconsistency

One important source of diffuseness in focus is inconsistency in the rendering of variables, especially the dependent variable. There are, first of all, differences from study to study in the way variables are measured. This phenomenon, however, is well known. Moreover, not only are critics' sensitivities to such things as measurement error and reliability already high, thereby reducing the mysteriousness of any instability, but to a great extent such variation should be encouraged rather than discouraged. If the measuring instruments are not vastly different, the variety in results should be intelligible, and it is not wise to cast a scale in concrete, simply to establish uniformity, before it attains a high degree of validity and reliability. Experimentation with a variety of scales at this stage is good tactics.

Beyond the ordinary differences in instruments, however, it is not uncommon to measure a variable by radically different methods or devices, and this practice, strangely enough, has not yet attracted as much attention. In particular, the same variable may be measured in different studies by the report of certain organizational members (managers, for example), by the examination of organizational documents, and by the researcher's observation or experimental manipulation. Pennings (1973, 1975) has shown with respect to structural and environmental variables that such differences in method can produce dramatic differences in results. The multitrait-multimethod matrix (Campbell and Fiske, 1959) is supposed to produce confidence by convergence. If the results diverge rather than converge, however, and if they appear in different studies rather than in the same matrix, then the result is not confidence but confusion. It is important to be aware of the differences in results that can be produced by such differences in devices. It is also well to recognize that in this kind of situation one is perhaps not faced with the same variable measured in different ways but rather with two or more entirely different variables.

Getting still further from simple measurement error, there are other sources of inconsistency in rendering the dependent variable. Sometimes two or more variables are so patently different from one another that they should not be called by the same name. Using a common umbrella concept to cover such heterogeneity leads again to instability. Time of adoption and extent of use, for example, are too different to be used indiscriminately to represent innovation (Downs and Mohr, 1976). In the same way, the early explorations of the idea of organizational structure as an effect of environment and technology used operationalizations of "structure" that were too disparate to represent a single concept (Mohr, 1971).

At times, a similar dilution of research energy and accompanying instability come about because the real center of research attention is an independent variable rather than a dependent variable. If the goal is variance theory, then the focus of attention must ultimately be the particular dependent phenomenon whose variance is to be explained. From time to time, however, the field becomes captivated by a cause rather than an effect, and there ensues an attempt to use that cause to explain all its interesting potential effects. This has occurred with human relations theory (participativeness, supportiveness) and may be occurring now with organizational environments (Osborn and Hunt, 1974). One cannot inhibit interest in causes, and it would not be desirable to do so. From the perspective of theory, however, there comes a point when particular dependent variables must be selected and pursued for their own sake, or one is left with a galaxy of partial results that are unstable from study to study because they have little or nothing to do with one another.

In much the same way, investigators have frequently been caught up in a labeling tide, so that instead of categorizing work by reference to a variance or process theory that would describe it conservatively and accurately, they use a much broader label. As is well known, such labels often have a certain fad value. Be that as it may, the label may apply in a general way to the subject research but is broad enough to permit the many projects so labeled to be quite unrelated to one another. From the standpoint of cumulative theory, the whole nonfield of interorganizational analysis is the result of this sort of labeling tide (compare Van de Ven, Emmett, and Koenig, 1974). Levine and White (1961), for example, studied the determinants of interactions among organizations; Litwak and Hylton (1962) studied the requirements for coordination among autonomous organizations; Evan (1966) emphasized the interorganizational determinants of the structure (centralization) of a focal organization within an interorganizational network and the determinants of conflict/cooperation among the units of such a network; Warren (1967) tried to determine the type of decision-making system used by groups of organizations; Turk (1970) sought to gain an understanding of both the activity level and the complexity of an interorganizational network; Hasenfeld (1972) explored the determinants of certain outputs of a focal organization in an interorganizational net; Jacobs (1974) analyzed the autonomy or dependence of such an organization; and so on. Rarely have any two authors studied the same thing, in spite of the common label. Thus, interorganizational analysis has not fulfilled the great and explicit expectations that were once held for its becoming a leader among subfields of organization theory (Lammers, 1974). Having failed to coalesce, it now appears to be dying out. In this process, the common label has not been and is not innocuous; it is a distraction, since the vague impression of a close and meaningful relation among studies (as evidenced by extensive citation of other studies within the scope of the label), without a clear perception of any compelling basis for the supposed mutual relevance, produces an underlying perplexity that makes creative thinking in the area more difficult than it might otherwise be.

Finally, there tends to be confusion or vagueness of intent as between process theory and variance theory. This issue will be analyzed and illustrated in detail in the next chapter and need be summarized only briefly here. In particular, there is some tendency to think process and write variance. I attribute the latter half of this combination to the fact that social science training has been dominated by the statistical approach; few students have been expected to produce process models of organizational behavior. There are two primary outcomes. One is the tendency to try ineffectively to see a process theory and a variance theory as being about the same thing when they are not about the same thing at all. For example, an explanation of the process of acquiring power within an organization—how this process works—is not the same as an explanation for the distribution of power—why one person or unit has more than another. There may be much to learn about one target of explanation from studying the other, but this learning unquestionably has a smoother road when the difference in focus is clearly in mind than when it is not.

The other outcome is to try to force process theory into the variance-theory mold, especially to bend it to the requirements of statistical testing and reporting. This tendency detracts mightily from the ability to derive full benefit from a process model and even nips some process models completely in the bud. It also leads at times to the massive outpouring and measurement of *variables* in order to make up for the real need, which is the observation of *events* in a process. In the popular area of the relations among size, technology, environment, and organizational structure, I think it possible that a small number of events and behaviors might begin to accomplish what large numbers of variables have simply failed to do. Instead of trying to explain all the cross-sectional *variation* in degree of centralization, for example, what is wanted is a model of the *process* by which change in contextual variables leads to change in the degree of centralization at a given hierarchal level.

Process models are used little in organization theory and even less in many other social science subfields. When they are used, they are often underdeveloped. There is a tendency to present and conceptualize the stages in the process but to omit the forces that drive the movement from one stage to another. The latter, however, are essential. On the positive side, the garbage-can model of organizational choice (Cohen, March, and Olsen, 1972) provides an excellent example within organizational behavior of a process theory in complete or classic form.

Sources of Interaction

The second source of instability to be considered is interaction—the dependence of the impact of one phenomenon on the presence or level of another. A term that will be used almost synonymously is *complexity* (see Brunner and Brewer, 1971, pp. 102–120; Downs and Rocke, 1981). The difference between the two is that *complexity* refers to the interdependence of influences in the world itself, whereas *interaction* refers to the same sort of phenomenon as it is formalized in one's models of the world—particularly statistical models. Sources of complexity or interaction may themselves be causes of a given outcome, but that is not what places them in this conceptual category; it is, rather, their role as amplifiers or contractors of the impact of other causes. Motivations may determine behaviors, for example, but only if the relevant resources are adequate. If the resources for carrying out the action are insufficient, then there is not likely to be much difference between the behavior of subjects who are highly motivated and those who are not, and hence we say that resources interact with motivation in determining outcomes.

The interaction problem cannot be solved simply by making sure to test for it or to include a product term in addition to main-effect terms in a regression model. This is frequently done, but there is a tendency to minimize the results of such tests even if they are noteworthy and to continue to make theoretical statements without taking account of them (Cronbach, 1975). However, even if such practices were to be reformed (see, for example, Bingham, Freeman, and Martin, 1980; Bingham and others, 1980), the problem would not be at all close to solution. The problem does not so much concern the variables that are measured and are therefore subject to test as those that are not. In practice, instability is mysterious. The impact of X on Y fluctuates from study to study in part because the Z upon which this impact depends is unknown, perhaps undreamed of, at least not generally measured. As the world is being conceptualized in some models, there are sources of complexity that are simply omitted.

The interaction problem appears to me to be the greatest single problem facing social theory at this stage of its development. Whether a hypothesis or model is of the variance-theory or the process-theory variety, it no doubt is valid only under certain conditions, but in social science the validity conditions appear to be so restrictive and so elusive for most hypotheses that have been offered that the value of these hypotheses must be seriously questioned. It appears to be almost impossible to make any important explanatory generalizations. Many writers have now taken note of this (Downs and Mohr, 1976, 1979; Cronbach, 1975; Medawar, 1977; Campbell, 1973). In particular, Cronbach's Distinguished Scientific Contribution Award Address to the American Psychological Association in 1974 (see Cronbach, 1975) emphasized and documented the formidable obstacle presented by interaction in several research areas of psychology. He announced with some dismay that first-order interaction terms will not solve the problem, since there is ample evidence of interactions of a higher order. Even *conditional* statements, in other words, are conditional on something else. The theory-building task in social science is apparently beset with so much complexity that its success, according to Cronbach, is in grave doubt.

Cronbach's conclusion, which is essentially to give up the hope of very broadly generalizable theory, depends on a view of research in which the same kinds of variables would be used to build the same kinds of theories in the same kinds of ways as previously, but with the addition of all the interaction terms that might be necessary. That is indeed a hopeless task. Before going down to defeat, however, it is appropriate to cast about for new departures. Cronbach may yet prove correct, but he perhaps concedes the battle a bit too soon.

Downs and Mohr (1976, 1979) sought to discover some of the factors that permit interaction to thwart generalizability so powerfully. If the responsible elements can be isolated, it is possible, though by no means certain, that they can be avoided or overcome. The group of such elements that is offered here is not exhaustive but is meant to cover a great deal of the ground, at least with respect to organization theory.

The first element is the *durability* of the theoretical variables and process events that are studied. By *durability* I mean the extent to which the variable as a theoretical element has constant meaning across actors and is relevant and significant to the human condition in all places and at all times (see Willer and Webster, 1970). The scale of durability is continuous, not dichotomous, but I will in general refer to certain variables simply as durables, meaning that they seem roughly to have sufficient durability to qualify them for inclusion in theories. My standards are not very high. I am much more concerned to rule out variables near the very bottom of the scale than to restrict admittance to those near the very top (compare Willer and Webster's theoretical constructs versus observables, 1970). Of course, the condition-specific variables near the bottom of the durability scale may justifiably be used in operationalizing a concept; the trouble comes in not specifying somewhere the durable being operationalized, with the consequence that the operationalization itself becomes in effect the theoretical construct. That is when interaction is invited and tends to become unmanageable. Unfortunately, the great nemesis of durables is the interest and curiosity of the investigator, because one tends to become interested in the world of experience rather than the more abstract concepts that are likely to qualify as durables.

Innovation is perhaps a durable, as it has constant meaning (namely, departure from habit, custom, or tradition) and is a potential behavior for all individuals and groups in all times, the lack of innovation being as significant theoretically as its occurrence. Adaptation is also a durable (Holland, 1975). Organizational structure is not a durable; it is multidimensional—too inclusive to have constant meaning and therefore to serve as a good theoretical construct. The decentralization of one's authority over an area of decision, however, is a durable and is manageably specific. Participativeness as a supervisory style might be irrelevant in some cultures or at some periods of time, but the conditions under which it is relevant are prevalent enough that many would consider it a durable. Percentage voting Democratic is not a durable; it is irrelevant to too broad a set of political conditions, and its meaning, even in the United States, can change from one election to another. Political tolerance, however, is a durable. Absenteeism is not a durable, nor is interorganizational interaction (that is, encounters of one sort or another).

Dependent variables should be durables because if the meaning of the dependent variable to actors changes over time or place, the forces that determine it will no doubt also change, resulting in instability. On this reasoning, cumulative theory is likely never to result from efforts to build models of absenteeism, interorganizational interaction, or percentage Democratic, whatever other value such models may have.

The use of durables works effectively on the independent variable side to limit interaction because of the association of durability with level of abstraction, or generality. Thus, a large number of highly condition-specific variables can generally be replaced in theoretical statements by one durable that subsumes them. Income might occur in one theoretical statement and professionalization in another. Neither one is a durable, but both might be adequately replaced by the durable "resources." "Supportiveness" can be used instead of all the ways in which supervisors can be supportive. As concerns the management of interaction, if the causes X and Z are durables, they may well interact with each other as they jointly determine Y, but alternatively, every condition-specific variable subsumed by X might very well—and probably does—interact with a large number of the condition-specific variables subsumed by Z. I once offered a framework for the study of innovation that had only two causal variables, motivation and resources (Mohr, 1969). These interact, but a single interaction is manageable enough. In the ordinary study of innovation there are thousands of lower-level interactions, most of them hidden. One difficulty with a simple motivation-resources framework (aside from the inappropriateness of the motivational component, which will be considered in Chapter Three) is that it is too sweeping and general to give good guidance for research or even, perhaps, to stimulate the kinds of ideas that will bring us closer to interesting, revelatory theory. Downs and Mohr (1979) improved on this framework by substituting and adding variables at a somewhat lower level of abstraction. In so doing, they increased the number of interactions with which one must deal, but they tried to keep it within manageable bounds by not decreasing the durability level too much from the level of motivation and resources. Furthermore, experience suggests that working with durables instead of highly condition-specific variables greatly enhances one's ability to deal with interaction in a theory, not just by limiting its quantity but by permitting one to see better what is happening—to grasp where the interaction lies and what kind of interaction it is.

Not only must the variables themselves be durable, but so must the relations among them. It will prove fruitless in the long run to try to express a process as a regularity or express an outcome as the result of efficient causes if one does not believe that the process is truly regular or the outcome the inevitable result of the causes. Innovation and effectiveness may be durables, but it is at least questionable whether there are durable variance theories to explain them. Unless one resorts to trivial or near-tautological explanations, some phenomena are too idiosyncratic to be susceptible to good, direct theory. The physicist would be unlikely to try to develop a theory of the heights of objects. In this same sense, can one expect that there is a small, well-behaved set of causes of the effectiveness of organizations? The physicist uses a law that relates the gravitational attraction between two objects to their masses and to the distance between them, but he or she does not attempt to develop a law that explains the variance in masses that exists or the variance in distances between objects. These are highly unlikely to be reducible to a law, although instances of each might possibly be explainable by a collection of other laws. In short, one does not try to develop a theory of everything interesting; one sniffs out the few, possibly enduring, true regularities of the world and expends scientific effort to expose them in their correct form. Social theories with an implicit foundation in brain physiology, sociobiology, or strong psychological or cultural conditions will be promising; those that depend on a variety of learned and circumstantial responses will be much more problematic, as Chapter Three will elaborate.

A second element that is important for interaction is *completeness*. A complete theory blunts the most troublesome effects of interaction by including them, at least implicitly, within the scope of the explanation. Interaction presents the greatest obstacle to cumulative theoretical development when the interacting variables are not juxtaposed, not examined in conjunction with one another, generally because one or more of the interacting variables is omitted entirely from the research or model. A hypothesis may therefore be strongly supported in one case, but only because the conditions under which it is valid happened to prevail in that case. The investigator is completely unaware of this contingency. The next time around, another investigator finds the hypothesis not to be supported. In some instances, he or she may take the trouble to find out why and may be fortunate or skillful enough to succeed (for example, see Haefner, 1965). In other cases—as prevails, for example, in innovation studies—researchers have rarely taken the trouble, and the situation is complex enough to make success improbable anyway. Thus, in constructing variance-theoretical explanations, it is well from this point of view to orient oneself around an explanation of all the variance. This does not mean to include the longest possible laundry list of condition-specific variables, which are undoubtedly so narrow that there will be gaps between them no matter how many there are, but to think in terms of an explanation that is logically or at least intuitively complete. If one begins with a complete set of variables, then most of the potential interaction is included in some form. Discovering it and expressing it in the proper functional form becomes a matter of manipulating, intellectually and mathematically, what is ready at hand. Of course, researchers cannot always be bothered with dealing in complete theories. One may well be otherwise motivated in a particular instance. A new determinant of Y might suggest itself, and one may want to go out and test that, without enduring the necessary time and expense of formulating and testing a complete theory (for example, see Hickson and others, 1971). Whatever good reasons may justify such strategies, they do unquestionably open the door to interaction and instability. Too much is left out.

It will be noted that in the advanced sciences incomplete theories or hypotheses are tested with great frequency and with eminent success. This is done prominently by means of experimental designs, in which the rest of the world beyond the causal variable of interest is neutralized. Social science may well aspire toward a state in which important theoretical advances will be made through experiments. As theoreticians in psychology have discovered, however (Cronbach, 1975), this is not to be expected at present; the strategy too frequently reduces to incompleteness and invites unmanaged interaction and instability. For the experimental strategy to be successful, either (1) conditions in the experiment (sometimes called the setting, or context) must adequately represent conditions of interest in the real world—when they do not, the difficulty of nonapplicability that results is simply a form of interaction; or (2) the conditions of the experiment must be precisely known and specified and must be of interest in themselves, so that validity can be established for at least that limited set of conditions. To specify the context intelligently, of course, is not easy; it means knowing the conditions under which the experiment might *not* produce the same results—that is, the sources of possible interaction. In social science, it is rarely possible at present to satisfy these requisites.

One cause of the tendency to incompleteness deserves to be singled out for special attention. It is the tendency, already noted, to make an independent variable the focus of inquiry rather than a dependent variable. This has occurred with great regularity in organization theory, perhaps the most recent prominent example being the idea of *loose coupling*. In an article on the subject, Weick (1976) discusses the concept thoroughly and eventually presents seven possible advantages of loosely coupled organizational systems as well as seven disadvantages. This is a singularly pure example of the tendency to focus on the independent variable, for here are fourteen hypotheses, each with a common independent variable (loose coupling) and a different dependent variable, and most with only the one variable on the causal side of the equation. What would happen if these hypotheses were investigated empirically as they stand? Probably loose coupling would be found to result in some of these advantages and disadvantages but not others, which would occasion some puzzlement, some creative thinking, and some talk of measurement error. Now what would happen if the same fourteen hypotheses were investigated again, but by different investigators and in different contexts? Unless loose coupling has only linear additive effects on these outcomes and interacts with nothing, which is highly unlikely, the results would be similar except that several *different* hypotheses would be supported this time while others would be unsupported, or the coefficients denoting support would vary a good deal from their levels on the first set of trials. This result would lead primarily to consternation, which is exactly what has happened and is happening in other branches of organization theory.

The human relations area, which has been sorely troubled by inconsistency in findings, has already been mentioned as a prominent example of focusing on an independent variable. Good human relations are hypothesized to result in organizational morale or commitment or effectiveness (which have been operationalized in a number of ways). It is highly unlikely, however, that supervisory practices will have the same impact on such dependent variables no matter what else is happening in and around the organization. This has been recognized in one way or another for a long time, and researchers have explored possibly interacting variables but have not been able to straighten out the discrepancies (White and Ruh, 1973). The difficulty that the field is in stems largely from its concentration on the independent variable. The proper interactions are not likely to be thought of and accounted for until emphasis is shifted to a *complete* theory of morale or effectiveness or commitment—until creative thinking is directed toward the general causes of the dependent variable rather than remaining on the consequences of supervisory practice or any other single category of independent variable.

To digress for a moment, organization theorists might discern the same problem more readily in medical and public health research. For example, considerable effort is currently being devoted to discovering whether exercise affects heart disease and longevity. It is well recognized that the results of studies are inconsistent and inconclusive, and will continue to be, because they are carried out in the absence of a comprehensive theory of heart disease (Fox and Haskell, 1968; "Exercise and Your Heart," 1977). Exercise may have an effect, but its effect depends on a host of factors describing the exercise itself, physiological condition, environment, genetics, and other risk factors. Experimental design might help, but this is an area in which experimentation is difficult, especially for long-term treatments. The experience with smoking and lung cancer has been similar (Cornfield and others, 1970). Eventually, after many, many studies, the impact of cigarette smoking has been found to shine perceptibly through the data, but the ups and downs of the research experience certainly support the common view that whether a person gets lung cancer from smoking cigarettes depends on a number of other conditions, many of which remain unknown. Although the findings are considered adequate to justify a warning label on cigarettes, the theoretical connection of smoking and lung cancer is still obscure.

Unfortunately, organization theorists are at least as far from a comprehensive framework for the study of effectiveness, for example, as public health researchers are from a theory of heart disease or lung cancer. It should be noted that like human relations variables, integration (Lawrence and Lorsch, 1967) and the consonance between environment and structure (Woodward, 1965; Burns and Stalker, 1961; Mohr, 1971; Pennings, 1975) have also served as focal independent variables, with the expectation that they, too, will be found to determine the effectiveness of organizations. Understandably, it is almost irresistible to discover variables that will increase organizational effectiveness. But unfortunately, looking at them one at a time will not prove the point. It is in fact overly optimistic, as will be shown in Chapter Six, to hope that there exists even a complex explanation, let alone a single universal nostrum, for the effectiveness of the human organizations of this world. Many kinds of forces no doubt enhance effectiveness, but only under certain conditions. Effectiveness, as Cronbach (1975) discovered with respect to the effectiveness of teaching, is highly interactive. It is brimming over with contingent conditions, especially in the usual case, when the independent variables examined are possible tactics or policies of management to improve operations. Either the search for a theory of effectiveness should be abandoned, which might well be the best strategy, or the kinds of variables used in the causal framework need to be remodeled, with an eye particularly for completeness.

A third contributor to interaction and instability is *ugliness,* as indicated particularly by length—the quantity of information that is explicit in a theory. Although this criterion for the quality of a theory is widely suggested, it is not widely analyzed. One exception on the social science side is a valuable text on modeling written by Lave and March (1975). The pleasures and usefulness of model building, they say, are enhanced by truth, beauty, and justice (p. 52). Justice aside, why should we care about the ugliness or beauty of a model as long as it is true or at least useful? The question is an important one for social science in particular, which at this stage is not noted for the esthetic appeal of its theory. To quote Kaplan (1964, p. 310): "The esthetic norm . . . has little bearing on behavioral science in its present state, which may be characterized—without undue offense to anyone, I trust—as one of almost unrelieved ugliness."

Beauty, I propose, is indeed an acceptable standard for the appraisal of theory because it is empirically related to truth, although not by logical necessity and not perfectly, and is often a convenient predictor of truth. Lave and March, for example, persuasively speak of beauty as being indicated in large measure by simplicity (1975, pp. 61–73), and therein lies the important connection between beauty and the likelihood of truth. Simplicity refers to parsimony and the absence of complexity (Kaplan, 1964, pp. 316–319). The claim here is that inadequacy on these two dimensions of beauty should cause wariness in social science on grounds of truth and utility, not on the basis of esthetics alone. The kind of ugliness expressed as a lack of parsimony invites instability. Few large collections of predictors can be additive. A great, motley laundry list of variables is an almost ironclad guarantee of bountiful and undecipherable interaction, including interaction with variables omitted. Similarly, the commonly encountered process model that is overburdened with a myriad of boxes and arrows is in general merely a complicated description of many alternative ways in which a class of events might unfold, not a theoretical explanation of anything. Complexity, the other criterion of simplicity noted by Kaplan, *means* interaction (see Downs and Rocke, 1981). If a model is able to cover its intended territory with a few clean interactions, then there can be no objection on the grounds either of truth or of beauty— quite the contrary, as demonstrated, for example, by Boyle's law. The usual case, however, is that the part of the world to be explained by the model appears to be full of complexity, and the model itself has great difficulty keeping pace in spite of a prodigious collection of *if*s and *but*s. Here there are both little beauty and little truth. There is, primarily, instability.

There is a counterargument—that some aspects of the world just happen to be complex and there is nothing that can be done about it, so that it behooves the scientist to seek complex models to understand such parts of the world. The problem with that philosophy is that complex models are difficult to construct and to work with; instability is rife, effectiveness of explanation is precarious, and expense is great (Kaplan, 1964, pp. 317–318). In the situation in which the world appears to be complex, rather than pile up variables, details, and contingencies, the wise course would seem to be either to keep looking for a different, simpler, *simplifying* theory or to abandon the particular program altogether. In the history of science, it has not been shown necessary from any point of view to reflect the world faithfully in theory, with all its manifest complexity. In fact, quite the opposite is true.

In sum, an attempt to explain an aspect of organizational behavior better by adding still more variables to an already large collection not only lacks beauty but is also unlikely to work. Unmanageable interaction is thereby ushered in. The attempt to account for such complexity or interaction mathematically is doomed both by the size and intricacy of the task and by the gaps that are inevitably left between the narrow-gauge variables in an overly large collection.

A final, major contributor to complexity and instability is the use of *motives*, both implicitly and explicitly, as elements of explanation in theories of behavior. Motives are explanatory, and they may even be considered causes, but whether they can contribute positively to theory is another question. Because of the importance and the scope of the topic, these issues, as well as the way they are connected to interaction and instability, will be treated separately and at length in Chapter Three.

Functions of Research

Having outlined a view of the obstructive forces that are seriously damaging the chances of developing organizational theory, I must now consider a sweeping counterargument—that requirements for cumulative theory are not being met mainly because there is little intent to accomplish that goal. There are, after all, many possible functions of social science research. It may be that academic productivity in this field is meant primarily for purposes other than theory as here defined.

The response must be largely subjective, but it is possible that there is substantial intersubjective agreement. First, it is unlikely that organizational research is heavily oriented around functions other than theory. When the various alternatives are considered, as they will be momentarily, theory appears to dominate the list. Second, to the extent that other serious orientations are in evidence, the goals appropriate to them seem to be no better attained than the goal of producing theory.

It is useful to examine the other alternatives to explore these two points and a third one as well—namely, the validity of the vague notion that seems to exist that any given piece of research is likely to be serving *some* scholarly function. Going down the following list of functions, one concludes that this is not necessarily true. It is quite possible for a piece of research to be serving no particular scholarly function at all. Research simply gets lost in the abyss because it does not meet the requirements for theory and is not seriously intended for anything else. Thus, in fact, a third impediment to theory, added to inconsistency and interaction, is vagueness of purpose.

The attempt will not be made here to provide an exhaustive and mutually exclusive set of purposes of social science research, and such an accomplishment would probably not be worth the effort. It is enough merely to identify any particular example of research with some commonly recognized function, without being overly concerned about the relation of this function to others. The following list has grown over time, and further additions are no doubt desirable. No hierarchy of the categories is offered, although some are subsidiary to one or more of the others. Rather than completeness or logical ordering, I have tried to emphasize the kinds of points noted earlier—the extent to which research may in fact be oriented around these alternatives, the extent to which the alternative goals are accomplished incidentally, and the indecisiveness that may be responsible for a drain on the resources needed for theory.

To Forecast. A certain amount of true, self-conscious forecasting research is quite appropriately carried out in management science and business decision making, but little has been relevant so far to organization theory or the study of organizational behavior itself. There is an exceptionally strong tendency, however, to confuse forecasting with theory by the exploration of models (actually just sets of independent variables) that stand vaguely between explaining or understanding a phenomenon and being able to predict it. A good theory is appropriately sought as a sound basis for a good forecast, but it is not necessary. One would want to judge a predictive, or forecasting, model by its accuracy and consistency over time. Therefore, even a motley collection of variables and processes should be given high marks if it performs well on these criteria; one need not pretend that the collection constitutes a theory. The statistical meteorologist might do well in predicting rain in Hartford, Connecticut, using the dry-bulb temperature in Sault Ste. Marie, Michigan, the north-south wind component in Oklahoma City, and fourteen similar variables (Miller, 1972, p. 377), but no one would claim that this amounts to a theory of precipitation. A theory has certain requirements for coherence, parsimony, and a sense of explanation. A variance model must in some way consist of *causes,* not just variables. Allowing a motley collection of variables to stand vaguely between two functional categories, theoretical development and forecasting, creates a danger of falling between the boards. If the collection is supposed to be theoretical, then it should not be so motley; if it is predictive, then it should be used to predict and should perform well at that task. The latter is rarely tried.

This does not at all imply that predictive models are a waste of time that might more productively be devoted to theory. On the contrary, forecasting may be the most profitable kind of thing that can be done in social science with the variance-type format, where the pursuit of theory, with its explanatory metaphysic and other exacting requirements, may just possibly be in large measure an endeavor of disappointment. But one needs to devote oneself self-consciously to the predictive mode of research; it has its own requirements and guidelines and is not merely a theoretical sidecar. One needs to begin the cumulative learning process of formulating within a subdiscipline the kinds of things that can and cannot be done with predictive models and how best to go about them, as has been done in meteorology and macroeconomics. The dependent variables tend to be different. One tends to address those that keep changing or recurring rather than those that are stable or that are either achieved or not. For that reason, one is more likely to develop forecasting models of morale than effectiveness, for example, and of goal priorities than of formal structure. This is not to say that models that are merely predictive have nothing whatever to do with theory, for clearly they may. They bring to light relations among variables, frequently at a low level of abstraction, and from that point the relations may be probed for the more durable, underlying variables that make up the true causal explanation for Y—if, that is, Y is at all amenable to theoretical explanation. The point to be made regarding theory and forecasting, as was made as well in regard to process theory and variance theory, is that more is to be gained through recognizing the distinction than through ignoring it.

To Contribute to Decision Making. This means to provide information for policy making and other processes of decision. In this case, the test of quality is utility for decision makers. This test is rarely carried out, even impressionistically. A good indicator of lack of interest in such testing is that organization theorists, and social scientists more broadly, have given little attention to developing the necessary measures of utility to decision makers (but see Patton and others, 1977). Theoretical models are not necessary for contributing to policy, nor is a model that contributes to policy necessarily theoretical. Forecasting models may be used, or simply a set of correlations or recurring processes that indicate some likely implications of organizational action. Certainly, if a study or model is supposed to have practical relevance but is not useful, one cannot by any means depend on its at least having theoretical utility.

Again, there is substantial danger that without a consciousness of purpose in this area, a potentially valuable research effort can end by being helpful neither for theory nor for policy.

To Describe. Any science profits by good descriptive data both for theory and for policy, and in organization theory there are few. The organizational Tycho Brahe has not yet arrived on the scene (and when he does, he probably will not get tenure). Descriptive data on dependent variables in which there has been abiding interest would doubtless be of great assistance. Researchers would benefit from mapping, on a large-scale basis by sector, industry, region, and time period, a variety of operationalizations of variables such as employee satisfaction (Blauner, 1970), organizational effectiveness, supervisory participativeness, structural characteristics, and, perhaps above all, empirically determined organizational goals. When purely descriptive studies are conducted, they will quite readily be distinguished for what they yield: raw materials rather than finished theoretical products. However, one common type of description that might be mistaken for theory is the mass of correlation coefficients. Studies that produce these are not necessarily theoretical in themselves, although they may be. Furthermore, they may be less helpful as raw materials in the long-term theory-building process than univariate descriptions.

Another sort of descriptive study is rare but worth noting. Some of the most important and seminal discoveries in the natural sciences have been univariate and descriptive rather than lawlike. These include, for example, the description of planetary orbits as elliptical and the establishment of the shape of the DNA molecule as a double helix. Sometimes, establishing just one such simple fact of nature can open the way to a host of significant theoretical advances. Indeed, the description itself is often called theory, although in a different sense than that in which the term is used here. Social science does not appear on the surface to be ready for studies of this sort; the lack of accurate descriptions of phenomena does not appear to present bottlenecks comparable to those experienced in the two cases cited. Few cases come to mind in which a field has proceeded far enough in the development of theory to perceive itself as stuck, to wish for an exact description of something that is confidently believed to be an important regularity.

One would not want to sneer at such a discovery if it were produced. The question is, rather, whether the sophistication exists either to produce it or to recognize its importance. The analysis in Chapter Five, however, leads to a somewhat different perspective on description as theory, or quasi theory, in social science. In one form, description does exist and will probably increase. It has more relevance for organization theory than appearances suggest.

To Evaluate. This is an extremely important function and one that properly evokes many of the same methods and the same degree of rigor as theoretical research. Most evaluation research, it is true, has to do with organizations, but it is rarely considered or proposed as mainstream organizational study. As a teacher and practitioner in both areas, I have, however, noted a somewhat exaggerated tendency to view evaluation research as potentially contributing to theory (see Coleman, 1972). The possibility does exist that evaluation research will contribute to real theory. Rarely, however, does research on education policy have a real chance of contributing to learning theory, or health policy to disease theory, or employment or welfare policies to whatever vague social theories are believed to be relevant. There are exceptions, but it is mainly theoretical research that leads to theory, while evaluation research at its best leads to company or governmental policy. Evaluation is a worthy end in itself that does not need a theoretical tab to justify the time and effort of social scientists. Societal support of both theoretical and applied research is ultimately justified by the intent, at least, to fulfill a constructive social role; neither one need be, or often can be, justified by the other. Fortunately, I see no evidence that the conspicuous tendency to pay lip service to theoretical value has actually impaired the quality of evaluation research. Still, as is widely discussed in the literature, evaluation research staggers under its own load of problems. It would be well to be single-minded and incisive about evaluation and, except in rare circumstances, to refrain from diluting the effort with theoretical concerns. Conversely, evaluation and other policy research cannot be trusted to lead to theory. If the latter is to be attained, then in some substantial measure it must be specifically sought.

To Generate Ideas. Another purpose of research is to propose and defend ideas. This category is, I fear, something of an escape hatch. These ideas are not necessarily of a form we would call theory. They need not even be embedded in a theory, nor need it be immediately apparent how they might be. Still, a good idea often becomes a well-used tool in moving toward both theory and policy, even in the short run. For example, Hirschman's *Exit, Voice, and Loyalty* (1970) in large measure gives us a fine idea—namely, that there are two significant and interesting ways of expressing dissatisfaction: to complain and to leave. Lindblom (1959) presented the dramatic idea that the goals of policies are chosen simultaneously with, rather than prior to, the means for achieving them. The quasi resolution of conflict (Cyert and March, 1963) is an idea. Critical decisions and the role of leadership in making them compose an idea (Selznick, 1957). In his early article on innovation, Thompson (1965) primarily gave us an idea that bureaucracy can be stifling and that a more progressive form of organization is possible. (In the book by Burns and Stalker, 1961, the same basic thought does not come across as an idea but rather as an element of theory.) The *idea* of cognitive dissonance (Festinger, 1957) has been useful and will remain with us for quite a while, no matter how many experiments cast doubt on the *theory*. However, although ideas can constructively stimulate theory and inform policy, not every idea is a worthy one. Good research of this sort is beautiful, but not every book and article whose sole claim to utility is an idea can be justified and encouraged. Fortunately, the field appears to impose high standards for ideas; very few acquire currency. Thus, if research is in general oriented around producing good ideas, there are a few notable successes and truckloads of failures, and one suspects that it will always be so.

To Understand Current Affairs and Institutions. Developing an understanding of specific recent affairs and institutions (for example, the Burger Court, the multinational corporation, the merger movement, the War on Poverty) can contribute constructively to important decision making. One can use it, for example, to benefit from past mistakes. To this extent there can be no quarrel with the research, but one must still explore how well the job is actually done—how helpful is the contribution, really, to the making of decisions? The answer to that question determines the value of the research. The same is true if the understanding function is considered to enable the members of the general public to deal better with the institutions studied. The question then is whether it seems to be having that effect on the public. If it is, few would dispute its worth, but if not, then many would be dubious. It is difficult to say how much research of this nature there is in the organizations field or how successful it is. On the latter point, however, it should be noted that success is extremely difficult because institutions and issues often change too quickly to allow well-designed research to be funded, completed, and written up and still be applicable. The successors to these institutions are often different enough in structure and context that it is not notably productive, frequently not even tempting, to apply the conclusions previously derived. Little effort has been devoted to the methodological question of the kind of research that is most useful in this situation. In general, institutions and issues are not durables—even while they last. When such research is considered a theoretical contribution, it may become more of a liability than an asset. A particular Supreme Court will soon disappear altogether, and the multinational corporation can change so rapidly that a behavioral law valid for multinational corporations today may no longer be valid just a few years hence. Under such conditions, the research may not be cost-effective. It is questionable whether what is wanted is theories about the Burger Court or rather about dispute institutions, about the multinational corporation or about economic diversification or national economic dependency, about the merger movement or about the explanation of economic size, about the War on Poverty or about signal input. To the extent that the less ephemeral, more durable concepts should be the objectives of theory in social science, studies of current institutions are in danger of being only case studies, samples of one, the validity of their conclusions so circumscribed by unnamed contingent conditions as to be of problematic theoretical value. There is a tendency to label such research as exploratory. However, without careful attention to the terms of generalizability, research on current affairs and institutions, even if considered exploratory research, may well be atheoretical. Thus, research that is not much help for practical affairs cannot, in general, be rescued by its contribution to theory. The facile assumption that it can be is unwarranted.

To Be Interesting to the Investigator and Other Social Scientists.
Almost anything can be justified on this ground, and the ultimate
subjectivity of the function makes assessment of the merit of individual examples difficult. Some would no doubt say that if this is all
that can be claimed for a piece of research, it is an inexcusable
waste of effort. Realistically speaking, it would be impossible to
demonstrate that no good has come from research that began by
fitting purely within this category and inappropriate to discourage
investigators from following their inclinations even when no
clearer objective is immediately in view. Still, it is likely that an
empirical discipline will suffer in prestige and accomplishment if
the major part of research within it is merely interesting to the
investigator and a few colleagues and goes no further in the short
run. In addition, contrary to what are apparently common though
vague beliefs, much presumably interesting research is not necessarily theoretical—not any more than it is automatically valuable
for social policy, forecasting, or evaluation. Theories of organizational behavior are specific and focused. They will not arise out of
interesting research quickly, perhaps not at all, unless some subset
of the discipline continues to address itself to the task self-
consciously. In more advanced disciplines, the permeation of academic training by *existing* theory makes such a preoccupation
largely spontaneous (a conservative force, but nonetheless theoretical); in organizational behavior, as in much of social science, there
hardly is such a phenomenon as existing theory. It is up to the
present generation somehow to set the theoretical machinery in
motion; future generations may then act in terms of it out of spontaneous individual interest.

In sum, the three concerns noted at the beginning of this
section are answered as follows: First, it is doubtful that all these
categories combined, with the possible exception of the last two,
contribute to a substantial proportion of the effort in what is generally considered to be research in organizational behavior. Second,
to the extent that these alternative goals may be prevalent, it is
important to ask how best to achieve them and how well they are
being achieved, but those questions are rarely asked. Third, if there
is an assumption that research standing vaguely in these categories

contributes to theory even if it does not serve the appropriate categorical goals, that assumption is almost certainly unsound.

Conclusion

The foregoing discussion has organized the chief sources of curtailed efficiency and effectiveness in the development of theories of organizational behavior. Fortunately, no single research area has all these problems, but unfortunately, each area seems to be beset with one or more. Given that interaction and inconsistency of focus are prominent, an explanation that might be considered for their prominence and for the frustration of theory is that theory building is simply not the primary goal of actual research activity. There are, we have seen, many things that students of organizational behavior could be doing and to some extent are doing, each with its own criteria of quality. These include forecasting events, describing important phenomena, and informing the making of organizational or governmental policy. It is always difficult and problematic to judge intent from product, but a reading of the scholarly literature suggests that for the most part, in spite of their substantial worthiness, these are not the goals being pursued. The research conducted is apparently interesting to the investigators and other social scientists, but it produces little actual forecasting outside of macroeconomics, only a moderate scale of contributions to organizational decision making, and a meager accumulation of solid description. It appears, rather, that the modal objective is indeed closely concerned with the production of theories of organizational behavior.

As a result of the enormous amount that has been learned through organizational studies about the contours of the subject matter, the investigative methods, and the fit between them, it is now apparent that a change in tactics is indicated. The marginal returns of the past approach are dwindling rapidly. In large measure, what can be learned from it is learned by stepping back, looking at the results carefully in broad perspective, and seeing what *cannot* be learned. Whereas the past approach has been eminently successful in revealing the nature and extent of the elementary problems of the discipline, especially the problem of unremitting complexity (Brunner and Brewer, 1971; Downs and Rocke, 1981), it is too diffuse an approach to solve them. With respect to theory, the change most likely to result is toward the statement of models with restricted generality but substantial endurance and toward a preoccupation with their modification, elaboration, and refinement. Some of the forms that these models will apparently take are suggested in the course of the discussion of specific problems in the ensuing chapters. I do not expect models that will have the sophistication, power, or utility of models in physics, but rather models which do have pretensions in that direction and which will serve well to reveal the problems at the new stages of theoretical development that will follow in the future.

❊ 2 ❊

Approaches
to Explanation

Variance Theory
and Process Theory

Practicing organizations scholars are apparently trying to produce examples of two highly significant types of product to which I would attach the label "theory"—process theory and variance theory. In distinguishing between these two, one is unfortunately not simply recognizing the prevalence of an exhaustive pair of categories, each with its own a priori instructions or guidelines. One does, however, detect in social research a striving, though implicit and imperfect, toward process theory and variance theory as distinct modes of explanation—a striving that deserves to be reinforced. Hypotheses, theories, and laws take on other shapes and other functions, especially in the natural sciences (for example, the specification of form or of composition; for an excellent typology of theories relevant to social science, see Rapoport, 1958). However, insofar as research and analysis in social science aspire toward explanatory theory as defined in the Introduction, they

appear overwhelmingly to aspire toward one of these two categories or the other. A problem that I will outline is that although the latent aspirations may, or at least should, clearly diverge
toward the two theoretical poles, actual products do not. There is a
tendency to miss either one target or the other, often by virtue of
trying, and inevitably failing, to mix the two together.

The basis of the distinction between process theory and variance theory is best conceptualized in terms of necessary and sufficient conditions as modes of explanation, or forms of theory. The
variance theory is a type whose characteristics grow out of a foundation in the necessary and sufficient, whereas the characteristics
of process theory grow out of a foundation in the necessary alone.

We imagine an outcome (Y) and a set of events and conditions considered as precursor (X), wishing to view the precursor as
a powerful explanatory generalization in connection with the outcome, so as to have a law, or a theory of Y.

If the precursor set is a necessary and sufficient condition
for the outcome, then this clearly constitutes a satisfactory theory.
It fits into the category of variance theory.

If the precursor is merely a sufficient condition and strives
to be nothing more, then it does not constitute a satisfactory theory
of Y, for if Y occurs quite commonly without X (since X is not
necessary), then one has not yet a good explanation. It lacks completeness. What makes Y occur when X does not? The precursor X
may surely be considered a cause of Y, and it may be extremely
important to know that X sometimes causes Y, but this falls somewhat short of providing a theory of Y. Strangulation, in these
terms, is a cause of death but not a theory of death. If one seeks a
more general cause or strives to add Xs in order to achieve completeness, then one's orientation moves toward a precursor that,
taken as a whole, is both necessary and sufficient rather than
merely sufficient. To try to cast an explanatory theory of a recurrent phenomenon in terms of the merely sufficient is to guarantee
instability. By its very nature, the merely sufficient condition will be
found to exert a strong influence in one context and little or no
influence in another.

Strangely enough, there is a special sense in which a precursor that is merely a necessary condition and strives to be nothing

more may constitute a satisfactory theory. This is the important category of process theory. It would appear, and it is partly true, that the ordinary necessary condition has the same sort of deficiency as the sufficient condition. For example, a warm climate may be a necessary condition for malaria, but this surely does not constitute a theory. We will see shortly, however, that one sort of necessary condition does become a theory. To characterize it briefly, it is the sort that consists of ingredients plus the recipe that strings them together in such a way as to tell the story of how Y occurs whenever it does occur.

Two propositions regarding variance theory and process theory are important for the present critique of theoretical development. The first, which is the subject of the next two sections, is that they may be and should be viewed as distinct types. For convenience in this discussion, the primary and secondary characteristics of variance theory and process theory are summarized in Table 1. The second claim is that confusion of the types and the attempt to mix them constitute a significant impediment, one source of the frustration of theory. The final section of the chapter takes up this latter claim in some detail, illustrated by research and theory building regarding the adoption and diffusion of innovations, an area that provides examples of the major ways in which process theory and variance theory are confounded. In later chapters, the analysis and conclusions are applied to several other areas of organization theory, as well.

Variance Theory

In variance theory *the precursor (X) is a necessary and sufficient condition for the outcome (Y).* In other terms, if X, then Y, and if not-X, then not-Y. This kind of explanation is likely to be a most satisfying one if it is well supported and if it also is intuitively appealing, or makes sense, given what one already feels one knows. Unfortunately, it has thus far proved extremely difficult to find powerful explanatory relations of this kind in the social realm. Nevertheless, the form of the theory is so straightforward and appealing that it generally serves as a model and a goal. If one's explanation happens to be as yet incomplete, one hopes that one

Table 1. Characteristics of Variance Theory and Process Theory

Variance Theory	Process Theory
The basis of explanation is causality.	The basis of explanation is probabilistic rearrangement.
1. The precursor (X) is a necessary and sufficient condition for the outcome (Y).	1. The precursor (X) is a necessary condition for the outcome (Y).
2. A variance theory deals with variables.	2. A process theory deals with discrete states and events.
3. A variance theory deals with efficient causes.	3. A process theory deals with a final cause.
4. In variance theory, time ordering among the contributing (independent) variables is immaterial to the outcome.	4. In process theory, time ordering among the contributing events is generally critical for the outcome.

has a part of a theory, at least, and that the precursor set will be filled out more satisfactorily in the future. A large amount of empirical social research is carried out in this tradition.

The logic of experimental design (Campbell and Stanley, 1963) is also that of the necessary and sufficient condition. The results of a true experiment are a variance theory in microcosm; instead of being an explanatory theory descriptive of the world in general, the results are descriptive only of what takes place for one set of subjects in one context. In an experiment, however, the precursor, instead of occurring naturally, is manipulated by the investigator. This fact suggests that the variance-theory format may be used conveniently in evaluating the effects of purposeful interventions. This use will become important when considering theories of the effectiveness of organizational designs or programs.

Because the precursor is necessary and sufficient, one of the prominent uses to which a variance theory can be put is prediction. Prediction without explanation is possible—quite common, in fact—but it is also true that an explanatory generalization can be both tested and applied by using the precursor to predict the outcome. In the same sense, if one can manipulate the precursor, then one has control over the outcome of interest. Prediction and control are powerful benefits, and the potential for attaining them helps to explain why variance theories are so commonly pursued.

We turn now to the characteristics, listed in Table 1, that arise out of the necessary and sufficient as a form of theory.

A variance theory deals with variables. In considering necessary and sufficient conditions, it is best to think of X and Y as defined states, events, or *values* (scores, quantities) and of not-X and not-Y as undefined states—simply the absence or negation or complements of X and Y. To say that X is necessary and sufficient for Y, therefore, is actually to deal with only those two defined states. With this form as a theoretical foundation, however, one may simply extend or enlarge the sufficiency statement "If X, then Y" to statements such as "If more X, then more Y" without contradiction of the premises denoted by *necessary and sufficient.* This is important because, as we will see later, the same extension cannot be made in the case of process theory. With the use of this kind of extension, the necessary and sufficient readily and conveniently accommodates *variables* rather than only single-valued states or events and their complements. A variable in explanatory theory is any quantified characteristic. It is significant for the attractiveness of variance theory that the necessary-and-sufficient basis of explanation accommodates variables; the interrelating of whole quantitative dimensions provides a fullness, a richness, and a parsimony that are highly desirable. Whether dimensions of this sort can actually be brought together to produce good social theories is another matter. It will be assumed at the outset that such is at least a possibility, while actual efforts to produce variance theories and the difficulties in the path to that goal become primary objects of attention.

It is of interest to note that the same sort of quantitative extension cannot be made in the case of multicategory nominal scales, such as type of ownership (public, private, nonprofit) and type of compliance structure (coercive, utilitarian, normative). Because the scales are not quantitative or even ordered, there is no possibility of extending X to the case of more X. The association of two nominal variables of this type cannot, therefore, be the basis of a single variance theory; separate theoretical statements about each of the defined categories are required.

It is also important to recognize that a variance theory has the form of a mathematical function; that is, with each value of X there is associated one and only one value of Y. This is simply a restatement of the sufficiency premise. If a value of X could occur without the occurrence of any corresponding value of Y, then that X, anyway, would not be sufficient for Y. Similarly, if a value of X occurred sometimes with one value of Y and sometimes with another, then it would clearly not be sufficient for either—that is, one does not have a sufficient condition for a certain value of Y if the precursor occurs but that value of Y does not.[1]

Typically, then, a variance theory, or, synonymously, a variance model, begins conceptually with an outcome that occurs within the theory as a variable—that is, in quantitative levels or amounts: for example, earliness of innovation, extent of innovation, presence/absence of innovation, amount of power, degree of effectiveness, level of morale, volume of gas, force of gravitational attraction. The theory consists of a general explanation for the occurrence of the phenomenon at all its different quantitative levels. If the phenomenon is Y, then the idea, in other words, is to explain the variation in Y. The explanation consists of a set of contributory conditions, each of which also has its own variance (and typically includes a stochastic error or disturbance component). For example, the level of innovation is a function of the levels of motivation and resources. It is a critical feature that explanation operates between the precursor variables and the outcome

---

[1]It would appear that if the sufficiency premise is violated when one value of X is associated with two values of Y, the necessity premise must be violated when one value of Y may be caused by either of two values of X, as in the legitimate function $Y = X^2$. That appearance dissipates when it is remembered that the concern is with a theory of Y; X must be a full explanation for Y, not the other way around. One may properly consider, for example, that the set comprising $\{X_1$ or $X_2\}$ is necessary and sufficient for Y_1, in the sense that when either of those two values of X occurs, Y_1 occurs, and one of the two must occur in order for Y_1 to occur. The value Y_1 is then fully explained by the values $\{X_1$ or $X_2\}$. It is of no importance for the explanation, the theory of Y, that Y_1 might occur and X_2 not. However, if one value of X may be associated with either of two values of Y, as in the text, X is merely necessary for each of these values of Y and, because it is not sufficient, may not be a complete explanation at all. True, X might simply be an erratic explanation for Y, just as warm weather might actually be the explanation, but an erratic one, for malaria. In this situation, however, there is lacking a vital element for satisfactory theory—namely, the explanation for this erratic behavior—as will be elaborated on in the section on process theory.

variable at all quantitative levels of their occurrence, so that, for example, early adoption is causally explained by the same causes and conditions as late adoption and in exactly the same way; only the levels of the explanatory variables are different.

Explanation of the gravitational force between two bodies by the mass of the bodies and the distance between them is a typical variance model, as is Boyle's law, in which temperature acts on volume and pressure, or Ohm's law, in which current is the result of voltage and resistance. Many variance theories are pursued in organizational research. In innovation research alone, for example, there have been attempts to build theories—primarily by connecting outcomes to precursors in regression or correlation models—that explain variation in the time at which different individuals or organizations adopt innovations, in the extent to which they commit themselves to innovations, in the extent to which different innovations are adopted within a population, and in the varying rapidity with which different innovations diffuse.

A variance theory deals with efficient causes. The concept of cause that is involved here was analyzed by Aristotle (1941, p. 241) and is generally called "efficient cause" by his interpreters and commentators. An efficient cause is a force that is conceived as *acting on* a unit of analysis (person, organization, and so on) to make it what it is in terms of the outcome variable (morale, effectiveness, and so on) or change it from what it was. It may be thought of as *push-type* causality. Each contributory necessary and sufficient condition in a variance model is an efficient cause. Furthermore, each such cause, whether standing alone as an additive contributor or combined multiplicatively with other causes, has a separable impact on the outcome; the extent of its impact is not lost in the intertwining of causes and conditions.

A necessary and sufficient association between precursor and outcome would not be an explanation, a theory, without this notion of causality. One is frequently warned in the methodology textbooks that X and Y may be highly correlated and yet X may well not be an explanation of Y. The explanation of Y, as of the observed correlation, may lie elsewhere. There are only two other possibilities: The relation might be *spurious*—that is, caused by some external force, as in the close relation between robins and baseball (Tashman and Lamborn, 1979, pp. 159–160) or the amount of fire-fighting equipment brought in and the damage found after the fire (Nachmias and Nachmias, 1976, pp. 8–9); or it might be pure *coincidence,* the result of sampling accident that will presumably right itself in time. It is sometimes possible to demonstrate satisfactorily that a relation is spurious, but most often not. Most commonly, either one believes that certain empirical relations are explanatory relations or one does not. If the necessary and sufficient precursor X is believed to explain Y—that is, if spuriousness and coincidence are ruled out—that belief will rest on the remaining possibility, the notion of efficient causality, the notion that it is X that makes Y happen or change recurrently. This notion is metaphysical or at least mysterious. Cultural background, existing beliefs, and accepted knowledge are the kinds of factors that no doubt determine whether one would see or feel or admit the possibility that a particular association involved causal explanation rather than being spurious or coincidental. Since causality is an abstraction and cannot be directly observed, it must be an article of faith, but it is logically indispensable to the acceptance of explanatory theory based on necessary and sufficient conditions. Thus, variance theory rests ultimately on the metaphysical concept of efficient causality. Despite the metaphysical nature of the concept, however, there is no doubt about its capacity to serve as an important guide in the development of the nonmetaphysical aspects of science.

The variance-theory model of explanation in social science has a close affinity to statistics. The archetypical rendering of this idea of causality is the linear or nonlinear regression model, but variance theories and regression models are not identical, and the relation between them is important for an analysis of theory.

The variables in a great many regression models are not conceived of as efficient causes. Take, for example, the regression model referred to in the previous chapter that predicts rainfall in Hartford on the basis of the dry-bulb temperature in Sault Ste. Marie, the north-south wind component in Oklahoma City, and fourteen similar variables (Miller, 1972). Few would quarrel with the utility of such models, but most would implicitly place them in a different category from variance theories; they are forecasting models or correlational models. They are rooted in spuriousness.

They do not have the same purpose as variance theories; that is, they are not causal or at least not directly so—they do not purport to explain why the outcome is what it is in each instance.

In variance theory, time ordering among the contributory (independent) variables is immaterial to the outcome. There are two senses in which this is true. First, there is no need to specify any variable to the extent that it merely functions as a conduit between variables already included in the precursor, on one hand, and the outcome, on the other. The outcome would not be affected at all. Since sufficiency is built into the theory, any conduit that needs to be there is guaranteed to be there, even if only implicitly, by virtue of the existence of the specified prior causes; one might in some instances wish to identify the conduit, but one is not required to be able to do so, nor would one be required to measure such intervening variables in order to make a proper prediction. One may always use what econometricians call a reduced-form, or one-stage, model (Johnston, 1972, pp. 350–351). If one's theory is correct, for example, one would not have to identify or measure *satisfaction* in the causal chain *employee participation in decision making → employee satisfaction → work-group effectiveness* (taking the arrows to represent causality). In fact, there almost always exists intervening mechanisms which are as yet unspecified but whose omission is of no consequence unless one decides to be puzzled about the *means* of bridging the gap between one included phenomenon and another. Sometimes it might be appropriate to be explicitly concerned with intervening variables and sometimes not. In the statement of Boyle's law, for example, it would complicate matters unnecessarily to include the molecular activity that intervenes between temperature and pressure.

The other sense in which explicit time ordering is immaterial is the following: In a variance theory, the independent contributors within the precursor are considered, from the viewpoint of the outcome, as though they all happened at once. Variance theory is state-oriented (Simon, 1969, pp. 111–112); it deals in snapshots rather than movies. The functional relation among the independent causes is important (for example, it may be linear or nonlinear), but the time ordering among those causes is unimportant because each contributor has an independent effect. Each cause is always sufficient, with the others held constant, to produce a given impact on Y. The very idea of holding *constant* demonstrates the irrelevance of time. It does not matter for the volume of the gas, for example, whether temperature precedes pressure or vice versa. If the variable called employee satisfaction in the earlier illustration had an independent contributory effect—if it were not merely a conduit—it would have to be specified in the model, but to the extent of its independent impact it would be viewed as occurring simultaneously with employee participation.

This is not to say that conduits do not appear as such in statements with the form of variance theories or that variables with independent effect are not assumed to be ordered (for example, the effects of parent and peer influence on educational achievement or occupational aspiration—see Duncan, Featherman, and Duncan, 1972; Duncan, Haller, and Portes, 1971). Multistage variance theories (or theoretical attempts) occur in social science particularly when variables are considered not only to function as intervening channels but to have independent effects as well. There is a considerable literature dealing with the expression of this theoretical form in structural-equation models (Goldberger, 1973) and path analysis (Duncan, 1966), and the advantages of specifying rather than ignoring time order have also been emphasized (Lewis-Beck and Mohr, 1976). But it is not essential to recognize time order in the necessary and sufficient explanation, and this fact allows a parsimony in the number of variables included and a simplicity in their arrangement without which it would be difficult to proceed.

Process Theory

In this section, the term *process theory* is given a highly specific meaning. At present, however, it is a common term with a variety of alternative meanings and connotations. The reader is therefore requested to put aside prior interpretations for the moment in order to allow the concept to be constructed here in its entirety for use in the present context. Loosely, a process theory is one that tells a little story about how something comes about, but in order to qualify as a theoretical explanation of recurrent behavior, the manner of the storytelling must conform to narrow specifications.

Process theories are quite different from variance theories in all the respects just reviewed. Paradoxically, however, although process theories as they will be described here are monumentally important in science and are at least as common as variance theories, their characteristics have not been articulated to the same extent. They have, in fact, only barely been suggested (see Kaplan, 1964, pp. 109–111; Simon, 1969, pp. 107–118; Lave and March, 1975). The variance-theory *outlook* dominates thinking about theory by scientists, philosophers, and the general public, even though the variance-theory *form* does not in practice dominate theory itself.

In process theory, the precursor (X) is a necessary condition for the outcome (Y). Again, we deal with some particular outcome, Y, as a descriptor of some focal unit, such as a person or object. The orientation is toward an explanatory theory of Y. Since the precursor, X, is necessary for Y, the basic logical statement involved is "If not-X, then not-Y." This statement, however, cannot be the most important thrust of a theory; to have an explanation, one must be heavily concerned with when Y does occur, not exclusively with when it does not. The precursor in a process theory contains three types of elements—(1) necessary conditions and (2) necessary probabilistic processes, which together form the core of the theory, and (3) external, directional forces that function to move the focal unit and conditions about in a characteristic way, often herding them into mutual proximity. Let us elaborate on these three components.

One crucial element of the precursor, as noted, is a set of necessary conditions or objects. These and the focal unit (for example, the person who may get malaria) are capable of changing over time and, particularly, of *combining* with one another in such a way as to yield the outcome. In the theory or story of malaria, for example, these necessary conditions are the malarial parasite, persons already harboring the parasite, and *Anopheles* mosquitoes. The combining of elements is of paramount importance. Process theory eschews efficient causality as explanation and depends instead on *rearrangement*—that is, on the joining or separation of two or more specified elements rather than on a change in the magnitude of some element. Whereas a variance theory explains a behavior or a characteristic of an object, a process theory explains the pairing or other rearrangement of mutually autonomous objects, such as the bets of the players and the number on the roulette wheel, whose individual courses are determined independently of one another by forces external to the core of the theory. One particular combination of the conditions and focal unit is defined, within the theory, *to be* the outcome. (For example, in the present context, the simple joining of the parasite and the focal person will be labeled "contraction of malaria," omitting all concern with the later appearance of symptoms.)

Because the precursor is not sufficient, there is no inherent force either within the focal unit or within the necessary conditions that makes them inevitably combine in such a way as to result in the state defined to be the outcome. Nothing about the prior malaria victim or the parasite is assumed to make the bite of another mosquito inevitable, and nothing about that mosquito makes it inevitable that it will later bite the focal person. Nevertheless, there must be something that leads to the occurrence of Y, even though it is not an efficient cause, or there can be no sense of explanation. If the joining of elements does not follow inevitably from any set of antecedent conditions, then it must occur by chance. What has not been sufficiently emphasized in this connection, however, is the degree of system, the regularity that may be then involved. The laws of chance, though based in randomness, do not necessarily imply disorder. On the contrary, those laws are *laws;* they can be used to construe powerfully some of our most profound insights into the nature and the order of things.

Thus, as the second element of the precursor, the role in process theory that is analogous to efficient cause is occupied by probabilistic processes—by random draws from simple or joint probability distributions of various shapes that are either explicit or implied. In part, it is occupied as well by the external directional forces, the third element, which are simply presumed to carry on in some generally accepted manner (for example, mosquitoes look for people and animals to bite), but the theoretical essence, the guarantor of the proper combinations of objects, lies in one or more probabilistic processes. For example, *Anopheles* mosquitoes bite people with and without malaria at random.

It is critical to recognize that from the viewpoint of the model, at least—and the model may attempt either to reflect faithfully or perhaps to simplify the physical world—*Anopheles* mosquitoes, no matter how many there are, need *never* bite any person without malaria. The fact that they do (and the rate at which they do) depends on the operation of the laws of chance. *Without those laws, there would be no basis for believing that new persons would ever contract the disease,* but given those laws, there is indeed a scientifically satisfactory explanation, and one that would be inadequate if it depended on efficient causality alone. In this way, probabilistic processes are crucial for explanation in certain theories and therefore become the basis for establishing a separate type of theory, the process theory.[2] A bit more must be said on the subject, but it will be well first to provide further examples of process theories in order to convey better the nature of the various elements and how they function. Five theories or models are described briefly in the following text and are set out schematically in Table 2.

1. *Contraction of malaria.* A certain proportion of the people in a population harbors the malarial parasite. Mosquitoes, following their natural habits, transfer the parasites about by biting people with and without malaria at random.

2. *Mendelian segregation.* This is the law that specifies how an individual organism acquires the two-element basis underlying a certain inherited trait. Each parent has elements in pairs (now

---

[2]One may observe that the disturbance term in a regression model also represents a random process, but that is functionally quite a different sort of mechanism. It is virtually univariate—a fluctuation of the single dimension Y on its scale of measurement. In a process theory, the process at issue is a probabilistic conjunction of two or more specified phenomena. Moreover, as will be discussed momentarily in the text, the essence of the metaphysic of variance theory is such that an outcome, some particular value of Y, is determined without the random process; the latter only provides a "fudge factor" by adding to or subtracting from the effects of the precursor. If only some *causes* were not missing from the model, pure functional form would be observed. There would be no random process in the theory. In the metaphysic of the process theory, however, there is no output at all without these probabilistic processes. The latter are not "disturbances" or something else that is otherwise conceptually complete; rather, without them all explanation and prediction comes to a halt, and there can be no bridge to *any* value of Y. Without the disturbance term in a variance theory, the outcome is completely determined; the theory is deterministic. Without the probabilistic processes in a process theory, the outcome is completely undetermined; the theory is indeterminate.

Table 2. Elements of Illustrative Process Theories

Theory	Focal Unit	Outcome	Necessary Conditions	External Directional Forces	Probabilistic Processes	Definition of Outcome
Contraction of malaria	Individual person	Has malarial agent	Malarial parasite; other people harboring the parasite; *Anopheles* mosquitoes	Mosquitoes look for people to bite	Mosquitoes bite people with and without malaria	Parasite combines with individual
Mendelian segregation	Individual, sexually reproduced organism (zygote)	Has specific genotype for one trait	Certain parental genotypes; gametes (units of transmission, such as sperm and egg)	Mechanism for distributing elements of inheritance to gametes; mechanism for bringing male and female gametes into contact	Segregation of elements; union of gametes	Two particular gametes combine
Diffusion	Individual organism	Has a given descriptor (for example, information, disease, innovation)	Other individuals having the descriptor	Business of daily living	Retention; individuals iteratively contact one another; transfer	Descriptor is combined with individual

Table 2. Elements of Illustrative Process Theories (Continued)

Theory	Focal Unit	Outcome	Necessary Conditions	External Directional Forces	Probabilistic Processes	Definition of Outcome
Garbage-can model	Choice opportunity in an organized anarchy with problems	Choice is made	Other choice opportunities; participants (energy)	Motivation to get choices made and problems solved	Participants (energy) and problems flow iteratively to choices	Quantity of energy relative to problems in choice is favorable
Darwinian evolution—the origin of species	Individual organism	Has new genotype	Parental genotypes; environment (niches)	Inheritable change in type (mutation); environmental change	Realization of niche (survival in environment); reproduction (mating)	Parental units of inheritance combine

known to be genes)—for example, AA, Aa, or aa. Within each parent, each pair is segregated and distributed randomly by a natural function to two units of transmission (gametes), one and only one element to a unit (zero or two may be seen as error). (The nature of this first probabilistic process becomes particularly important when the distribution of elements of one trait is considered relative to other trait elements carried by the same unit of transmission.) Through the sexual reproduction process natural to the organism (pollination, copulation, and so forth), one unit of transmission from the male parent unites at random with one unit of transmission from the female.

3. *Diffusion.* There are a great many variants. Basically, some proportion of individuals in a population bears a descriptor, such as a disease, innovation, or rumor. Retention of the descriptor for a certain length of time may be an external directional force or may be included in the model as a probabilistic process. Following their natural habits of life, individuals with and without the descriptor contact one another at random. To say at random, here and elsewhere, does not necessarily mean that all individuals have an equal probability of being contacted, or selected, but rather that all individuals in the same category (however categories may be established) have the same probability and that the probability of being selected depends on one's category. At any contact between a have and a have-not, all or part of the descriptor may or may not be transmitted, depending on random draws from a frequency distribution.

4. *The garbage-can model of organizational choice.* There are many choices or decisions to be made over time in an organizational setting that includes a number of problems. Energy imported by participants is required to make each choice. Under certain constraints of access, and with higher probabilities attached to choices closer to than further from solution, problems and participants transfer iteratively and at random from one choice to another. A choice is made when its balance of energy relative to encumbering problems is favorable.

5. *Darwinian evolution—the origin of species.* The question addressed is how any given type of biological individual comes about. The theory deals with the parental generation. Poten-

tial parents describable as various types (genotypes) exist, as does an environment. External natural forces independently create changes in aspects of the environment and also in the inheritable composition of some potential parents (the latter forces culminate in mutations). Each potential parent is selected at random either to survive or not survive to reproductive age within the environment (to combine with a compatible niche), with higher probabilities of survival conferred on some types than others. For sexually reproducing organisms, each surviving potential parent is then selected probabilistically for a rate of reproduction through mating, with zero, high, or low probabilities conferred on types according to biological traits. A given type of offspring then results from mating and reproduction; it may be a type with brand-new traits or not, depending on the earlier processes.

In sum, it is clear from Table 2 that the precursor is not sufficient to produce a "successful" outcome (such as malaria) on any given trial, but if one has faith in the laws of chance, it is sufficient to produce that outcome some proportion of the time. Just as variance theory rests ultimately on a belief in the metaphysical notion of efficient causality, so process theory rests ultimately on a metaphysical belief in the operation of the laws of chance. Some airborne seeds do find favorable soil. In the wondrous Rube Goldberg machinery of protein synthesis, it is conceivable that the completed polypeptide might never be produced simply because the right bit of transfer RNA might never happen to come along. But it does come along; the system thrives. Mosquitoes might bite only people who already have malaria, but they do not. In short, the proposition of a specific probabilistic process is a strong hypothesis, because otherwise there is no reason to suppose that certain things would ever get together in the world or would get together more often than not. A process theory is only as strong as the clarity and compelling nature of the probabilistic processes hypothesized to make the connections. These processes, together with the external directional forces, bring a definite action into the theory, which is thus an action hypothesis about the world in areas of the absence or irrelevance of efficient causes. An important observation coincident on the prevalence of process theories in science is that the shape of human understanding of the world may be considerably affected by our particular ability—perhaps unique in the animal kingdom—to interpret much of it in terms of probabilistic processes, the interpretation being much more important than the "true" nature of the phenomena.

The view just elaborated is in sharp contrast to the usual view of probabilistic events in science and the philosophy of science. There, random processes are error; they cover ignorance. Here, random processes are explanation. This is not at all to say that there is no ignorance, no missing variables or hidden causes. It is possible to suggest, however, that at least some occurrences that would automatically be ascribed to hidden causes might indeed be inherently probabilistic instead. The discussion of probabilistic occurrence is almost always conducted with a causal metaphysic as backdrop (for example, Hempel and Oppenheim, 1948; Suppes, 1977, pp 266–283; or the discussion of Bohr's views on quantum theory in Suppe, 1977, pp. 180–191), and in such a perspective, tendency statements, or nondeterministic hypotheses, will always be in a certain amount of conceptual trouble as theory. Tendencies are an admission that the causal picture is a bit obscure. The difficulty evaporates, however, when a probabilistic metaphysic itself is applicable. Not all recurring events are causal, especially because what is considered an event depends on how reality is construed. The explanation of a roulette wheel's stopping with the ball on number 23 may be causal, subsumed by covering laws from Newtonian mechanics, but the explanation for the fact that somebody wins is not causal; it is inherently probabilistic. It depends on the ball's happening to come to rest on a number that happened to be covered by a bet, each phenomenon being governed by its own set of forces. Similarly for the genetic composition of the sperm that fertilizes a given egg: To the egg, it is a turn of the wheel.

Without external forces and probabilistic processes, alleged, tentative, or incipient process theories are anemic. They may be of value in clarifying the nature of certain developmental and other procedures that exist in the world, and they may eventually be developed into theory. In order actually to be theory, however, in the sense of being an explanation for a recurrent Y, a compelling flow of action is required. It is not sufficient merely to name a succession of necessary stages or events—for example, to say that

organizational innovation proceeds through a process of unfreezing, moving, and refreezing (Zand and Sorensen, 1975); one must
also supply the external forces and probabilistic processes constitut-
ing the means by which that sequence of events is understood to
unfold. Either the causes of the development inhere in the initial
state (as the infant inherently becomes the adult), or the progres-
sion depends on encounters of the focal unit with factors that
spring from elsewhere. Moreover, there is a tendency for the outcome in such incipient theories to be an individual behavior or
characteristic rather than a combination. In such cases, merely in-
terjecting probability does not help, for it is not a satisfactory explanation. One may always ask, "Why?" Why did this organization
refreeze instead of retrogressing, as many do? Any seriously explanatory answer must be in terms of either some form of causality
or some form of motivational reasoning. Probability simply begs
the issue. Unless the precise probability is universal and immutable,
the theoretical understanding of refreezing is not enhanced by reporting the probability—that is, the relative frequency—of its
occurrence in a certain study or organization. When outcomes are
successfully conceptualized as a combining of independently developing entities, however, probability becomes not only a meaningful
response but generally the only response. It is, no doubt, often true
that an outcome of interest is capable of being seen either as a
characteristic that has a cause or as an encounter that is probabilistic, but to be a process-theory outcome it must somehow be conceptualized as the latter. Unfortunately, as will be illustrated in this and
later chapters, process-oriented ideas in organizational behavior,
and in social science more broadly, tend to be primarily of the
stage-naming variety. They are incomplete from the standpoint of
theory in that they simply rehearse a series of steps; they lack
the lines of action—either causal or probabilistic—that must be
present to convey a sense of explanation.

Whereas in variance theory, use, testing, and theoretical
modification proceed largely by direct prediction and control of
outcomes, the procedure is more varied in process theory. Much
emphasis is still on the future—that is, process theories can predict
that an outcome will occur some proportion of the time. Similarly,
they may be used to prevent the occurrence of phenomena (for

example, diseases) or to enhance their occurrence (for example, the diffusion of innovations). But the fertility of a process model may also be extremely strong and significant in the direction of reconstruction of the past. The Darwinian theory of natural selection has been incredibly rich in increasing understanding by "predicting" what must be there or must have been there; it continues to inform and assist growth throughout the many branches of biology and in other sciences as well, such as geology. Similarly with the elementary laws of Mendelian genetics; they not only predict and explain proportions of progeny by type but have helped to establish the necessity of genetic linkage, recombination, and so forth. In fact, as will be evidenced in later chapters, there is a tendency to overemphasize prediction of outputs as a means of verifying and exploring what are really process-type theories in social science, probably because of the prevailing variance-theory orientation. Often, that is not what process theories do best, particularly with respect to a given trial. Output checking can be distracting and even misleading. It would be better simply to look into the process itself to see whether it occurs as alleged and, as Lave and March (1975) highlight so successfully, to concentrate on fertility, to look for implications of the model for phenomena other than the outcome.

With this introductory elaboration of process theory as involving the necessary but not sufficient precursor, let us now turn to the resultant characteristics, which stand in marked contrast to the characteristics of variance theory.

A process theory deals with discrete states and events. The predominant flavor of a process model is that of a series of occurrences of events rather than a set of relations among variables. With variance theory, one is permitted to extend the statement "If X, then Y" to cover the case of infinite, continuous variables—"If less-or-more X, then less-or-more Y"—but a similar extension cannot be made with the process-theory statement. As noted earlier, to say that X is necessary for Y is to say that if not-X, then not-Y. The extension of this statement would read "If not-less-or-more-X [that is, if X], then not-less-or-more-Y [that is, then Y]," which, as indicated by the bracketed expressions, ends in a violation of the nonsufficiency requirement. In other words, the merely necessary cannot be transformed into a functional relation between *variables;* it must simply deal with a given precursor (although possibly one that involves many events and processes) and a given outcome. (The term *function* is still being used here in the strict sense of one and only one value of Y for each value of X.) In general, if one desires an explanation for a different state of Y, or for not-Y, one must produce a second process model. It might be quite similar to the first one, but it might be quite different, or it might not exist at all.

Exploring this issue a bit further, it is possible that a process theory about the specific events X and Y also holds for the similar specific events X′ and Y′ and for X″ and Y″ even though the theory still may not be extendable to a functional relation between variables. Each connection, such as that between X′ and Y′, is a special, discrete case, without any implications for other connections. It is not uncommon for a single model to be a linkage between varying initial conditions or inputs (for example, X, X′, X″) and varying outcomes in such a way as to resemble a variance theory but not actually to be a variance theory, to differ in some critical way. In particular, if it is a true process model, one input will be capable of leading to more than one outcome. Consider Mendelian segregation. A necessary condition for a given outcome in terms of offspring genotype—the genotype AA, for example—is the set of initial states that can lead to it, in this case at least one *A* in each parent. Within the same general model, an *a* in each parent is necessary for the offspring outcome aa, and so forth. But putting these together does not yield a variance theory, because the latter would adhere to functional form and this does not. For example, the single initial condition Aa/Aa can yield both AA and aa as outcomes, and Aa as well, depending on the operation of the probabilistic processes. The issue may be in doubt if the initial conditions and outcomes seem to look and act like ordinary variables. It can be important to examine the essence of the theory in such instances to determine which of the two types it is. Knowing the category, knowing whether to rely on functional form or multiple outcomes, can make a large difference in how one states the theory, works with it, applies it, tests it, and develops it further in the light of research.

A process theory states that X is necessary for Y. Does this at least provide, by extension, a process theory of not-Y? Not even that. The original statement cannot be extended in variablelike fashion to the theoretical statement that not-X is necessary for not-Y, because that again, and even more clearly, would imply the unacceptable sufficiency conclusion "If X, then Y." We do not say, for example, that the absence of prior victims, or of mosquitoes, or of the parasite, is necessary in order that A not get malaria. These are not the *only* ways to avoid the disease. The random processes are such that many individuals may remain free of the parasite amid all the dangerous conditions simply because they happen not to get bitten, or at least not by the right mosquito.

Since one cannot have, then, that not-X is necessary for not-Y, what does constitute a good process theory of not-Y? In some instances, where not-Y is a specific Y', it may indeed happen to be the same basic model with different initial conditions supplied, as in the Mendelian segregation case just reviewed. In others, however, what is truly and merely necessary for not-Y or for a given Y' may constitute a new and quite different process model. Innovation theory presents an excellent illustration. The current literature contains several attempts to model the process of innovating within an organization (Eveland, Rogers, and Klepper, 1977; Yin, 1977; Zand and Sorensen, 1975). These will be explored more fully later. The work of Charters and Pellegrin (1972, pp. 5–11), however, presents in process-model form exactly the opposite event—that is, how not-innovation takes place, or the failure of an innovation to become established. Their model is a model of fizzle. What is interesting in the present connection is that their model bears little conceptual resemblance to any of the models of innovation. This provocative treatment, being oriented much more toward the neglect and resistance of a new idea than toward acclimation and reinforcement, uses entirely different imagery and terminology, entirely different events, than do models of the more commonly treated phenomenon, successful innovation. It is not the same theory with different states of the events; it is a different theory.

The true and general way to frame a process theory is to specify the necessary conditions and processes, as in Table 2, and allow for various outcomes, only one of which is Y. Another tempting possibility, however, might be to specify only the successful results of the probabilistic processes, instead of the processes themselves, and posit this whole specific chain of events as being necessary and sufficient for Y. For example, if an *Anopheles* mosquito bites a malaria victim and later bites A, then A gets malaria, and if any event in the chain fails to occur, then he or she does not. An underlying process theory may in this fashion be stated as a degenerate variance theory, degenerate in the sense that a rich precursor has been reduced to one dichotomy in which the result of any possible failure or breakdown along the line is that the whole precursor must be categorized as not-X.

What such a theory calls to mind most is a sausage machine—a program or mechanism whereby one specific event follows another and a given output always results. An *artifactual* (man-made) mechanism of this sort is not a theory because under the axiom for artifacts that there is more than one way to skin a cat, which in this context must be accepted as both true and profound, the mechanism specified is not *necessary* for the outcome. I will elaborate on this subject in a later chapter on possible theories of organizational effectiveness. A *natural* mechanism, however, can be a theory, in the sense of a belief that the specified mechanism constitutes the only way in which Y does naturally occur. Indeed, there are many such theories in the natural sciences, but note that this explanation of the occurrence of Y—that is, a belief that the specified mechanism constitutes the only way—has precisely the form of a process theory. Almost all machinelike theories that I have reviewed have in fact unequivocally been process theories, but stated so as to emphasize the chain of "successful" events rather than the external directional forces and probabilistic processes that are the backbone of the true explanation. To be a true variance theory rather than a degenerate one, the machinelike series must be strictly causal as it exists in nature, which is possible but apparently rare; that is, each dichotomous event must trip the next in domino or billiard-ball fashion, and the end result must be foreordained when the first event occurs. This criterion is a useful one. One asks about a proposed theoretical chain of events: Is the end inevitable once the beginning has occurred? The answer might sometimes lie in an area of doubt involving the proper specification of contextual or boundary conditions. But, in general, an answer of no must lead to the recognition that the process-theory approach to the question is probably appropriate, that one or more nodes of probability interrupt the causal sequence—that in the true chain of events, one must halt periodically for a random draw.

In general, the mechanism as a degenerate variance theory is inferior to its true underlying process theory for two reasons. The first is that it must somewhere, probably at the very end, involve not an inevitability but a tautology; otherwise there could be no guarantee that an outcome would follow on its precursor. One overlooks a probabilistic process, in other words, instead of recognizing and allowing for it. In the malaria example, for instance, we have *defined* malaria for our purpose as being the uniting of parasite and focal individual (recognizing but omitting for convenience the immunological battle that is waged from that point). To say "If an *Anopheles* mosquito bites a malaria victim and subsequently bites A, then A *gets malaria*" is simply to say that if the parasite is transferred from victim to mosquito to A, then it is *transferred to A*. The second reason is that the reduction achieved by evading all the external directional forces and probabilistic processes becomes a bit simple-minded. The theory then necessarily contains no account of how the intervening events occur; they simply do or do not. In short, rather than be content with a mechanism, which may well be a degenerate rather than a true variance theory, it will generally be of value to push beyond it to the process theory that is probably implied. Variance or process, the proposed manner in which the connections in the sequence are made should be stipulated. Otherwise one has merely presented an observation on the manner in which events have occurred or might have occurred, with no basis for belief that they will ever occur in that fashion again.

A process theory deals with a final cause. The concept of efficient cause is essential to the definition of variance theory, its true counterpart in process theory being the probabilistic processes that account for combinations of objects. There is no inherent necessity to pursue Aristotelian terminology further, and in that light the present section is provided largely for the sake of symmetry, yet the perspective in which it places the contrast between variance theory and process theory is important.

To say that X is necessary for Y is to say that Y is sufficient for X: If Y, then X.[3] This by no means implies that Y is a theory of X, but it does suggest that Y may in some sense be taken as a cause. In using this terminology I am asking the reader to set aside the common tendency to equate *cause* with *efficient cause*. Since Y comes after X in time, to say that it is a cause of X is plainly to use that term in an unusual sense.

It is by analogy with or extension of Aristotle's reasoning (1941, pp. 241, 250–251) that one may say that process theory deals with a final cause. Basically, a final cause, to Aristotle and his interpreters, is an end point whose existence connotes the occurrence of certain prior events. Aristotle uses the term essentially, it seems to me, with implied reference to a state that gives the purpose (divine, human, or animal) for which events occur. He places special emphasis on the development of organisms, on the adult form as the final cause of the earlier stages. Clearly, however, the same reasoning can be applied to other natural processes, aside from organic development. Aristotle does not explicitly make this extension, but he appears to strive toward it and to avoid it only with difficulty. That is the sense in which the term *final cause* is used here. Thus, not only is the adult the final cause of the prior developmental process of the organism, but so is malaria the final cause of its precursor, a new species the final cause of its precursor in Darwinian theory, and so forth. All are natural processes consisting of steps that we know must have occurred if we see before us the phenomenon we have been calling the outcome.

In this sense, a process model involves *pull-type* causality: X does not imply Y, but rather, Y implies X.

In process theory, time ordering among the contributory events is generally critical for the outcome. It is not critical in the sense of a universal. It is not true, and does not follow deductively from the

---

[3]Picking up a thread from the previous section, the statement "If Y, then X" cannot be extended to "If more-or-less Y, then more-or-less X" without the unwanted implication that X is sufficient for Y. The reason clearly is that "If more-or-less Y, then more-or-less X" implies that "If not-more-or-less-X [that is, if X], then not-more-or-less-Y [that is, then Y]."

definition of process theory, that in any precursor consisting of two or more events, those events must be ordered in time. However, what comes out of a probabilistic process depends on what goes in, and what goes in almost always depends on what came out of a former one, so that their order must be faithfully rendered within the model.

Recall that in a variance theory the time ordering of two direct causes, X_1 and X_2, is immaterial in the sense that each has an independent effect on Y with the other held constant. In a process theory it is rare for two events to have this kind of independent connection with the outcome. Rather, one tends to pick up where the other left off (for example, after acquiring the parasite, the mosquito then bites person A). In this circumstance, the order of events clearly matters; if the mosquito first bites A and then acquires the parasite, malaria does not occur in A.

As long as the necessary conditions are merely necessary, their role is that of ingredients. Ingredients alone do not convey a sense of explanation (for example, victims, mosquitoes, parasites; so what?). There must also be some instruction for mixing them—a recipe. Recipes generally mandate activities that occur over time and in a prescribed order. They do not necessarily have to; a martini, for example, can be arrived at by adding the vermouth first, then the olive, and then the gin, or indeed by adding all three at once. The same sort of recipe could logically exist in the natural world. Nevertheless, the rarity with which it apparently does exist makes the flow of time a striking and pervasive feature of the process model as a theoretical form.

Moreover, probabilistic processes themselves are part of the precursor; they cannot be omitted without the loss of vital information. Recall that in a variance theory, intervening or conduit variables need not be specified, since the flow of causality from prior variables ensures that the bridge will be crossed, whatever it might be. In a process theory, however, the same is not true. The second event might never occur. Thus, if a probabilistic process intervenes between two events, it is necessary to allow a place for it in time—generally a place in time over which two objects (male and female gametes, malaria victim and parasite) begin within the theory as separated and end as united.

Variance Theory and Process Theory in Action

The foregoing has delineated and described the two categories of theoretical orientation that predominate in organizational behavior. As noted in the introduction to the topic, however, it is not that simple. As ideas in the literature are in fact presented, it is not always easy to know to which category they belong. Even more important, theoretical propositions may sometimes not be recognizable as being in either of the two categories because they are actually somewhere in between. This tendency to blur the distinction, as will be seen repeatedly in later chapters, contributes to the frustration of theory. It becomes an obstacle, a distraction, a derailer of purpose. The following, using examples from innovation theory, illustrates the tendency and suggests that curtailing three practices would help to eliminate it.

Three Caveats on Peaceful Coexistence

1. A process theory may easily be overly encumbered by the intrusion of conditions that are thought to make it or its events more or less likely.

Such conditions represent an intrusion of variance-theory thinking that a process theory cannot easily tolerate. One example may be based on Hagerstrand's (1968) spatial, or geographical, model of the diffusion of technical innovations. Here, the major events in the precursor are the sending and receipt of messages and the level of resistance to adoption. One probabilistic process governs the geographical aiming of a message by a past adopter. Another utilizes a probability grid that governs the successful transmission of messages over space. A third connects the receipt of a message with the lowering of resistance to the innovation.

Consider the following commentary on the work of Hagerstrand: "Hagerstrand appreciates the limitations of his 'neighborhood effect' model and acknowledges that there are 'receptivity factors' which affect the spatial patterns and rate of adoption of innovations. These factors include cost, returns, attitudes, predispositions, and value systems. Although these latter characteristics are not as amenable to simulation techniques as physicial space, they are modifiers of the 'neighborhood effect' and hence must be considered in any multivariate theory of the diffusion process" (Kelly and Kranzberg, 1975, p. 307). A diffusion theory is, of course, *not* a multivariate theory, because it is not a variate theory at all. Hagerstrand's model is a true process theory. The problem encountered is that of error. That is, when the definition of *adoption* given in terms of rearrangements within the model is attained, sometimes a person in the empirical world adopts, but sometimes he or she does not, and the same is true when the definition is not attained. These conditions which bothered Hagerstrand and which are noted by Kelly and Kranzberg, then, bear on the likelihood that people will adopt, which is a variable. They are part of a presumed variance model. Such conditions may be integrated into a process model by specifying that the distribution from which a random draw is made is nonuniform—that is, that some people have a higher probability of, say, receiving a message or reacting favorably to it than others. The spatial probability grid is just such a nonuniform distribution based on one trait, geographical distance from the adopter. One might introduce further conditions by using a joint distribution based on two or more traits—for example, distance and favorableness of attitudes. In the latter case, those nearby with favorable attitudes (if there are any) would have the highest probability of adoption, those far away with unfavorable attitudes the lowest, and so forth. Some models can perhaps tolerate two or three such conditions while still communicating something and remaining manageable; most, however, including the spatial diffusion model, rapidly lose their meaning and their applicability when they lose their simplicity.

A similar example occurs in the work of Brown (1977). He presents a three-step rendering of the *process* of the propagation of innovations: Propagating agencies are established, they contact potential adopters, and the latter adopt. Immediately, however, this is qualified by the notation of several *variables*—strategies of persuasion, types of agencies, and categories of local infrastructure—that influence the likelihood of acceptance by individuals (Brown, 1977, pp. 27–31). These greatly complicate, if not destroy, the implied statement of the process model: When do the three stages occur as specified, and when do they not? Because the events and the variables are unmarriageable, the result is a limbo; there is no process model, and there is no variance theory. There are, to be sure, "factors" that may have heuristic value, but it would be better to be able to use them systematically. Adding the results of this research on innovation behavior to those of all other research, there are simply too many factors to be used well heuristically.

The felt need to add such conditions in the form of variables arises out of dissatisfaction with the universality of a process model or some of its events as they now stand. The model is supposed to convey how something works, but (so it seems) it might not work that way all the time. Therefore, the model needs to be qualified. Some small number of qualifications of certain kinds can sometimes be absorbed, but both conceptual and mechanical limits are reached very quickly. For example, thousands upon thousands of vectors representing combinations of the variables may become possible, such as old, nearby, progressive, rich; old, nearby, conservative, rich; and so on. In general, there will be no objective basis for deciding which vectors to use in simulating a population and in what proportions. The decision must be arbitrary, but the generalizability of the model, or its relation to empirical reality, is determined entirely by such decisions. For the model builder as theorist, the prospect is intolerable. Thus, *process models abhor givens in the form of variables*. The geographic model of diffusion can distinguish among individuals in the model's population in terms of how far away they are from an adopter, but it is destroyed as a spatial model, and hopelessly derailed, by the need to distinguish among them, in addition, by their attitudes, predispositions, and value systems. Evolutionists, it may be observed, almost always talk about fitness in terms of one trait—never the possible combinations of twelve or thirteen.

In both the Hagerstrand and Brown examples, however, as well as in connection with many other suggested process models, conditions of this type appear to be extremely important. The validity or applicability of the model seems to depend on the kinds of conditions that prevail—on the cost of the innovations, the predispositions and value systems of nearby potential adopters, the type of infrastructure, and so on. Such conditions do not seem to admit of being ignored and, once considered, require that the model take specific account of them or be abandoned. Sometimes it might indeed be wise to abandon the process theory and take up the implied variance theory—for example, the more favorable the attitudes, the more likely the adoption, and so on.

It should be noted that we have been speaking indiscriminately of two types of conditions, one that applies to all units or individuals or trials of the theory and one that differentiates one unit from another. If the cost of an innovation is the same to all potential adopters, then "cost" in a theory about the innovation is in the first category. If predispositions differ among potential adopters, then that factor is in the second category. It is the second one that must be assiduously avoided in process models. The point to be made is that the first category is not quite so troublesome and, in conjunction, that any condition can be brought into the first category if one is willing to narrow the scope of the theory so that it applies only under that condition. There are two potential strategies for dealing with such conditions. The first (to which one is tempted to succumb because of the influence of variance-theory thinking, which pushes one to cover all the ground) is to extend one process model to become two or more models. One model, for example, might apply to the diffusion of high-cost innovations and another, differing more or less markedly from the first, to low-cost innovations; or one to a population with X-type values, another for Y-type, and a third for Z-type; or one to propagation under infrastructure-constrained conditions and another under infrastructure-independent conditions; and so forth. Clearly, if there are a great many simultaneous conditions, the investigator faces the need to create too many models. The impossibility of providing an understanding of diffusion or propagation under *all* conditions then suggests the second basic strategy—namely, to stick to one model and *specify carefully the conditions under which it does apply.* This alternative, it seems to me, has the greatest merit for the geographical diffusion model. Not all theories aspire to cover all contingencies. The garbage-can model, for example, does not apply to all organizations but is specified, rather, to apply to organized anarchies—that is, to organizations in which goals are unclear, technologies are uncertain, and participation is fluid. If the specified set of conditions is too limiting, the model may not be very useful. However, it will presumably be of some utility, and in its favor, it is definite and comes with a sense of closure.

2. Stalemate may result from the attempt to use a phenomenon in the sense of final cause and dependent variable simultaneously. The two functions have competing requirements. The same factors cannot usually serve as events leading up to the final cause and as independent variables determining the dependent variable. The attempt to improve efficiency by accomplishing both tasks at once can end by serving neither.

I will illustrate with two examples, the first taken from the intriguing recent work of Eveland, Rogers, and Klepper (1977). These authors deal with a concept that is coming to be known as *reinvention*. When treating this phenomenon as a final cause, the authors begin to elaborate an innovation process model, a model of what might be characterized as the process of amalgamation of a foreign and irritating substance into the procedural structure of an organization. The key events in the process are agenda setting, matching, redefining, structuring, and interconnecting. This is not a full-fledged process model as yet, because even though the events are specified and elaborated verbally to an enlightening extent, the model is still confined essentially to a rehearsal of the events and arrangements, while lacking the external forces and probabilistic processes that make them occur. The process could not yet be simulated, for example, with this model.

A distraction enters into work toward this goal when the authors take up a second strand. They note that reinvention occurs with variance. They view it at times not as a discrete kind of event but as a scaled dimension, such that the innovation that actually results in any given instance may differ (which is what makes it a reinvention) in five or fewer degrees from some core, or basic description, of the idea that was originally up for adoption. They view reinvention as a dependent variable rather than a final cause when they become interested in the *degree* of reinvention and speculate on the determinants of its variance—for example, the degree to which it must find problems in the organization that it can solve and the closeness of the relationship between the propagator and the user (Rogers, 1978).

It is difficult to proceed from this point if one tries to integrate the two strands. The total effort may easily bog down. The events in the process theory (agenda setting and so on) will not make good independent variables at all. Agenda setting is simply done; one does not easily deal with it as coming in scaled values from high to low. But neither will the predictors of variance in reinvention make good events for the process model; the attempt to insert them as conditions would simply be a complicating and unproductive diversion precisely along the lines discouraged under the previous caveat. The only safe way to proceed in circumstances such as these, which occur frequently, is to consider each undertaking as a completely separate enterprise from the other—that is, with no attempt at mutuality.

The kind of tension referred to here arises more obviously and with greater damage in a recent study by Zand and Sorensen (1975). These authors posit a process model of innovation with the following phased events: unfreezing, moving, refreezing, and success of the innovation. To follow the example, let us understand and illustrate these terms. *Unfreezing* means to cease to view one way as the established and immutable way. For example, the way nursing-home patients receive dental care is to be transported on appointment from the home to their private dentist or to the public health clinic. *Moving* means to entertain and perhaps try out one or more new ways. For example, one uses portable dental equipment on loan from the manufacturer and brings private dentists into the home periodically to provide this service. *Refreezing* means to settle on a new way as established and as accepted as a matter of course. For example, a home now operates under contracts with two group dental practices that have purchased the portable equipment. *Success* of the innovation refers to its efficiency and effectiveness for the organization.

Actually, the authors have no direct measures of the occurrence of these events, but rather some scaled variables that indicate the likelihood of their occurrence. This fact leads them into a muddle in which success of the innovation becomes a dependent variable simultaneously with being a final cause. As a partial test of the process model, the authors report correlations among all the variables. This strategy is totally inappropriate. If variance-theory logic applied, one would indeed expect high correlations, but it does not apply. There is clearly no belief in push-type causality here; unfreezing is not viewed as an efficient cause of moving, because moving is still problematic. Nor is moving an efficient cause of refreezing, nor is unfreezing-moving-refreezing an efficient cause of success. The innovation may be a failure. Rather, the true logic is that success, when it occurs, implies the prior occurrence of these other events. To expect a high correlation, in other words, is to deny the logic of the process theory. Conversely, to affirm that logic is to confess to having no basis for expecting particular magnitudes of the correlations. Although not-moving, for example, does indeed imply that there will be no refreezing (because moving would be a necessary condition for refreezing), the occurrence of moving implies nothing definite; refreezing may subsequently occur or not occur. The nursing home could always go back to the former way or perhaps keep experimenting indefinitely. How strong, then, should the correlation be between moving and refreezing? There is no way to tell from the theory. If one abandons correlational logic, what then determines whether refreezing occurs? The answer should be in terms of certain forces and probabilistic processes, but these are as yet unsupplied to the model.

If success of the innovation is to be the dependent variable in a variance theory, then one must develop a model consisting of independent variables that are true efficient causes and drop the idea of staged events such as unfreezing and moving. If it is to be a final cause, then one must measure the events and evaluate the model in some other way than by making variables out of the events and running correlations among them.

3. Process theories and variance theories may surely be mutually informative. In general, however, odd bits and pieces of research results cannot be integrated or interchanged from one theoretical type to the other; the effort produces confusion

and stagnation—the frustration of theory. Sorting the two out and keeping them separate, however, produces clarity and the basis of progress.

Consider the following convenient summary of the research of Coleman, Katz, and Menzel (1957). Material in brackets is added.

> The physicians were divided into two major groups. Doctors who were more profession-oriented (that is, were more in communication with their colleagues) adopted the drug earlier than those who were patient-oriented (that is, more isolated from their colleagues) [*variance theory*]. Adoption of the drug by the profession-oriented physicians followed the logistic or S-shaped curve, since the physicians were themselves propagators, while that of the more isolated or patient-oriented doctors, who were not propagators, was exponential [*process theory*]. Additionally, Coleman and others found that the rate of adoption by the patient-oriented doctors differed between those practicing alone and those in partnerships, with the latter adopting earlier [*variance theory*]. However, both groups of patient-oriented physicians followed the exponential curve, thus lending support to Hagerstrand's assumption that the S-shaped curve implies a stable communications and influence network [*process theory*] [Kelly and Kranzberg, 1975, pp. 324–325].

What theory of innovation is suggested here? How do propagators, professional versus patient orientation, earliness of adoption, and shape of curve fit into a theory of innovation? The answer is that they do not; we are dealing here with two different theoretical issues: (1) a variance theory of earliness of adoption and (2) several process models of diffusion and the conditions under which each applies. However, if one but reads the four factors in the order 1, 3, 2, 4 instead of 1, 2, 3, 4, with a clean break between the two sets, perplexity dissipates and the direction of progress is clarified.

Similarly, consider the following summary of Mansfield's research (1968):

> A number of significant findings emerged from this massive undertaking. First, the length of time a firm waits

before using a new technique tends to be inversely related to its size and the profitability of its investment in the innovation . . . [*variance theory*]. Second, twenty years or more are often required for all the major firms in an industry to adopt an innovation . . . [*process theory*]. Third, the number of firms adopting is positively related to the rate of adoption, which is in keeping with the previously described S-curve of growth prior to the saturation stage [*process theory*]. Finally, "the personality attributes, interest, training, and other characteristics of top and middle management may play a very important role in determining how quickly a firm introduces an innovation" [*variance theory*] [Kelly and Kranzberg, 1975, pp. 316–317].

What theory of innovation is suggested in this case? How do size, profitability, time frame of diffusion, number of firms adopting, rate of adoption, and attributes of management fit into the theory of innovation? They simply do not; two issues are again at stake: (1) the determinants of variance in innovativeness among firms (size, profitability of investment, management characteristics) and (2) parameters and outcomes of the process by which an innovation diffuses throughout a population of firms (rate of progress, total time required, cumulative adoptions, form of the curve). The potpourri represents confusion and stagnation. If the points are taken in the order 1, 4, 2, 3, however, and if a resolute separation is maintained between the two halves, they will not *interfere* with one another, and progress along both lines may be pursued with some chance of success.

In short, borrowing and lending back and forth between variance theory and process theory leads to a situation in which neither is as well served as it truly deserves, although further work along either track by itself, more purely conceived, might well pay handsome dividends.

All this is not to say that process theory is never relevant for variance theory or vice versa. Variance-type predictions, for example, if not variance theory itself, may often be based on process theory and may serve to test it. For example, the natural selection model might allow a prediction that as an environmental characteristic varies from place to place, so will a certain trait of organisms found within those places. The foregoing examples indicate, however, that when results are derived from research in the two different theoretical categories, although they may appear on the surface—quite disarmingly—to relate to the same subject, they in fact do not. They are like the intermingled pieces of two different jigsaw puzzles. When one realizes that one is dealing with a mixed collection, the two types of bits must first be sorted out; then assembly can go forward in earnest.

Application. There is one perspective in which process theory and variance theory function similarly and in which their elements may be intermingled without the danger that more will be lost than gained. That perspective is application: intervening in the world on the basis of theory in order to affect outcomes. From the perspective of the change agent or policy maker, both types of theory in a field where both exist can indicate factors that enhance or depress the probability or level of some occurrence. If there were three or four advanced theories from which to choose, it could well be immaterial to the policy agent how many were variance theories and how many were process models. The agent could pick and choose among them according to how well the situation he or she contemplated in the world seemed to translate itself into the logic and terms of the theory. But even more, the agent could pick and choose one or two elements from each and operate with them simultaneously, just as engineers or physicians need not utilize whole theories in blocks from the basic sciences as they set about solving a particular applied problem. Although each theory must be an integral, inviolate whole as theory, splintering and recombining is eminently possible and desirable in application.

Few research results can be used with confidence, however, if there are no advanced theories at all. Clear and acceptable theory in organizational research, if it is to be attained, will result from the pursuit of process theory and variance theory separately and distinctly.

✳ 3 ✳

Explaining
Motivated Behavior

Motivations are prominent in hypotheses about organizational behavior and no less so in other branches of social science.
This assertion will be clarified in the pages that follow as numerous
examples are reviewed. There is substantial doubt, however, that
the theoretical role that tends to be accorded to motivations can
possibly be a legitimate one. In truth, a weakness is connected with
motivation as an element of theory, one that will be seen to relate
directly to nonconstructive instability due to interaction. Although
motivation is therefore a special case of an issue covered previously,
it is so special as to require an extended discussion of its own. Three
questions will be considered in the present chapter, reflecting the
fact that the issue of motivation as theory lies at the very heart of
social science as it currently exists: (1) Can an explanation of behavior in terms of motivations be a general, truly theoretical explanation? (2) Can motivated behavior be theoretically explained in any

way *except* in terms of motivations? (3) Is anything left of theoretical social science if the first two questions should be answered in the negative?

Unfortunately, it is not possible to report a consensus on the theoretical status of motivations and motivated behavior. There are some fairly sharp differences in view among interested scholars, and there is also a certain amount of candid perplexity. To reach a conclusion, it will be necessary to dip into arguments and findings in the philosophy of science. Nevertheless, the perspective and the priorities of the practitioner of social research will remain the most influential guides in the discussion.

The conclusion on the central issue will be that motivations are on very shaky ground indeed as elements of theory in social research. There is, in fact, an even stronger position—namely, that motives may be excluded peremptorily and categorically because their use as explanatory precursors of behavior is tautological. This view is based primarily on the idea that it is behavior that proves motives, not direct measurements of the motives themselves. I will show in the first section to follow that an argument of that degree of strength and finality is not valid. In the second section, however, I will present another case, which, although somewhat weaker, is almost equally damaging.

Practical Syllogism and Causal Law

The issue of motives as explanations of human behavior is usually approached through treatment of what is called, after Aristotle, the practical syllogism (Brunner, 1977, p. 438), or the purposive explanation (Malcolm, 1969, p. 335). The practical syllogism contains two premises and a conclusion, as in the following paradigm example (after von Wright, 1971, p. 27, and Malcolm, 1969, p. 335):

> Person P desires prestige.
> P believes that adopting a certain innovation is necessary for attainment of the prestige goal.
> P adopts the innovation, or at least tries.

In the present discussion, a motive will be defined as the conjunction of the two premises, so that if P both desires prestige and feels that innovation is required for prestige, one may say that P is motivated to innovate by prestige or that P has a prestige motive for innovation.

Almost all who study the practical syllogism in some detail point out that the relation between the premises and the conclusion (that is, between motivation and behavior) is not in a category such as causal, empirical, lawlike, synthetic, or separately verifiable, but is rather in a category such as logical, analytic, tautological, definitional, or a priori (Brunner, 1977, pp. 438–440; von Wright 1971, pp. 110–118; Lasswell and Kaplan, 1950, pp. 69, 70; Malcolm, 1969, p. 337). If the practical syllogism truly is analytic in character, that fact may have considerable relevance for theoretical social science as well, for it may signify that motives cannot function as causes of behavior in general empirical laws. The difference between the practical syllogism and theory, after all, is in a sense not great, since the practical syllogism uses motives to explain individual behavior, and theories would use motives to explain the behavior of people in general or under certain conditions—for example: Organizations innovate for the sake of either better task performance or prestige (see Downs and Mohr, 1979). The potential threat to theory inherent in the comparison with the practical syllogism is formidable; it appears that an impressive share of the theoretical hypotheses investigated in organizational behavior, and in social science as a whole, do indeed seek to use motives to explain behavior. If motives are illegitimate elements, such hypotheses are disqualified as theory.

Returning to the practical syllogism set out earlier, suppose that one's measurements attribute a prestige motive to P but that P does not innovate. In this situation, Lasswell and Kaplan (1950, p. 69) suggest that because P's behavior is the best guide to his motives, one is inclined to suspect that one has measured inadequately; either P did not feel that innovating would bring him prestige, or some contrary motive was more important, or he did not desire prestige in the first place. At this point, the social scientist interested in the pursuit of valuable research uses the behavior as a point of entry to explore P's motives further, to amplify or clarify them, and, in essence, to produce an amended practical syllogism (Brunner, 1977, pp. 438–439; von Wright, 1971, p. 119; Lasswell and Kaplan, 1950, p. 70). What is learned directly may be of great interest, especially in comparison with the motives of others, but is nontransferable; not only may it not apply to Q, but it may not even apply to P at a different time (Brunner, 1977, p. 442). It is in the sense of this procedure that the practical syllogism is said to be nonfalsifiable, or logically true (although it may still have great value). The motivation has no operational status independent of the behavior; rather, the behavior is always used as a verifier of the measurement of the motive.

That being the case, suppose that one wanted to offer a general, lawlike hypothesis linking the prestige and task-per-formance motives to innovation among organizational decision makers. There would not appear to be any particular reason *besides* the possible logical, or analytical, status of the connection that such an explanation should not be legitimate. In fact, Mill (1969, pp. 26–28), Hempel (1969, pp. 308–313), and Popper (1969, pp. 47–53) have suggested that such explanations are legitimate and can be lawlike in the same way as theoretical explanations in the natural sciences, although these writers are not as specific and thorough about the precise role of motives as one might desire. Can motivational explanations be theoretical and lawlike or not?

Many other philosophers of science who address the issue have argued in depth against any possibility of general, explanatory social theories on the grounds that in not using reasons and motives as the basis, such theories would inevitably fall short of complete and satisfying explanations of purposive behavior (Malcolm, 1969; Peters and Tajfel, 1969; Peters, 1960; Winch, 1969). In the main, these treatments are concerned with demonstrating the invalidity of neurological, mechanical, or purely environmental explanations, as though those were the only kinds that could be lawlike, and they tend to end on this negative note. Few have troubled to deal with the claim of Hempel and others that theoretical explanations do become possible when motives themselves are included as part of the theories (but see Scriven, 1969a, pp. 102–103). This particular aspect of the issue has for some reason not been salient for philosophers of science, yet it is unquestionably salient for researchers in social science, because a proscription on motives in explanatory theory would undermine an incredible amount of work. To take just one illustration for the moment, when Brown (1969, pp. 240, 246), arguing in favor of the possibility of laws in social science, offers what he calls a random list of hypotheses of the appropriate sort, almost all the entries may be seen, with a bit of thought, to involve motivational explanation, either explicitly or implicitly. For example: (1) Magical belief and ritual fortify confidence and reduce anxiety. (2) The higher the cohesiveness of a human group, the higher will be the correlation between popularity rank and perceived leadership rank. (3) Industrial workers strike for higher wages only if (a) they believe that they can maintain themselves during a period of unemployment and (b) they believe that their employers are able to pay higher wages. (4) The strength of the drinking response varies directly with the level of anxiety in society. (5) Labor turnover increases directly with the distance of workers' residence from work and inversely with the level of unemployment. (6) If the price of a good rises, the supply of that good will be increased, other things being equal. (7) A country can improve its deficit on the balance of payments by devaluing its currency.

Thus, some writers have argued against the possibility of laws that govern purposive human behavior on the basis of the proposition that motives are necessary for the proper explanation and understanding of such behavior. Others have suggested, however, and without extensive rebuttal, that the motives themselves may be included in the laws. One rebuttal, however, has been offered on precisely the grounds under discussion here: von Wright (1971, pp. 110–118) argues that the connection between premises and conclusion in the practical syllogism is a logical rather than an empirical one and therefore that motives cannot be proper causes of behavior within the framework of general empirical models. If von Wright is correct, then his extension of reasoning from the individual case, the practical syllogism, to the general case, the causal law, places much potential social theory in jeopardy.

Let us, then, briefly examine this extension. Consider again a theoretical hypothesis connecting innovation with the two motivations of improved task performance and prestige. Suppose that the two motives were found in abundance in a population but that the people who had these motives did not innovate. If von Wright is correct that there is a logical, or analytical, relation between motive and behavior, then the conclusion must be that the measurements have been either inaccurate or incomplete. Although that perspective may at times be useful and may fit handsomely the role of the practical syllogism, it is not in tune with the usual perspectives and practices in the pursuit of general theory. In that tradition, inaccuracy is separated from incompleteness. It is much more to the point to grant the possibility that the measurements of motives may be reasonably accurate as far as they go but that there may be a specification error; the initial hypothesis as a potential causal law may be demonstrably incorrect because of incompleteness. It is possible, for example, that people tend to be safety-conscious, that individuals in this population perceived innovation as threatening to safety, and that this third motive overpowered the other two and led to a low level of innovation. In this perspective, the original hypothesis was like ordinary, legitimate scientific hypotheses. It was falsifiable on the basis of whether the selected motives constituted the complete and correct set of independent variables. Legitimate behavioral theories with motives are possible, in other words, but their validity depends on selecting the right motives.

We will leave this reasoning for the moment but return to it in the next section, for although it saves the motivation-based theory from one perspective, it undermines it seriously from another.

Although it may appear to be a digression, it will be of value to return for a moment to the practical syllogism and ask the obvious question: Is the practical syllogism not empirical rather than logical as well, on the basis of the preceding demonstration? In the precise form in which it has been discussed to this point in the present chapter, almost all scholars who have concerned themselves with the issue would agree that the practical syllogism is indeed empirical rather than logical. If one chooses to accept the measurements as accurate, still, a practical syllogism specifying only one motive, for example, may surely be incomplete. They would add, however, that it will in general be necessary to consider the premises, or motivations, in the context of a more complete personality or set of values or in the absence of countervailing factors (see Lasswell and Kaplan, 1950, p. 69; Malcolm, 1969, pp. 335–336; Winch, 1969, p. 322). In other words, it is part of the essence of the practical syllogism to take account, ultimately, of all the motives, a *summary* of the motives, pertinent to a potential behavior for a given individual. The essential or ultimate syllogism in effect reduces to "If the individual is motivated, all in all, to perform behavior Y, he or she will perform behavior Y." In this form, the practical syllogism would surely appear to be an analytic statement. It is important to reiterate, therefore, that this conclusion in no way detracts from its value. The purpose of the practical syllogism as a research paradigm is not to predict or control behavior but rather to understand it, and the latter would be achieved, for example, by searching further into the individual's goals and expectations if his or her behavior were inconsistent with the motives already revealed (Lasswell and Kaplan, 1950, pp. 69–70; Brunner, 1977, pp. 441–442). Furthermore, as historical method amply demonstrates, there is often more to be gained from extracting and describing the operative motives themselves than from seizing on some subset of them to try to explain a particular behavior.

But it is also important to note that even in this inclusive form the practical syllogism is really not an analytic statement. It may perhaps not be falsifiable, although even that is problematic, but it is not analytic, definitional, or tautological in the sense that the conclusion has the same meaning as the premise. That it is not seems to be evident in the felt need of all who write on this subject to interject a qualifier such as "provided that she is not restrained" or "if he possesses the ability." That is, the motivation and the behavior are indistinguishable provided that the motivated individual is not prevented somehow from behaving in accordance with his or her motives. But the very fact that he or she can be prevented demonstrates that the two are not indistinguishable! Imagine a man tied to a railroad track in the path of a train. He is apparently strongly motivated to stand up and move out of the way, but he does not do so because he cannot. As the train rounds the bend, we cut the rope, and he leaps up and moves quickly aside. We must accept by all reasonable signs and measurements that his motivation to stand up and move aside was exactly the same before and after the rope was cut, yet his behavior at the two times was different. If so, then the motivation and the behavior are not indistinguishable in principle. Moreover, the restraint need not come from external forces, either artificial or natural, but may emanate from within. Imagine an elderly woman who is strongly motivated to scale a wall for food but does nothing because she is thoroughly convinced that the effort would be futile, that she cannot scale a wall. It does not even occur to her to decide that she would rather sit in place than try to climb; she merely sits there because she has been sitting there. Again, the motivation is different from the behavior, and the belief in futility is as strong a restraint in this case as the rope was in the previous one. In short, motivation is not sufficient for behavior. Resources are also necessary. Thus, motivation can exist without the corresponding behavior, and in that case, certainly, the two are in principle distinguishable.

It is not necessary to demonstrate thoroughly here whether summary motivation (the algebraic sum of all motives and motive strengths, positive and negative, bearing on a behavior) and behavior are separately identifiable, although the foregoing discussion indicates that they are. Philosophers have in recent years already proposed that analytic and synthetic statements are not the only kinds, that some concepts in science are bound so tightly together as apparently not to be separately verifiable, as is the problem with motivation, yet their meanings are not mutually dependent. The paper by Putnam (1962) has been of substantial importance (see also the discussion by Hempel, 1969, which deals with the issue directly in the context of the practical syllogism; the discussion of "normic" statements by Scriven, 1969a, pp. 109–113; and the discussion of Ohm's law by Kuhn, 1977, p. 469). Putnam suggests that many of the important principles and laws in science, such as $e = \frac{1}{2}mv^2$, are not empirical statements, since they are not subject to refutation by isolated experiments, but are not definitional or analytic, either. The elements of such laws Putnam calls *law-cluster concepts*, the point being that such concepts (for example, energy, mass) take their meaning not from one relation but from a whole cluster of relations in which they appear. Thus, they do not depend on the other concepts in any given statement for their meaning, and so none of the individual statements in the cluster is analytic. Summary motivation is not now a law-cluster concept, although it may well eventually become one as behavioral science progresses. It is similar to the law-cluster concept in essence, however, in that whereas it is difficult to separate empirically from behavior, it appears to take its identity at least partly from sources other than behavior; it is seen as a phenomenon of mind. The connection between summary motivation and behavior in the practical syllogism, then, is not analytic.

We have already seen that a lawlike causal hypothesis containing a set of *specified* motives, such as prestige, task performance, and safety, is empirical and falsifiable. Shall we now say, in view of the foregoing analysis of the practical syllogism, that even a lawlike hypothesis relating *summary* motivation to behavior is a valid empirical hypothesis in principle? Perhaps—and I will return to this notion when the potential theoretical use of specified rather than summary motivation has been shown to evaporate. For the moment, however, one must give the obvious response—namely, that such a hypothesis, whether legitimate or not, is trivial. It would yield a most uninteresting theory to propose that when people are motivated, all in all, to perform a certain behavior, they do so unless prevented. Even if not analytic, such a "theory" does not seem to be valuable.

To summarize, the practical syllogism may be considered empirical rather than logical in the specified-motivation case, and it is at least not tautological even in the summary-motivation case. Whether empirical, logical, or otherwise, however, it is valuable for certain kinds of research purposes. The generalized or lawlike motivational hypothesis, in contrast, is apparently trivial in the summary-motivation case, even though not analytic. It does, however, appear to be a valid form of empirical proposition in the specified-motivation case, and that is precisely the form in which social scientists have wanted to use it—to explore hypotheses such as the ones listed by Brown (1969) and cited earlier or the illustrative hypothesis that innovation is a function of the motivations for approval and better task performance and of other specified motivational and nonmotivational factors.

Weakness of Motives as Theory

Although the specified-motivation hypothesis may be legitimate in form, it must be presumed in principle to be deficient in content, and for the very reasons that make it falsifiable. Once the summary form is abandoned, one is thrown on the necessity of supplying the specific reasons that people do certain things. The specified-motivation form links specific motives with a given behavior. As such, as a theoretical statement, it makes the extremely strong proposition that the given behavior is motivated identically in all instances and in all people, or in all instances and people of a specified type. Such a proposition is nearly a denial of what must be generally accepted as a fundamental assumption on motivation and behavior, namely:

Any motive may, in principle, be a condition for any behavior.

In principle, we must be prepared to accept that some may innovate for wealth or to isolate themselves or to ensure a place for their mothers at the right hand of God. Under such conditions, how can the link between a given behavior and a limited set of positive and negative motives be offered as a general theory, a natural law?

The phrase *nearly a denial* was used just previously rather than simply *a denial* because the fundamental assumption does not logically preclude the possibility that some behavior does have connected to it only one limited set of motives. Although in principle any motive could be influential, perhaps the empirical fact as indicated by research seems to be that for a given behavior, only one set actually is influential. The possibility must be admitted, but it seems to me that the appearance must be questioned. A motivated behavior of interest is performed or not performed all over the world by people of infinitely variable background in an infinite variety of circumstances. Given the fundamental assumption, it is possible that any uniformity in motivational determinants observed is not law but coincidence, a strong correlation that has emerged in a population owing to particular circumstances and is destined to weaken again before long for other circumstantial reasons. To believe the opposite, one must ask oneself: What could it be about the possibility of performing this particular behavior, as distinct from nearly all others, that would evoke motives A, B, and C alone and would rule out wealth, love, fatigue, revenge, patriotism, and so forth? On what basis may it be decreed that people do not perform behavior Y out of motive X?

On the contrary, a more defensible position would be to begin with the expectation that the generalized determination of a given behavior by motives is indecipherably overburdened with interaction, or complexity, as these terms were elaborated in Chapter One. Motive A may be important for some people, but only under conditions B and C, which may be blunted by the effects of D or E, and so on. In this view, one would assume not only that any motive *can* condition a given behavior but that a very large number of them do, in one instance or another. If there is a conceivable manner or circumstance in which a behavior may be construed as contributing to the attainment of a goal, there is no logical basis for ruling out a priori that someone will perform it toward that end. In thinking about social theory, in other words, the position is vulnerable that admits that all motives *can* influence a particular behavior but rejects, without strong reason, the possibility that they *do*.[1]

[1]This reasoning, for example, greatly weakens Hempel's (1969) claim for covering-law status for certain kinds of explanation of motivated behavior. Briefly, the "law" would say that *rational* people in situation C do X. It is clear from the paper by Dray (1963) on which Hempel's comments are based that situation C includes the motives of the actor. The difficulty comes in specifying situation C so that doing X would indeed follow as a rational universal. To whatever specification is made, unless it quite artificially excludes all motives except those specified and thus renders the "law" a pure triviality, a further motive could be added that would make doing not-X more rational than doing X. Returning to an example in the text, if situation C is defined by the prestige and task-performance motives and X is innovating, a concern for safety could make not innovating, rather than innovating, the rational behavior. To say that this would no longer be situation C is, as noted, to render the original point too trivial to be a productive contribution. The only meaningful application of Hempel's proposed form would be to a situation C for which no additional motives would change the rationality of doing X, but such situations do not, in principle, exist.

Here is perhaps the heart of the matter. A theoretical behavioral hypothesis involving a particular set of motives might be offered, but its claim to validity would be empty unless it were accompanied by reasoning that made the irrelevance of all other motives plausible. It is conceivable, in fact, that valid hypotheses could be offered with the required reasoning based, for example, on strong biological forces. Such a hypothesis would plausibily describe a system of factors or variables that is not affected by the variation in its remaining environment. However, without the reasoning to support such *decomposability* of the system from its environment, as Simon (1969, pp. 99–103) would call it, it seems to me valid to categorize the ordinary motivational hypothesis not as theoretical but rather as simply a belief in the circumstantial empirical association of certain motives with a behavior in a certain population at a certain time. Such a hypothesis is not to be derogated — quite the contrary — but it is different from theory, and one of the recurrent themes of this volume is that matters can only be helped by recognizing it as such.

Before proceeding to consider how motives might appropriately function in research, it is desirable to take a closer look at the distinction between circumstantial associational statements involving motives and theoretical statements. The kind of nontheoretical associational statement considered here is not uncommon, but it is different from many others, such as the association between rainfall in Hartford and the dry-bulb temperature in Sault Ste. Marie. In the latter case, the causal connection between the variables is vague and distant. In the case of motive and behavior, the causal link, if that is what it should be called, is clear and immediate, but one knows that it is not general. The set of motives specified may not be the explanatory precursor of the behavior in other times, places, or populations. Where the explanatory links are vague, as in the rainfall case, it is clear that one has not yet a reasonable claim to theory, but where they are quite clear, as is the case with the motivational precursor, the distinction between theoretical relations and those that are merely associational might possibly be seen as problematic (see the summary treatment in Kaplan, 1964, pp. 93–94). How can one tell the difference between a circumstantial associational hypothesis with causal overtones and a true theoretical hypothesis?

To some who are not in social science, this problem would appear to be exaggerated. One might suggest that the hypothesis be offered, without feeling obligated to decide whether it is theoretical or merely associational, and allow time and further research either to support its theoretical nature or to produce the counter examples that will reveal its associational nature. The distinction between the theoretical and the merely associational, in this light, would not seem to be productive. In social science, however, the counter examples are always abundant to begin with; models are, in fact, presented as tendency statements, and the error terms are usually large. Assuming the model to be a true theory, only non-deterministic in its present form, investigators can and do, I fear, proceed to pursue it indefatigably across data sets, modifying it continually in the light of new contextual circumstances, without ever reaching the unreachable goal of true explanation. Knowing and believing from the beginning that the model is not theoretical but merely associational, while not necessarily obviating the research area entirely, could possibly modify its content and direction and change the customs of many researchers and critics.

As noted earlier, Mill (1969, pp. 26–28) has taken the position that a motive is clearly the cause of a behavior (also see Collingwood, 1940, p. 285) and that associations between the two are in the nature of causal laws having the same standing as laws in the physical sciences. What is particularly noteworthy for the present discussion is that Mill recognizes that such laws are not totally accurate but sees that as no obstacle, since many laws of physics are not totally accurate, either. In other words, the difference between theoretical and associational relations is merely one of convenience or degree. This again appears to undermine the distinction that has been made.

The word *cause* presents something of a distracting problem here. For the present discussion, I shall construe Mill as proposing (but will myself oppose) that motives may be explanatory, theoretical precursors, an interpretation that I believe is faithful to his meaning of *cause*. The issue, it seems to me, is not whether the motive is in some sense responsible for the behavior—all agree that it is—but whether the kind of responsibility is the same as with mass, distance, gravity, and so on. I suggest that there is a distinction and that it is based on the difference between an abstract and general link or a real-world instantiation of it, on one hand, and, on the other, a link that is merely observed and not necessarily *construed* as an instance of one that is abstract and general.[2] The world *cause* is used in both senses, and I will not quarrel with that, but the distinction is an important one that deserves not to be obscured. I will not attempt to resolve the terminological problem, but rather to concentrate on the essence of the issue involved.

I suggest that we must disagree with Mill and agree with Winch (1969, p. 322), who commented in his critique of Mill, "I am not denying that it is sometimes possible to predict decisions; only that their relation to the evidence on which they are based is unlike that characteristic of scientific predictions." The individual motive as cause in the sense of theoretical precursor fails because, unlike laws of classical physics that are inexact, it must be considered to be *intrinsically* momentary and circumstantial. The difference inheres in the acceptance of the fundamental assumption—of the belief that, intrinsically, the relation can *never* be revealed to be a deterministic law. One can never adduce the perfect set of qualifying, contributing, and interacting conditions that will eliminate the error. Given the fundamental assumption, one must accept that changing conditions will undoubtedly change the strength of the individual associational parameters observed (such as regression coefficients), vary the accuracy of forecasts, and in some cases make the relationship disappear altogether. Furthermore, one accepts that a large number of alternative motivations can substitute for the

[2]The observational/theoretical distinction is in deep trouble in the philosophy of science and justifiably so, but I have not meant to make that particular distinction here. I suggest that without in any way bearing on the observational/theoretical issue, a distinction may legitimately be made between theoretical terms, which I have called abstract, and phenomena (specific motives being categorized here as phenomena) that are not construed as instantiating an abstract term involved in a theoretical relation. Nevertheless, if I have not run afoul of an untenable distinction, I have come close, and that is lamentable. It is lamentable that the tenability of classical positivist philosophy of science has been undermined but nothing has taken its place that approaches its utility in the analysis of theory. Until that happens, one must, in the effort to be constructive about one's science, attempt to get along in something like the old manner as best one can without transgressing in the particular ways that have been shown to lead to invalidity.

given motive under *any* conditions. It is as though one could view the relation from the standpoint of the behavior; the latter does not care *what* motivation is present as stimulus, just as long as there is *some* motivation. This is unlike the case of a physical law that holds only under certain conditions (in a vacuum, for example), since there the theoretical precursor is not arbitrary; it is not as though 100 other precursors would do just as well.

In conclusion, a specified motive may be a cause, but only in the individual case and not in the general, theoretical sense, at least not for the vast majority of behaviors. No specific motive, nor even set of motives, is a necessary condition for the performance of a behavior. Impact parameters (such as regression coefficients) relating the motives to the behavior must be expected, in principle, to vary in magnitude from one application or population or time period to the next, and no lawlike statement can be a true law or theory if, even with perfect measurement, its parameters vary without stable explanation from one context to another. The fact that motives are often used as theoretical precursors, even implicitly, has the significance for research that is emphasized in the present treatise—namely, unmanageable instability. Moreover, the fundamental assumption, the essence of the reason that motivation should generally not be used if durable theory is the object, signifies that the source of the instability is again interaction. In ordinary language, generalization is defeated by the high probability that the impact of any motive on behavior is indeed infinitely contextual; it depends on the essentially unique array of other motives and environmental conditions that may bear on the same behavior.

Roles for Motives

Although the argument of the previous two sections undermines the use of specified motives as elements of explanatory theory, I have not meant to suggest that motivation is not a concept of value in social research, even beyond its central position in intensive analysis, where it anchors the practical syllogism[1] (Brunner, 1977). It is possible, for example, that sociobiologists and similarly oriented behavioral scientists, whose numbers appear to be rapidly increasing, will find that certain motives with a genetic base do indeed figure in a specifiable way in determining certain recurrent behaviors. Beyond the potentially important possibilities of that nature, the following roles for motivation, which represent something of a shift in perspective but perhaps not quite so much as turning toward biology, would seem to me to be constructive.

Summary Motivation as Focus. It is overly hasty to dismiss summary motivation with the idea that a theory of behavior in which it figures prominently would be trivial. It is not a foregone conclusion, obviously, that motivation itself leads to behavior. As I have pointed out in connection with innovation as a behavior, for example, the concepts of resources and of barriers, or obstacles, are also critical (Mohr, 1969). Others have conceptualized it differently (for example, Atkinson, 1957), but the idea is common that purposive behavior is determined simultaneously by both motivational and nonmotivational forces. With emphasis on the importance of measuring summary motivation rather than a short list of presumably pertinent specified motives, there should be much to learn from a comparison of the relative importance of the motivational and environmental components in determining different behaviors or different behavior types.

But that rather blunt sort of attack fails, perhaps, to give proper credit to the importance of the motivation/behavior relationship for social and behavioral science. The obviousness of that approach should not necessarily be grounds for disparagement; this is precisely the kind of powerful, near-tautological relationship that can potentially become the cornerstone of grand theory, the unassailable core around which is constructed a network of other relations, laws, and processes. The problem in this light is not so much triviality as it is overcoming the formidable conceptual and operational obstacles that block the path of nontrivial motivational theory. These appear continually in the work of psychologists (for example, Peters, 1960); I have collected a few to give the flavor of the point:

1. The problem of conceptually separating motivated behavior from volitional but nonmotivated behavior, such as habit, unconscious acts, programmed routine, and the apparently unreflective following of internalized authority, including im-

personal authority, such as written signs, rules of behavior, and norms of conduct.

2. The question of the effects of strength of motivation on behavior. The theoretical place of threshold values and of continuous, scaled values. The true meaning of the idea of a balance of positive and negative components.

3. The conceptualization of expectations as a component of motivations. The appropriateness of *would contribute to,* which is a weak rendering of the expectation premise, instead of *is necessary for* in the practical syllogism. The clarity of expectations—the role of fuzzy ones as opposed to clear ones. The location of perception of futility in a motivational theory.

4. The place and function of time in the relation between motivation and behavior; the proper conceptualization of a lag between motivation and behavior in relation to the instantaneous following of behavior upon motivation.

5. The question of fluctuating aspiration levels—the rapid changing of motivation as it follows feedback from the results of ongoing behavior; the conceptual relation of this sort of motivation to the development of motivation before behavior begins (see Simon, 1977, p. 281).

6. The relation between motive and *act meaning* (Kaplan, 1964), or *intention in* (von Wright, 1971). Does motive simply persist into behavior with all its complexity and become act meaning and intention, or are those other concepts something else again?

In short, to say that if a person is motivated, all in all, to innovate, he or she will innovate, is not so much trivial as it is vastly oversimplified. The extent to which substantial inroads can and will be made on questions such as those just listed is not settled, but if tangible conceptual progress can be made and supported by research, the understanding of purposive behavior will probably begin to have a sound theoretical basis, comparable to theory in more developed disciplines. Notice that the kind of theorizing implied in the detailed working out of the relation between summary motivation and behavior does not closely fit the thrust of applications of the practical syllogism, nor does it appear to bear most

directly on the quest for explanations of variance in the world—
why these persons or organizations behave in a certain way whereas
those do not. What is suggested is a conceptualization of how certain things work in the human being and, thus, process theory or
process description. Probability, random draws, may accordingly
play a larger role in motivation/behavior theory than has been expected heretofore.

Ceteris Quietis Models. The preceding has dealt with motivation in its summary form and is pertinent largely to psychology.
Moving to the specified-motivation case, and broadening the
perspective toward the kinds of studies that have already been
common among organization theorists in all the relevant disciplines, I would suggest three additional modes of motivation-based
research.

For theory building, one may recognize a modification in
approach whereby motives cease to be independent variables or
process events and instead are used only one or a few at a time as
constant conditions, assumptions, or givens in connection with
which a theoretical hypothesis not including motives is proposed.
The hypothesis could be of either the variance- or the process-
theory variety. To illustrate the format: "Given the dominance of a
prestige motive (or a material-gain-acquisition motive), then dependent variable Y is determined by the following factors." Or
"Given an anxiety-reduction motive (or a status motive or a
stability motive), then outcome Y is produced by the following
necessary process." I will propose an illustrative model of this type
in Chapter Four in connection with the centralization and decentralization of authority upon cues from the environment.

The change from variable or event to condition or assumption appears, from my own review of the organization-theory literature, to be an important one. The reason is that holding all
motivations constant—one or two in the active state, the rest
inactive—may be holding constant the main factor by far that produces interaction and instability in the social and behavioral
parameters of interest to organization theorists. The different concerns and values that are activated are the major sources of contingency shaping the importance of other factors in determining a
behavior. If one were to view the world, so to speak, as though

prestige were the only motive anyone ever had for adopting an innovation, or as though status were the only motive relevant to authority-decentralizing acts, or as though task effectiveness were the only motivator of supervisory style on the democratic/ autocratic dimension, then one's models could be much more finely honed. Numerous ambiguities, dependencies, and competing behavioral programs and processes evaporate when other motives are assumed out of existence. Obviously, that would be choosing to view a complex world as simple, but that, in a strong sense, is the function of theory.

Such models would be *ceteris quietis* models—other motives inactive. They are unrealistic in the sense that they assume other motives to be nonoperative when in fact that is quite rare. However, to the extent that a certain motive does tend in reality to be a dominant force, the model would provide an explanation for some amount of clearly manifest behavior. Insofar as a variety of motives may be influential simultaneously, the model would provide insight into a part of what is always happening beneath the surface—it would contribute to a more general understanding through the distillation of important contributory elements (see Mayhew, 1974, where the desire for reelection is taken as the precursor of certain behaviors of elected officials, *ceteris quietis*). Utility will be greater the fewer the motives that are of substantial importance to a behavior of interest, but my own research does indicate to me, at least, that certain motives in connection with certain behaviors would indeed be valuable to understand, such as prestige and task performance in connection with innovation, affiliation needs and decision quality in connection with supervisory style, and status and security in relation to the centralization and decentralization of decision authority. No doubt, the problems of the social scientist in *testing* such models would be formidable, but perhaps not more so that similar problems that have been faced successfully in more advanced sciences. It is perhaps more difficult to isolate the operation of some motives from others than to create a vacuum in a bell jar, but the natural scientists have clearly found the isolation of systems to be a great challenge, as well. Ingenuity, lab experiments, and mathematical techniques are available, and for a start, of course, one may simply look for test instances in which there is a strong presumption that one motive is dominant. The payoffs of a *ceteris quietis* approach are great; to the extent that it is feasible, it preserves specified motivation as an element of social theory.

Summary-Motivation Models. Another avenue for theory is only a slight departure from the previous one but a departure that results in a different tone. It is similar in that one simplifies the motivational aspects of the precursor and concentrates on the remainder. Instead of assuming a given motive, such as status or decision quality, one assumes a certain level of motivation in general to perform a particular behavior. Or, in place of assuming, one might actually measure the sign and perhaps the strength of the summary motivation. Instead of thinking in terms of the desire for prestige, for example, as a foundation for theorizing about innovation, one would think in terms of the strength of the desire to innovate in itself, for whatever reasons or motives, and proceed with the nonmotivational aspects from there. The tone is different because the theory would then not have an appeal to one's understanding in terms of the peculiar effects of well-known motives, such as the desire for status or for good decisions. It would simply highlight the nonmotivational circumstances that are essential to the explanation of the subject behaviors. One thinks of the effects of structural factors such as centralization and formalization, for example, in connection with innovation theory (Hage and Aiken, 1967; Zaltman, Duncan, and Holbek, 1973) or of the revenue constraint in connection with municipal budgeting theory (Crecine, 1969). As with *ceteris quietis* models, stability becomes possible in reducing the threat of infinite interaction by homogenizing the motivational component.

Models of Limited Generality. Finally, and briefly, specified motives have a critical role in associational models—models and hypotheses designed for such uses as forecasting, providing an informational base for policy decisions, and contributing to an understanding of current modes of behavior. This is one direct translation of the practical syllogism to a higher level of aggregation. Always, one of the best ways of explaining behavior in a given population at a given time will be with reference to the reasons people seem to have for engaging in it (or not), and much creativity may be required to conceptualize such a model most usefully. As in the case of the practical syllogism, the measured set of values may rarely be considered complete and may even more rarely be considered permanent, but it could be of substantial value nevertheless. Such studies are not in the category "theoretical" as that term is used here, and the results may not have a high degree of durability but research that is self-consciously in this class is underemphasized in social science.

Nonmotivational Theories of Motivated Behavior

To this point I have addressed only one of the three questions that introduced the chapter, the question whether motivations can be theoretical elements, and have given a qualified but worrisome no for the answer. It then becomes important to examine the second question—namely, whether theoretical explanations are possible without motives as elements.

This issue has been treated by several philosophers of social science; Malcolm (1969) and Peters (1960), for example, have presented particularly thorough analyses (see also Winch, 1969). To a great extent, their treatments, which reach negative conclusions (that is, that explanation without motives is impossible), are responses to the position of Hull (1943), who argued for a theory of human behavior based on neurological and other physiological states. However, one might entertain the possibility of environmental or circumstantial causes as well, or explanations based on past experiences and behavior, or on the values of reference groups or authority figures, or on traits (for example, considerateness, punctuality, vanity), or on neuroses, or on instincts, and so forth (see Peters, 1960, pp. 32–33; Krimerman, 1969, pp. 207–213). Is satisfactory explanation of motivated behavior possible on these grounds alone?

It appears to me that Peters, Malcolm, and others who have treated the subject, though providing important insights, have not yet completed the case. They emphasized over and over again that when behaviors are intentional, no explanation other than an intentional one will capture their essence, but they do not say precisely why not. They do not have a demonstration that would rule out all other possible explanations, including the ones that they do not explicitly consider. Yet I believe that they are correct in the central orientation of their claim.

There would appear to be two reasons that intentional behavior, which I take necessarily to connote motivated behavior, cannot be satisfactorily explained without taking account of its motivational aspects. The first is that without the motivations that infuse it with meaning, the behavior itself would probably have a different value on a scale of measurement—even a dichotomous scale—so that explanations that did not take proper account of the motivations would be quite inaccurate. The second is that even in the almost unimaginable event that the behavior would in general be the same with or without the motivations, an explanation that ignored the motivational aspects still would not be acceptable within the science.

To expand on these reasons and to provide what appears to be the missing element in much prior explanation, it is essential to conceptualize and to use as an assumption what intentional behavior would be without the intentions—that is, if it were explained by factors that categorically excluded the motivational component. Only in that way can one see whether one is missing something essential by withholding the motivational component from explanation.

If one were to strip from people, in connection with certain behaviors such as innovating and supervising, all the explicit positive and negative motivations and intentions that might be connected with those behaviors—the reasons people have for doing or avoiding them—then people would be left to perform the behaviors or not as a result of the kinds of nonmotivational or quasi-motivational forces that govern most of the behavior of nonhuman animals: habit, reflex, compulsiveness, instinct, neurosis, force of circumstances, and so on. Animals, after all, particularly birds and higher animals, do innovate, supervise, impose structure, initiate aggression, and so forth with considerable frequency, although it must clearly be seen that we anthropomorphize to some extent as observers, infusing these behaviors with more act meaning (Kaplan, 1964, pp. 32–33) or intentional character than they probably have, simply in giving the behaviors these human social labels. In people, and no doubt to some extent in animals too, specific motivations may then be added to the balance of these forces, thus giving the behavior (or its absence) the special *intentional* character that makes it interesting to us as social scientists and as analytical human beings.

Returning to the reasons that nonmotivational explanations are deficient, one sees first that the recurrent behaviors that one measures on a certain scale—say, an innovation scale—would be different without the explicit motivations. As they occur in the world, they would therefore be incorrectly predicted if one applied in the precursor everything else that was pertinent but excluded this motivational component. The acts themselves are what they are to some extent *because* of the specific motivations involved. There would presumably be much less innovation in the world than there actually is, for example, if prestige and task-performance motives were kept out of the picture, leaving it like the setting for fish. Therefore, models based on fish assumptions would predict, incorrectly, that there would be a good deal of *non*innovation. However, *more* aggression might be predicted than is actually found, and so forth. If the models took absolutely no account of the motivations involved in purposive behavior, they simply would not fit the data.

But that is not all. One might consider for the sake of logical completeness, if nothing else, that the motivations brought to bear on the potential for a recurrent behavior always either canceled each other out or merely reinforced the inclination stemming from other sources. What then? Predictions based on nonmotivational models in this hypothetical case could be accurate, but one must agree with Peters (1960), Malcolm (1969), and others that *explanation* would not. It is not necessarily that the intentional behavior itself could not be explained, as these writers have argued, but that the explanation would not be satisfying, would not be satisfactory within the science, unless it captured the motivational component. To say that people innovate reflexively or out of instinct and neurosis, for example, when in fact they also have many substantive positive and negative motives that cancel each other out, is to provide an explanation that would be regarded as wrong in its incompleteness. It would be considering people only as lower animals when one wants to consider them as people. It does not adequately describe the current problem set of social science to accept as a constraint on explanation that it must be confined to the instinctual, circumstantial, neurotic, habitual, and so forth. The scientific domain, as Shapere would call it (see Shapere, 1977, and Suppe, 1977, pp. 682–704), has at least to the present time very prominently and emphatically included the purposive aspect of purposive behavior. Thus, it is probably vain at present to pursue motivation-independent real-world explanation, not only because it would be inaccurate, which it surely would be, but because when it happened to be right or nearly so, it would not be accepted as enlightening.

I would emphasize, however, that this leaves open a course for the future. Even if the theory were to predict and explain overt behavior incompletely and inaccurately, it might come to be considered enlightening to provide models of certain behaviors *insofar as* these behaviors are determined in general by submotivational programs. This, for example, is one appropriate goal for human sociobiology.

Physiological Explanations. I have argued that a complete explanation of motivated behavior that excludes the motivations is not feasible. Yet this does not necessarily mean that the motives themselves must be included. It is well to consider whether there might be a path to theory through the implicit incorporation of motives rather than their explicit invocation. For example, is a neurophysiological explanation of motivated behavior possible? My own answer, unlike that of Peters (1960) and Malcolm (1969), would be: In principle, yes, although not one that is independent of the motivations. I can easily imagine a causal-chain model, for example, in which motivations of the sort that result from prior experience cause a neurophysiological state, which in turn causes a behavior—in both its physical *and* intentional or meaning-conscious aspects. If one utilized the neurophysiological precursor alone, one would have a nonmotivational model of motivated behavior, but one that entailed in summary form the specific motivations that are implicated, whatever they might be in each case. If the behavior would have been different without those motives and if the physiological equation is correct, then the motives must necessarily be implied. In other terminology, to which we shall return, the physiological-state description is an intervening variable, a factor between the motivations and the behavior.

The problem with such an explanation, as with the explanation of motivated behavior without any reference to motivations whatever, is that it does not tell practicing social scientists what they want to know. The model might be of central interest to the neurologist or the endocrinologist or the philosopher of science but only of incidental interest to the organization theorist. The latter will not be satisfied to have an explanation for the decentralization of authority in terms of nerve X and gland Y, for example, if *motives* are in fact responsible for that physiological state. Even if a motive were *defined* by a physiological state, such as brain cells number 1023 and 964 being in the "on" position, still the social scientist would need to call the state by its motivational name and leave the neurological description to the neurologist. In short, a nonmotivational explanation is possible if it entails the operative motives, although a physiological one that does so is not going to be satisfactory to the social scientist.

Entailing Motives by Means of Other Social Science Concepts. The more important case, it seems to me, because it comes up often in current research, is that in which not physiological but social terminology is used that entails motivations while not being very explicit about them. Consider the hypothesis of Hickson and others (1971) that the variance in influence among organizational subunits is explained in part by their varying control over uncertainties. No motives are named, yet it seems clear that the influence in question would result from the fears that people would have about what might happen—what confusion and inefficiency might result—if the uncertainties were not properly managed. These concerns to avoid a bad situation are motivations. Here, however, it is the motivations (rather than physiological states) that are viewed as the proximate causes of behavior. There is an underlying interaction model in which a perceived organizational circumstance involving control over uncertainties triggers a relationship between a specified motive and a behavior. The fully stated motive is a desire to avoid confusion, along with an expectation that ruffling or crossing those who control uncertainties will bring confusion, and these conditions lead to behavior as influenced by those other persons. In just the same light, consider the hypothesis that environment determines structure (see Chapter Four) or that compatibility enhances innovation. A careful look shows that each depends critically on quite specific proximate motivations, even though none is named—in the first case a desire for organizational effectiveness, with a belief that harmony between environment and structure will achieve it; in the second a fear of disruption, with an expectation that innovations not very compatible with existing activities will lead to disruption.

That being the case, the same factor that defeats specified motives considered explicitly—the fundamental assumption on motivation and behavior—defeats them when they are implied by surrogate terminology. This is not simply a logical exercise but a factual obstacle. Parameters on uncertainty control estimated in various applications of the hypothesis of Hickson and others just noted, for example, will be inherently unstable because other motives—infinite other motives—are involved here and there in the determination of influence besides the motives connected with uncertainty control. They may even be such as to cause uncertainty control to have a zero correlation with influence in certain settings; it would not be at all surprising.

This same reasoning illuminates the relation of Skinner's (1953) highly influential thesis to the present discussion. Skinner argues that it is not only possible but preferable to view prior experiences as predictors and determinants of behavior rather than the intervening mental states, such as motives. The critical distinction to recognize is that Skinner has reference to the individual case, the practical syllogism, not to general theoretical explanation. His view is controversial even at that level (see, for example, Scriven's critique, 1969b). If one grants, nevertheless, that the motives of a person that lead to a behavior may be ignored in favor of the experience that led to the motives, the attempt to *generalize* this insight comes abruptly against the fundamental assumption. If a certain behavior, such as innovation, cannot be stably explained by one particular set of motives, then it defies explanation by one set of prior experiences all the more, since a host of different experiences can lead to the same fears, desires, and so on.

Nor does it help to turn to process theories, in which the precursor is only necessary rather than necessary and sufficient; the foregoing analysis applies to these as well as to variance theories. Some necessary conditions in a process theory of motivated behavior may surely be nonmotivational, as resources might be in an innovation model, for example, but the motivational conditions must also be there. These are subject to the fundamental assumption in process models just as they are in variance models, as also are surrogates that might entail them without naming them explicitly. Because process models are models of rearrangement and motives are not readily conceptualized as objects to be rearranged, there may be a tendency simply to ignore them altogether, as in most diffusion models, but this would in the ordinary case be at the peril of the validity of the theory.

It is immediately clear that this is precisely the source of the difficulty that was experienced in connection with Hagerstrand's (1968) spatial model of the diffusion of innovations. Kelly and Kranzberg pointed out (see "Variance Theory and Process Theory in Action," Chapter Two) that one appeared to need to bring in receptivity factors such as cost, returns, attitudes, predispositions, and value patterns, but these are clearly motivational considerations. Because of this and because of the fundamental assumption, no accurate distribution of the important motivational determinants could ever be supplied to the random processes in such a model. An obvious major difference between a diffusion model of innovations and of communicable diseases, for example, is that the former is a model of a motivated behavior, subject to the fundamental assumption, while the latter is not. This means that diffusion patterns will be different for different innovations in different situations. For some reason, an inordinate amount of attention has been devoted to a few instances in which the cumulative adoption pattern in the diffusion of innovations has followed a sigmoid curve, but nobody truly believes that this is the typical pattern. It is difficult to document (because of what social scientists happen to have chosen to publish about), but the truth of the matter appears to be, at least in part because of the complexity of motivations, that adoption patterns follow every curve known. What is the cumulative adoption curve followed by nuclear power plants? By pince-nez, contact lenses, chemotherapy units in hospitals, do-it-yourself blood pressure devices, soft whisky, 45-rpm record players, democratic republics in the world, programmed instruction, prohibition among counties, the city-manager form of government, or compact cars in the United States? Many different motivational settings are represented here, and therefore many different diffusion processes. If one looks at the universe of diffusion curves, nothing appears to be stable but instability itself. In short, the motivational component cannot simply be ignored for a general theory of this sort.

The garbage-can model, however, is again instructive as a process theory. It is rather successful at what it tries to do, largely because it does not try to do too much. As a model of decision making, it surely covers intentional behavior, but in a special distillation rather than as a theory of complete reality. It is, in fact, a *ceteris quietis* model of the sort mentioned in the previous section, in which one or a few specific motivations are taken as given and all others are assumed not to operate. In this case, however, the motives are not very explicit. Readers familiar with the model know that the absence of the usual sorts of decision-making goals is one of its most striking features. The goals that are implied are ultra simple: Problems want to be solved and choices want to be made. The power of the model lies not in its realistic portrayal of what actually occurs but in its persuasive suggestion that under certain conditions, systems with a tremendous profusion of goals behave much like a system with almost no goals at all.

In sum, nonmotivational theoretical explanations of intentional behavior, at least as social rather than physiological science, fare only as well as those that consider motives explicitly.

Implications for Social Science

The third of the questions posed at the beginning of the chapter was whether it would be a devastating blow to theoretical social science if the first two questions should be answered in the negative. Now that the first two questions have indeed been answered in the negative, not categorically, but in the main, the third requires attention.

There can be no doubt that a great many hypotheses now offered and investigated in organizational behavior, and in social science more broadly, are of the type that, because they use specific motives as explanatory elements, should not be expected to produce theory. Usually, the form is not one in which the motives are explicit, but rather, as elaborated in the previous section, one in which the hypothesis ultimately makes sense only in specific motivational terms. The hypothesis that influence is affected by control over uncertainty was used as one illustration and the prominent idea that organizational structure is determined by such forces as environment and technology as another. Similarly, divisible innovations—ones that can be adopted incrementally—are supposed to diffuse faster than nondivisible ones (Rogers and Shoemaker, 1971, p. 155) but this must depend on the imputed motivation to avoid heavy losses should the innovation not work out and have to be discontinued at an early stage. Such examples are multiplied profusely throughout organizational behavior. Beyond the borders of organizational studies the same is true, as is clear from a close look at the hypotheses mentioned illustratively by Brown and cited under "Practical Syllogism and Causal Law," earlier in this chapter. In short, there can be no doubt that considerable tonnage of social science is touched in a serious way by the problem of the unsuitability of motives to theory.

However, it seems to me that there need be absolutely no fear of running out of productive things to do on this account. Without attempting a logical categorization, since researchers will no doubt repeatedly invent unforeseen examples, one may list a few of the possibilities to bolster the claim.

As noted repeatedly, not all good, rigorous, sophisticated, useful research need be theoretical in the sense used here. Research based on the practical syllogism is one type of case in point. Forecasting research is another. Purely descriptive research or classificatory research can undoubtedly lead to theoretical payoff as well as practical—for example, the continued search for useful classification schemes for environments or for organizations themselves or surveys of empirically determined organizational goals. Normative theory is also important—studies and treatises on what roles within the social system should be occupied by organizations, for example, or studies to determine the proper levels and forms of worker participation in decision making from the democratic-theory perspective or from others.

On the empirical-theory side, the directly conceptual research on the concept of summary motivation outlined earlier represents a large program. *Ceteris quietis* models, which take a few motives as given and ignore the rest, also constitute an area of promise. A good deal of economic theory, after all, is in precisely this category. Then there are summary-motivation models, which assume or measure the motives in general form and focus on other forces, such as environmental constraints and conditions. Further, one should not omit theories that explain the operation of artifactual, as opposed to natural, systems. These may assume that certain motives are attached to the actors in the system or not. Formal organization is itself a class of such systems, as may be the interorganizational network. The object in this category is to elucidate the properties of the system, mathematically or otherwise. The *ceteris paribus* theorems of Simon and his colleagues (see Simon, 1969, pp. 99–103) for hierarchal systems are one kind of example, network theory is another, and comparative analyses of voting or choice systems another. One may also consider explanations of traits and attitudes, insofar as they may possibly be conceptually regularized. Intelligence and morale, for example, are not motivated behaviors and so are not debilitated as objects of inquiry by the fundamental assumption. Motivations themselves may be attractive as dependent variables or process-model outcomes rather than causes (March, 1976) and theoretical explanations sought for their form of occurrence. And lastly, because the fundamental assumption is not a logical necessity, there is always the possibility that certain motivated behaviors will in fact be explainable by a stable model that includes or entails specific motives.

There is, in short, an abundant array of possibilities, depending at bottom only on the inclinations and creativity of researchers. One must only avoid attempts to give or imply—without adequate theoretical justification—specified motives as the stable causes of recurring behaviors. In the history of social science, this was naturally an extremely tempting way to proceed because motivated behaviors cried out so conspicuously for explanation, and motives, being clearly the reasons that people do things in the individual case, offered themselves so obviously as explanatory forces. Instability, however, has closed that potentially quick and easy road. It will not be a devastating blow, it seems to me, but a great relief to accept this, to banish motives from precursors in general theoretical hypotheses, to be relieved of the burden of chasing the uncatchable, and to be free to view the social world more in terms of isolated motives, limited models, under-the-surface mechanisms, evolutionary forces, constrained situations, probabilistic rearrangements, and other concepts that lead in theoretically amenable directions.

✳ 4 ✳

Organizational
Structure

Centralization
and Participation

Having dealt with the obstacles to theory in principle, let us now turn to specific research areas in organizational behavior. It is not within my capacity to cover knowledgeably each of the large number of theoretical areas in which organization theorists have shown an interest. I will instead devote several chapters to selected topics of major long-term theoretical concern in order to illustrate the application of the previous discussion to the practical issues of cumulative theoretical research.

Centralization and Decentralization

In the early days of organization theory, roughly the first sixty years of the present century, the structure of an organization was viewed as an artifact. The early theorists, such as Taylor ([1911], 1967), Fayol (1949), and Weber (1947), saw the importance of structure for effectiveness and efficiency and assumed without the slightest question that whatever structure was needed, people could fashion accordingly. Organizational structure was considered a matter of choice. Throughout the entire period from the First World War to the Second and beyond, management consultants and organizational scholars concentrated on the kinds of charts, rules, and principles that came to be known in various versions as organization and management, public administration, and bureaucratic theory (see the insightful review and critique by Perrow, 1979). When, in the 1930s, the rebellion began that came to be known as human relations theory, there was still not a denial of the idea of structure as an artifact, but rather an advocacy of the creation of a different sort of structure, one in which the needs, knowledge, and opinions of employees might be given greater recognition.

Suddenly in the 1960s a different view arose, one meriting close attention because so many perceptive and influential organizations scholars conceived and emphasized it at about the same time (Woodward, 1965; Perrow, 1967; Burns and Stalker, 1961; Lawrence and Lorsch, 1967; Blau and Schoenherr, 1971). This view maintains that to some important extent, organizational structure is an externally caused phenomenon, an outcome rather than an artifact. Human choice may surely play a role, but one that is almost passive, that consists in bending to the demands of the forces that always put spontaneous pressure on organizational structuring: the organization's technology, environment, and size. From the first tentative adoption of this theoretical view to the present day, there has been a certain amount of difficulty in specifying just which dimensions of technology, environment, and size are important, but there has been widespread agreement with the basic idea, emphasized by Thompson (1967), that the key ingredient is uncertainty: The more these three forces present the organization with difficulty because of continuing uncertainty over the best means of coping with them, the more the organization will compensate by departing from traditional hierarchal or bureaucratic structure toward a looser and more decentralized mode of operation.

Structure in this area of developing theory has been expressed mainly in terms of dimensions of bureaucracy. There has, however, been even more difficulty in conceptualizing bureaucracy for the sake of this theory than technology and environment. With much justification, scholars have turned to the definitions of Max Weber (1947), but the attempt to interpret Weberian bureaucracy for conceptual duty as a dependent variable has run into trouble on at least two significant grounds.

The first problem concerns the levels of the organization on which the theory and the research must focus. The seminal works in this area focused primarily on whole organizations (Woodward, 1965; Burns and Stalker, 1961). A company or agency was conceptualized as falling into one technological category or having one sort of environment, and it therefore had one given type of structure, as well. Early instability in research results, however, suggested that organizations may have many technologies, highly divisible environments, and heterogeneous structures (Hickson, Pugh, and Pheysey, 1969; Mohr, 1971). The point has been reemphasized more recently (Comstock and Scott, 1977; Dewar and Werbel, 1979), but it has been difficult to determine the proper level within the organization on which to focus, the level at which the concepts are homogeneous enough for the theory to be meaningful and valid. Some researchers have used the work group (Mohr, 1971; Comstock and Scott, 1977); others have used departments or whole but small organizations (Dewar and Werbel, 1979; Pennings, 1975). At first glance, those levels seem almost too small to capture the spirit of a theory of organizational structure. Yet, because of the discovery that heterogeneity of structure within a given organization is common, the theory simply may not be valid when applied to greater aggregates. The fundamental theoretical idea does not, after all, concern average uncertainty and average bureaucratization, but a particular occurrence of bureaucratization or decentralization that is an exact response to one source of uncertainty. Whether one is giving up the spirit of the theory or not, and I think not, the proper focus indicated in this perspective is a single manager at any hierarchal level and the subordinates to whom the manager might delegate authority and responsibility. This focus avoids ecological fallacies—inferences based on inappropriate aggregation—and preserves the basic idea.

But even this focus does not avoid all aggregation. A single manager, especially one at a high level, might be concerned with several types of environment and technology and should therefore be expected to structure the flow of authority differently for different tasks or decisions. Following this reasoning, executives, even in quite uncertain environments, are expected to operate on the basis of a centralized authority structure for the most part or in principle and to defer systematically to specialists with more expertise or information only in those specific areas in which it is necessary to do so. One recent study (Wyszewianski, 1980) does use the task level as the unit of analysis for exploring the relation between technology and structure. Thus, recent research has covered the gamut of levels of aggregation from whole, large organizations to individual tasks.

The second problem has to do with a pivotal concept in the definition of bureaucratic structure—centralization. Decentralization of authority is accepted as the key structural result of the need to cope with uncertainty from a given source. Authority is diverted to the points in the organization that are especially equipped to deal with that uncertainty—to Kremlin watchers, for example, or sales forecasters, equipment specialists, lawyers, labor relations experts, electronics engineers, legislative liaison personnel, experienced artisans, and so forth, depending on the type of organization and the source of continuing uncertainty. This decentralization is interpreted as a departure from bureaucratic structure. Somewhat surprisingly, however, empirical research has rather consistently revealed a *negative* correlation between centralization and other important dimensions of bureaucratic structure, such as specialization and formalization. That is, the more bureaucratic the organizational structure is in other ways, the more decentralized it is rather than centralized (Pugh and others, 1968; Child, 1972a; Reimann, 1973; Pennings, 1973).

Child explained this result persuasively in 1972; he showed that Weber did not suggest that all decisions would be made at the top of a bureaucratic structure, but rather that responsibility would be successively delegated outward and each lower official would have his or her own area of authority, subject to the guidance of rules and policy directives from above and subject to appeal in the event of dispute. Decentralized decision making is therefore expected in a bureaucracy. It is a critical component of what Child called the *bureaucratic strategy of control.* An executive would quickly lose control if he or she tried to make all decisions personally. Control is maintained by the delegation of authority, along with clear guidelines for its exercise, to lower officials with clearly defined spheres of operation. In other words, control is maintained by the strategic and rather natural integration of decentralization with rules and a specialized division of labor. (One implication of these findings for research on uncertainty and structure is that the relatively noncommunicative term *structure* should be dropped in favor of *strategy of control,* which is far more meaningful from the standpoint of lucid theorizing.) When the technology is routine and the environment stable, a bureaucratic strategy of control will be implemented, including normal delegation, or decentralization. When there are continuing sources of uncertainty, it is no longer possible to delegate with clear guidelines for decision, and a different strategy of control must be employed—an organic strategy, perhaps (Burns and Stalker, 1961), in which one depends on known and uniform training within professions to ensure that tasks will be carried out in an effective manner, consistent with organizational goals. In truth, not enough attention has been given either to the kind of strategy of control that must emerge under conditions of technological and environmental uncertainty or to whether a nonbureaucratic strategy is always of the same type, even though there are many kinds of uncertainty (but see Galbraith, 1973). Instead—and here the problem comes to a focus—organization researchers have relied on the rough idea that uncertainty will generally result in some sort of decentralized structure. But given the hypothesis of a variance-theoretic relation between uncertainty and structure, this reliance forces one to expect that under more certain or stable conditions—calling for a bureaucratic strategy of control—there must be far less decentralization, whereas it has been known for a long time that that is simply not true.

The way out of this predicament is obvious enough. It is clearly possible to decentralize two kinds of authority. One is *operational authority*—the delegated right to carry out a certain assignment without close supervision but with rather detailed guidelines for action and the possibility of intermittent effective oversight from above, as well as the possibility of effective appeal from the sides and below. The other is de facto ultimate authority, or appeal authority, or what for brevity I will call *true authority.* This latter kind of decentralization occurs to the extent that the hierarchal official cedes or loses the capacity to exercise effective oversight. Political struggles aside, this occurs in the normal course of organizational life when subordinates at any level possess critical skills or manage critical information whose use the executive cannot or at least does not effectively control. In this situation, subordinates will often have some amount of complete autonomy. Even more commonly, governance will proceed in part by joint decision of supervisor and subordinate, teamwork, consensus, democratic process, and so forth.

It is worth remarking in this connection that Weber did not use the terms *centralization* and *decentralization* at all; he spoke only of being "organized in a clearly defined hierarchy of offices" (1947, p. 333). One may now recognize that the term *hierarchy* as used by Weber means the structure in which operational authority is successively delegated, while ultimate, or true, authority is always retained by the delegating official. The hypothesis relating uncertainty to structure, therefore, must not deal with operational authority, since that will generally be decentralized even under routine conditions as the basis of the bureaucratic strategy of control, but with true authority in given areas of task or decision, which would presumably be decentralized as a strategy of control only under conditions of uncertainty resulting from technology, environment, or size.

With these conceptual caveats in mind, let us make a few summary observations on the research carried out to test the hypothesis of a connection between technology, environment, and size, on one hand, and structure, on the other. First, to the best of my knowledge all the research has been variance-theoretic in form. Second, the results, the parameters of relationship between uncertainty and structure, have been seriously unstable across studies and even within studies, and the instability has been widely recognized (see Child and Mansfield, 1972; Mohr, 1971; Pennings, 1975;

Comstock and Scott, 1977; Kimberly, 1976; Dewar and Werbel, 1979). Sometimes the hypothesis is sturdily supported (this was especially true in the seminal studies cited earlier), sometimes the results are ambiguous (Leifer and Huber, 1977, report a relation between environment and structure, for example, but based mainly on quite low levels of a statistic that typically is inflated), sometimes they are mixed (Dewar and Werbel, 1979), and sometimes they appear to reject the hypothesis rather resoundingly (Billings, Klimoski, and Breaugh, 1977; Hickson, Pugh, and Pheysey, 1969; Child and Mansfield, 1972; Mohr, 1971; Pennings, 1975).

Here one has in rather flagrant display the undomesticated sort of instability that characterizes so much research into theories of organizational behavior, as well as other kinds of social behavior. What are the reasons for it in this case? In part, it results from focusing too heavily on independent variables; it is probably true not only that other variables contribute to structure besides technology, environment, and size but also that the two sets interact. In part, as well, it results from inconsistency in focus; operationalizations probably have been hit and miss with respect to the true dependent variable. The outcome conceptually targeted by the theory is true authority over aspects of certain decisions or task areas. Because empirical research typically has not differentiated between operational and true authority, however, some of the many measures used in these studies may possibly have captured the true concept fairly closely, while others have been wide of the mark. But with this outcome in better conceptual focus, it is also clear that incompleteness and operationalization are not the only problems. More serious than these is the high probability that one is addressing an inherently nondurable relationship. There is no set of variables, no matter how large or clever, that will explain with stability the variance in the state of decentralization of true authority across organizations. The phenomenon is thoroughly complex and cannot be made simple.

There is, for example, a certain inertia to structure that maintains it in a temporarily steady state after formative changes in the environment. The changes will eventually have their effect, but the lag times vary and can depend on many factors. There is the matter of executive succession, or simply executive variety, such that some managers are better equipped to deal with particular forms of uncertainty themselves—that is, without decentralizing—than others are. There is the matter of democratic values, which impel the managements of some modern organizations to enforce a certain amount of decentralization even under stable conditions but in no reliable pattern. There is the important question of whether the organization is in a period of growth or decline (Freeman and Hannan, 1975; Kimberly, 1976, p. 580). There are also politics and charisma, which mean that the impact of technology, environment, and size will depend on the kinds of people in positions of hierarchal authority and the kinds of people around them. One cannot help recalling Dalton's classic book in this connection, particularly his comparative organization charts showing significant differences between the distribution of official authority and the distribution of true authority (Dalton, 1959, pp. 20–27).

Above all, it has been pointed out that an executive can cope with uncertainty in many ways, only some of which involve decentralization, and that the strategy selected may depend on pressures coming from elsewhere than technology, environment, and size. Galbraith (1973, pp. 39–44) elaborates a situation in which there are as many as five alternatives in response to one particular augmentation in uncertainty: The executive might use an econometric forecasting model, tighten up organizational slack, create autonomous product-oriented groups, computerize his or her decision process, or use a more frequent and more lateral decision process. Note that two of these alternatives involve increased centralization, two mean decentralization, and one requires no change. Child (1972b) has argued this sort of principle at length, demonstrating persuasively what he calls "the role of strategic choice," and Galbraith's example illustrates it well. In brief, managers make many structural decisions, and they make them for many reasons. Decentralization is not the only way to cope with uncertainty, coping with uncertainty is not the only consideration in regard to effectiveness, and effectiveness is not the only goal of executives. The manager assesses all the forces with which he or she has to deal, either in a stabilized or in an uncertain situation, and makes a strategic choice; there is no single force that determines it.

Child's proposition is a particularization, almost precisely, of what in the previous chapter was called the fundamental assumption on motivation and behavior, and from this one can see that complexity in this area is inevitable. The hypothesis relating uncertainty to strategy of control says, in essence, that the structuring behaviors of centralizing and decentralizing are caused by particular motives—the desire to avoid uncertainty and to enhance organizational effectiveness. But the fundamental assumption, recognizing that centralizing and decentralizing are motivated behaviors, signifies that any number of factors, not some constant subset, may determine when those behaviors are performed and when not. The motives that are activated depend on the person and the situation (this is well demonstrated for one case in Wyszewianski, 1980, pp. 224–260).

It is clear, then, from the empirical research, from the kind of observational experience reported by Child, and from the more deductive sort of analysis based both on Child's 1972 article and on the previous chapters of the present volume, that the ordinary variance-theory approach to the explanation of structure cannot succeed. I would judge, in fact, that a variance theory of organizational structure was not truly the vision at all of those who have been impressed by the structural dependence hypothesis. It is overly enthusiastic to propose that all the variance in the state of decentralization in organizations, or even a substantial portion of it, can be so simply explained. The seminal insights, it seems to me, did not have to do with the causes of variation in the state of organizational structures in the world, but with *what happens* in organizations when there are technological and environmental changes in the direction of long-term uncertainty (and also what *should* happen, but that question will be considered in Chapter Six). The course of past empirical research probably reflects the variance-oriented training of social scientists more than it reflects their ideas of how the world truly operates. What is wanted instead is a process-theoretic approach of the *ceteris quietis* variety—that is, one that assumes, and does not generalize beyond, the operation of specific motives.

It is important to preserve the original insight, not to allow it to be compressed out of existence under the weight of unstable research results. However, there is no escaping the fact that organizational structure truly is a human artifact and, as such, is the result of motivated behaviors. The solution is to express the basic insight of a strong regularity linking uncertainty and strategy of control in such a way as to avoid attributing all structure to technology and environment and to tap into motivational roots, which are powerful and ubiquitous even if not always dominant. I have the sense that this can be done in several quite different ways. I present here the one that has occurred to me, both to illustrate the particular point and also to illustrate working with this theoretical approach in general.

A Status Model of the Centralization of Authority

The model elaborated in the following three sections is a process theory of the manner in which true authority comes to be decentralized and recentralized by those who hold it ex officio. In its present form, it is the verbal outline of a simulation applying to almost any individual manager.[1] By no means does it try to accomplish the same purposes as the uncertainty/structure hypothesis just explored, yet it is relevant to many of the same kinds of issues and is a theoretical realization of the same basic insight. At its core, the model yields decentralization automatically upon the probabilistic encounter of executives with uncertainty.

The Model Itself. The focal unit is an executive—that is, a person in an organization who has official authority within a hierarchy and has the potential for delegating it. The executive is characterized by a state vector of three variables: (1) a primary variable representing the proportion of his or her *true authority* that

---

[1]The simulation is also available from the author as a FORTRAN program to assess the effects over time of different job environments on the authority of different managers.

is decentralized, (2) a variable, *attention strain,* almost always taking a value close to 1.0, which represents the proportion of the executive's total possible attention that is regularly demanded by his or her duties, and (3) a variable, *qualifications,* which represents the extension of the executive's cognitive skills beyond (or short of) the norm for his or her job. This third variable has an important special meaning in connection with status. It means the extent of the cognitive domain, or fields of competence, in which the executive feels he or she can perform or truly supervise work without losing status by appearing inept or performing ineffectively. The three descriptors in the vector have assumed initial values and are updated as output at the end of each successive time period, or iteration of the model.

It is assumed that all of an executive's actions with respect to centralization and decentralization are motivated by status and status alone—that is, by the desire not to lose and even to gain in social standing within the organization. The model is thus in the category referred to in the previous chapter as a *ceteris quietis* theory. The claim is not made that no other motives affect decentralization, but rather that the theory explains what occurs insofar as the behavior is governed by status concerns. Nevertheless, the model would not be a very useful or important one unless the status motive did indeed have considerable prominence in the totality of decentralization behavior and unless it operated quite independently of the other motives that might also be active. Some of the infinite alternative motives that might have some importance for decentralization are money, democratic or authoritarian ideologies, altruism, orderliness, organizational effectiveness, and job performance. The last of these would no doubt have frequent salience— and, indeed, it is not excluded from the theory, since the desire to be perceived as performing well as an executive is intimately related to the desire for status. It is assumed, in other words, that the status motive is causally active in an executive's concern for his or her own effectiveness; one may lose status by being ineffective. (It is assumed for simplicity that one's status will not be increased by an improvement in performance that results from decentralizing true authority to someone else; rather, whatever status increment there is would accrue to the latter person.)

It is given by definition that when an executive does not participate in any one or more aspects of a decision that fall within the scope of his or her official authority, including decisions about what information will be brought to bear, and also lacks either the capacity or the time to review the correctness of those parts of the decision, then authority flows outward. The further, key assumption of the theory is that when authority does leave the executive, status flows outward as well. Thus, since the executive is motivated by status, he or she behaves, within the theory, so as to try to retain full authority.

The necessary conditions for change in decentralization are represented by one or more environmental fields containing demands. One might metaphorically imagine the demands as particles within the fields. To simulate some kinds of organizations, one field may be adequate, but executives in other organizations may exist in two or three highly salient environments, such as a market environment, a technical-economic environment, and a scientific environment (Lawrence and Lorsch, 1967). The term *environment* here is not meant to be restrictive. It relates to the individual executive more than to the organization as a whole and therefore comprises factors within the organization as well as outside, and it includes uncertainty emanating from technology and size as well as from environment in the narrower sense. The environmental fields change after each time period, in the following ways: The number of demands decreases when the latter are absorbed by executives, as will be elaborated in a moment. They may also increase, simulating the rate of organizational growth and the rate of appearance on the scene of new demands. The number of demands assigned to the field may vary, so that the investigator may place some organizations in a crowded environment and others in a relatively empty one, or, to borrow terminology from Emery and Trist (1965), the environments may vary from placid to turbulent.

The demands in the environment are of two basic types, positive and negative. The most numerous are positive—those that would increase the strain on an executive's attention. The negative demands would reduce the strain; that is, they would make the job more easily manageable by making the environment more certain. The demands have three additional descriptors whose individual values are drawn from three probability distributions supplied. The first is the space in the environmental field occupied by the demand, which governs how likely it is to be encountered. The second is cost, the coin of payment being executive time and attention; some sources of uncertainty are more demanding of attention than others. The third dimension is relatedness—that is, relatedness of the demand to the usual skills and duties of the executives on whom it might be imposed.

Without operationalizing them, the model presumes that three forces are at work in the natural world (these are external directional forces, a required functional assumption in any process theory). The first is the status motive itself. This exerts a constant upward pressure on attention strain by causing a tendency in the executive to retain all possible authority. It operates in two ways: (1) It is the criterion that determines what happens when an executive bumps into a demand. (2) Whenever the executive's available attention exceeds a certain threshold for a given number of time periods, the assumed force of the status motive causes the value of the executive's centralization variable to be automatically increased. It causes, in other words, the recentralization of decentralized authority. The second force is the group of factors comprising technology, environment, and size, which are in turn related to general economic conditions, scientific developments, demography, international affairs, and so on. These operate through their assumed influence on the density of demands in the organization's environmental fields over time. The third force is executive learning. This causes the manager's job to become easier through experience and operates in the model by reducing the strain on attention automatically at the end of each time period.

Finally, the operation of the model simply has each executive moving through the relevant environmental field and colliding with demands on occasion, the probability of collision based on the number of demands in the field and their sizes. Collision with a negative demand results in a lowering of the strain on attention— the job becomes easier. Each collision with a positive demand results in one of three possible decentralization outcomes: do nothing, decentralize operational authority only, or decentralize true authority. The actual disposition is based on a comparison of descriptors of the executive with descriptors of the demand encountered, a comparison that yields values indicating (1) whether the executive has enough available attention to manage the demand without decentralizing and (2) whether the executive's cognitive skills are extensive enough to cover a demand as unrelated to the normal, traditional duties as the one encountered. (When the latter question is answered no, the model is representing the common sort of situation in which, for example, a federal executive must deal with economic theory and cost-benefit analysis in order to comply with program planning and budgeting requirements, an electronics engineer must deal with a national union because the company employees have just been organized, the chief of an armed service must deal with a secretary of defense who has brought in a lot of "whiz kids," a farmer must deal with his son, who has formal education in the agronomic techniques that are proving successful in the district, and so on.)

The status-controlled dispositional rules are uncomplicated: If there is enough available attention and the demand is within the executive's cognitive range, the *do nothing* outcome occurs; that is, the executive absorbs the demand by adding it to his or her own duties. If the demand is covered by the executive's skills but there is insufficient attention, the executive delegates operational authority but retains true authority—the standard bureaucratic response. If there is sufficient attention but an insufficient cognitive range, the attention cost is first multiplied by a parameter greater than 1.0, and the comparison is then made again. If there still is adequate attention, the bureaucratic option is selected, signifying that the executive tries to retain status by making up in time and energy what he or she lacks in training and experience. If there is neither the attention nor the cognitive skills, then and only then is true authority decentralized. Bearing in mind that the cognitive range is determined in part by status concern, this decentralizing outcome may be interpreted as depending on a balance of evils: The status loss from appearing inept or from ineffective performance is balanced against the status loss from decentralizing authority.

The probabilistic operation in the theory that directly determines the outcome has executives colliding with demands in the same sense as organisms collide with niches in the first stage of the Darwinian model. In fact, the present encounters may be seen precisely as an extract of the basic Darwinian model, one in which the probabilistic encounters of certain kinds of human beings with certain kinds of environments help determine the Darwinian fortunes of individuals, or what biologists call their "inclusive fitnesses" (Hamilton, 1964). That is, colliding with demands that can affect status is part of life for executive organisms, contributing in various ways, perhaps even significantly, to the success of some genetic lines relative to others.

Observations on the Model. The difference in motivational foundation between the theory just presented and the uncertainty/structure hypothesis is noteworthy. The latter relies on managerial concern for organizational effectiveness as the motivational link between uncertainty and structure (Child, 1972b), whereas the status model relies on concern for status, conscious or otherwise. The underlying proposition of the status model is that the status motive as it impinges on structure is strong and does not interact significantly with other motives; human beings would have to force themselves, with difficulty, or have unusually powerful alternative motives to behave in a manner contrary to the logic of the model. If the theory is valid, then there exists a true regularity in the world with an aspect of organizational structure as outcome, whereas under the effectiveness motive there is no such regularity or at least not one that has made itself clear to students of organizational behavior. That is, the desire-for-effectiveness linkage allows a fundamental ambiguity about what sort of structure must be attendant on particular increases in uncertainty; the problem is that sometimes centralizing or doing nothing would seem to be as effective as decentralizing, or more so. Using the status linkage, however, makes the appropriate outcomes quite straightforward, at least theoretically. With a few simple assumptions, the structural requirements for the maintenance of upward pressure on status are clear. Whether behavioral reality reflects the theory is, of course, yet to be decided.

It is worth taking further brief note of the point, made in passing, that the status model leads to a concrete definition of the decentralization of true authority. The latter occurs when a manager's nominal scope of authority includes the supervision of activities that he or she cannot control by review, because of either lack of expertise or lack of time. Thus, the *legitimate* structure of an organization—that is, the structure as it stands apart from the acquisition of power by political and charismatic means—is not indicated by the organization chart alone but by the organization chart in conjunction with a description of the extent to which important tasks and information are managed at subordinate hierarchal levels and cannot be adequately controlled from above, at least not without a shift of scarce attention that would only result in the relinquishing of true authority elsewhere.

The object of explanation in the status model is circumscribed. First, the theory refers directly only to the two-level managerial unit—to a manager and his or her subordinates—and nothing organizationally more complex. Equally important, the idea of decentralization is made to refer only to specific task or information areas—legal decisions, hiring decisions, titanium technology decisions, and so on—not to an administrative unit as a whole. As a theoretical outcome of interest, a dimension of organizational structure such as the extent of decentralization is made up of discrete subject matter components. To describe and understand it well, one needs information at the level of the components—that is, at the level of the particular decisions being decentralized. This has been recognized operationally in measures such as the Aston group's centralization scale, which documents the locus of decision making in a large number of individual subject areas (Pugh and others, 1968). To try to understand structure in amorphous chunks may be to lose the explanation irretrievably in the artificial melding of components (Hickson, Pugh, and Pheysey, 1969, pp. 394–396).

Centralizing and recentralizing forces impinge on organizations as well as decentralizing ones, and these cannot safely be ignored in theoretical explanations of structure. One facet of the recentralizing tendency, labeled by Hickson and others "the decay of expert power" (1971, p. 224), is particularly important in any consideration of structure as outcome. It means that even some turbulent environments become much more manageable by generalists over time as the executives catch on to the most applicable preoccupations, analyses, and strategies of the experts. When they do catch on, they recentralize—recapture decentralized appeal authority. The structural process is a dynamic one.

Implications of the Theory. The core of the meaning of the theory is that to a powerful extent status drives the distribution of true authority in formal organizations. Moreover, the tendency with respect to any given executive is, for this reason, always toward centralization and always toward strained attention. Many implications of the theory and expectations based on it may be examined in connection with general observational knowledge and information contained in the literature. I believe that this information, although nowhere conclusive, is favorable to the theory.

The particular skills of the executive are seen to have great importance in determining the response to increased uncertainty. The executive who can construe a demand as requiring only the application (or more intense application) of skills that he or she happens to possess in some measure is expected to do so. The executive will be seen to opt for the delegation of operational authority rather than true authority to the greatest possible extent.

This tendency to retain true authority whenever skills permit serves to emphasize the importance of many, if not most, instances of managerial succession. When one manager leaves and another takes his or her place, the current distribution of authority and autonomy is vulnerable to substantial disruption. If the relevant skills of the incoming and outgoing managers are identical, there is no expected change. The subordinates concerned may or may not find this constancy satisfactory. If the skills of the two managers are quite different, however, the succession can have far-reaching, deeply felt, and troublesome implications. Each subordinate may be subject to two kinds of pressure. Some subordinates who have enjoyed a measure of autonomy or influence may find their information or skills to be no longer esoteric; they can be supervised. They may therefore experience a degree of status loss, and they may be moved to fight somehow to preserve what they formerly enjoyed. However, if the new executive is of the same profession or the same experiential background as they, there may perhaps be an offsetting status gain for them in being better understood by and more closely allied with the top person. Other subordinates may in the past have been quite thoroughly understood by the executive and perhaps socially and stylistically close to him or her and may now find themselves outside the inner circle, on one hand, but with esoteric and therefore potentially authoritative skills and information, on the other. These are the general implications of the theory in connection with succession. The individualized implications for such things as affective relations and political behavior after succession will be different, depending on the mix of personnel and nuances of context. One illuminating example occupies almost the whole of Gouldner's classic study, *Patterns of Industrial Bureaucracy* (1954).

The distinction between staff and line as it applies to decentralization must be reconsidered. The traditional view categorizes the authority that resides in staff personnel, or the service arm of the executive, as centralized and that delegated to line personnel, or the production arm, as decentralized. It has always been clear that operational authority may be delegated either outward (staff) or downward (line), but the conception has been that true authority never is delegated to staff; the latter, in the persistent textbook perspective, is simply an extension of the cognitive and sensory organs of the executive. But that view is obviously false; the staff, as much as the line or even more, may perform critical tasks or manage critical information that the executive cannot control. When staff positions are occupied by esoteric experts, such as econometricians or medical advisers, performing in important areas, the unit around the executive may be decentralized rather than centralized, only laterally rather than hierarchally on the organization chart.

This being the case, assume for the moment an organization in which the addition of administrative, or staff, personnel tends to result in decentralization of true authority outward, whereas the addition of production, or line, personnel results only in delegation of operational authority downward. If the organization's volume of activity increased but without changing in character, the model would not predict a disproportionate increase in staff—that is, an increase in the ratio of administrative to production personnel (A/P). The model would probably yield such an augmentation, however, if there were increases in uncertainty from environmental and technological sources.

This is essentially what was found in a variance-theoretic study by Freeman (1973)—that is, zero to negative relationships between the A/P ratio and organizational size but positive relationships between the A/P ratio and environmental and technological uncertainty. Although it is my impression that the model does explain these findings in the manner just suggested, too many questions remain unanswered to adduce Freeman's study as strong support for the present theory. What is suggested at the least is that the status theory of decentralization might help to explain the bewildering and rather paralyzing instability found in studies using staff or administrative ratios as dependent variables (see Freeman, 1973; Kimberly, 1976). Basically, there will be a strong tendency for the A/P ratio to depend, among other things, on the comparative potential of staff and of line for capturing true authority from the executive concerned.

The model suggests that subordinates, particularly subordinates who are themselves managers, will tend to develop their functions in esoteric directions or in volume or preferably in both, in order to increase their own status by forcing decentralization of true authority toward themselves. When applied to democratic organizations such as certain unions, political parties, and voluntary associations, in which true authority supposedly resides in the membership, the same operation of the model dictates the tendency for the paid executives to become what Michels ([1915], 1959) called "oligarchs" and proposes also the general manner in which this is accomplished. Thus, the model is a process-theoretic underpinning for Michels's famous "iron law of oligarchy." Any such organization has a massive demand in its field—the need to hire a full-time executive—to which the membership is likely to have neither the attention nor the skills to respond except by decentralizing true as well as operational authority.

In certain organizations—those in which professionals are supervised by officials outside their fields or in which there has been substantial past decentralization—executives with time on their hands will be a source of tension and trouble. The model portrays them as meddling—attempting to hurry the decay-of-expertise phenomenon by using their time to try to catch on to esoterica and regain lost authority on a decision-by-decision basis. The motive will draw them into the areas of the experts by virtue of their available attention. Organizational growth and operational demands in the field may save the day for the professionals (and perhaps for the organization) within the model; politics and clever devices to keep the executives busy may be additional factors at work in the real world outside the model.

The model predicts that in the category of organizations with little possibility either for the introduction of esoteric skills or for narrowly based control of important information, there will be extreme centralization of true authority at all levels—that is, with respect to each executive.

An important concept in the human relations approach to organizational behavior is the potential existence of participativeness, or democracy, across hierarchal levels—that is, shared authority between supervisor and subordinates (assuming the absence of a Workers' Council mechanism or similar legal requirement for shared authority; see Dachler and Wilpert, 1978). The status theory implies that if there have been no encounters with demands in which the executive has come up short on both skills and attention, all such participativeness is only advisory. The executive may listen, may be persuaded, may opt to please employees as part of an integrated goal strategy, and so forth, but he or she does not decentralize true authority. Unless imposed from outside the superior/subordinate relationship, there is only one sort of democracy across hierarchal levels in formal organizations, that based on the nonoverlapping distribution of required cognitive skills or critical information.

The theory predicts that there will be a movement toward centralization, perhaps radical centralization, following certain accessible advances in information technology. One example bearing out the expectation is cited by Simon (1960, p. 44): radical centralization of diplomatic decision making in the foreign offices of nations following the invention of wireless transmission. This is a rather dramatic instance of encountering a negative demand in the field; most are not so conspicuous or far-reaching. Insofar as computers can accomplish the same feat, they should also bring about a centralization of decision making in organizations, but the outcome there may easily be problematic. Whereas the wireless frequently enabled the secretary of state to command key information rather than zero information, computers primarily enable executives to possess complex rather than simple information, and the status implications of having to deal with complex information can themselves be quite complex.

Last, consider a scale in which cognitive activities or areas are ranked according to their importance times inaccessibility, that is, their perceived importance for organizational effectiveness as weighted by their inaccessibility to nonprofessionals—by the difficulty an intelligent but untrained person would have in figuring out what is being done and why. The model implies that the higher the rating of a specialist's area on this scale, the higher will be his or her rating on ceded authority and consequently on status. What is required for authority is to be both needed and impenetrable. Mathematics, for example, should be a primary source of successful claims to authority, although one must first make it appear that the mathematics is needed. With respect to organization theory, Fayol understood this in 1916, when the first edition of *General and Industrial Management* was published, and elaborated on it with his usual directness and eloquence (Fayol, 1949, pp. 84–89).

The Consonance Hypothesis

The status theory deals exclusively with structure or strategy of control as outcome. The original uncertainty/structure hypothesis, however, slipped easily into other subject matter. The motivational basis on which the validity of that hypothesis rests is clearly effectiveness, or good performance. It is that motive which would cause the managers of an organization to bring its structure into harmony with its technology, environment, and size. Another hypothesis, therefore, that flows through almost all the uncertainty/structure literature previously cited, is the variance-theoretic hypothesis that organizational effectiveness depends on this harmony, or consonance, between structure and the forces that presumably impinge on it. Uncertainty may not *force* one to decentralize, but one had better do so or else pay a serious toll in poor performance. In this second hypothesis effectiveness is the outcome rather than structure.

Because this proposal incorporates so much of the conceptual apparatus of its parent, it labors under many of the same difficulties, particularly the difficulty of being hard pressed to specify just what is consonance between uncertainty and structure and what is dissonance. It also suffers from the kind of interactive incompleteness that frequently plagues models that focus on the independent variable; organizational effectiveness is a highly involved phenomenon that, if it can be explained with stability at all, is unlikely to be explained to any constant degree by one cause. In neglecting the other kinds of forces that may also be important for effectiveness, one neglects important variables and therefore invites instability. Indeed, research results in this area, as in so many others, have been characterized by what appears to be a rather hopeless instability (Mohr, 1971; Pennings, 1975; Dewar and Werbel, 1979). Other difficulties contribute as well, such as a failure to escape the effects of dealing theoretically with motivated behavior.

Let us postpone these issues for the present, however, so that they can be integrated into a broader treatment of the question of a theory of organizational effectiveness in Chapter Six.

Participation

Perhaps the most prominent of the organizational behavior subareas in terms of effort to develop explanatory theory has been the human relations area. The outcomes studied are divisible into three categories: dimensions of organizational well-being and performance, such as organizational effectiveness, innovativeness, growth, acquisition of resources, and worker productivity; characteristics of individual organization members and groups, such as job satisfaction, fulfillment, absenteeism, and cohesiveness; and lastly, the style of human relations itself. In the third category, which represents the smallest amount of research effort, ways of behaving toward human beings in the organization have the role of outcome, whereas in the first two they have the role of precursor. The term *human relations* has referred in research to numerous types of behavior, but few of them have been examined repeatedly in such a way as to represent a possibility of cumulative theoretical development. One that has, however, is participativeness, or democratic tendency as a style of supervising subordinates. I propose to focus here on that dimension, as have most others who have stood back to review theoretical progress in the human relations area (Blumberg, 1968; Lowin, 1968; Stogdill, 1974; Filley, House, and Kerr, 1976; Locke and Schweiger, 1979).

Subordinate participation in decision making may easily be seen as a form of decentralization, and it has, in fact, been used to operationalize decentralization in research on uncertainty and structure (see Pennings, 1975, for example). But it has, for the most part, been operationalized neither as the delegation of operational authority nor as that of true authority. Rather, participativeness and democratic supervision have generally meant only the opportunity for subordinates to have some input into managerial decision making at the level above them (or higher) and to have their views be allowed to count to some degree in the decisions made. This has been true both in experimental manipulations and in measurements by survey questionnaire (see the listings in Locke and Schweiger, 1979). There have been some prominent exceptions in research on the Workers' Council type of mechanism in Yugoslavia, West Germany, and Israel, where the concept presumably means a sharing of final authority, but in most theoretical research by far, the participation referred to has been only consultative, informational, and advisory (Dachler and Wilpert, 1978, pp. 9–20). Even in studies of Workers' Councils, it is clear that de facto ultimate authority is not always shared with the workers (Mulder, 1971). Since the consultative meaning is the one given to participativeness overwhelmingly in actual research settings and measurements, let us accept it for the purpose of theoretical review at the conceptual level, as well. It is difficult to impose true democracy on an ordinary hierarchal organization in any case, and at least some attempts to push too hard in that direction have had unhappy outcomes (Adizes, 1971, pp. 159–164; Malone, 1975, cited by Locke and Schweiger, 1979, pp. 325–326). In truth, it is difficult even to guess theoretically at what kinds of outcomes to expect from the pure democratization of industrial organizations and government agencies, and in spite of the frequent consideration of such terms as *power equalization* (Leavitt, 1965), I conclude that the less extreme operational rendering has been, roughly speaking, the intended conceptual dimension of the theory.

As noted, one of the prominent hypotheses is that participation enhances effectiveness, or the achievement of organizational goals. Like the consonance hypothesis just reviewed, this one would best be explored in the context of a general examination of the possibility of developing a theory of organizational effectiveness, which is the subject of Chapter Six. By this point in the analysis, however, some observations are obvious and need not be reserved. Here is one of the most prominent examples in all of organization theory of an overriding concern for the independent variable. The energy of human relations researchers has gone not so much into explaining effectiveness as into explaining it with human relations variables. All would be well if participative supervision did not interact extensively with other forces in its role as precursor, but it apparently does. Furthermore, to the extent that effectiveness depends on the effort of employees, that effort is in the category of motivated behavior, and the degree and kind of effort exerted is determined by many other motives, in no constant pattern, besides the need to participate or to feel valued. One's prediction would therefore be that the cumulative emergence of a theory of participation and effectiveness would be frustrated by instability in the research results, and indeed the instability has long been recognized and has long troubled investigators of the hypothesis (see the excellent review and analysis by Perrow, 1979, pp. 58–138). There is some reason to believe, moreover, that participation enhances performance only under a variety of rather special conditions that do not occur with great frequency. In the most recent systematic review of empirical research on this question, Locke and Schweiger (1979) report on a large number of individual studies, twenty-seven of which can be categorized as correlational studies or controlled field experiments on participation by adults in true, organizational work situations. Of these twenty-seven, a significant positive relation between participative leadership style and performance was found in only eight (30 percent). In three of the eight a significant positive association was not found in the study group as a whole but only in some particular subset of the group. The effects of participation on effectiveness, then, appear to be highly contextual.

Accepting this and proceeding to the next step, the precise effects of different contexts, one of the salient observations that Locke and Schweiger make on the state of knowledge in this area is that for a number of reasons, the workings of context remain obscure. One still knows very little about when participation will have the desired effects and when it will not. An even more fundamental question, however, is whether one can ever hope to know much more—that is, whether one can hope to develop research along these same lines to the eventual achievement of a true variance theory. Since the answer to this quite fundamental question has considerably more to do with the concept of effectiveness than with the concept of participation, its further exploration is deferred to Chapter Six.

Participation and Satisfaction. The variable that vies with performance in the extent to which it has been studied as an outcome of participative management is satisfaction. Here, I will consider only satisfaction with the supervisor and overall job satisfaction. I will exclude the welter of results on measures whose theoretical relevance to participation is more tenuous or problematic, such as satisfaction with higher managers, with the organization, or with the work itself or behavioral indicators of satisfaction, such as absenteeism and turnover. The question is whether the human relations approach is yielding a theory of job satisfaction, or at least part of a theory. In answer, we will see that persistent instability is to be expected in connection with this outcome just as it is in connection with effectiveness, but the expectation of instability is not as straightforward. The complication was suggested to me by the analysis of data reported in an earlier publication (Mohr, 1977).

Many of the same difficulties would appear to arise here as in the hypotheses treated earlier in the chapter, and in fact these problems do apply, inviting instability in the usual ways. There is, first, the problem of incompleteness resulting from a focus on the independent variable, with the danger that the incompleteness is of the interactive variety. Job satisfaction depends on more than leadership style, and it is a good guess, moreover, that the impact of leadership style on satisfaction will vary unpredictably because of the infinite variety of contexts in which leadership is exercised. It is also true that satisfaction, though not a behavior, is intimately bound to the idea of motivation and subject to the fundamental assumption treated in Chapter Three. (The first definition of *satisfaction* in the *American Heritage Dictionary* [Morris, 1969] is "The fulfillment or gratification of a desire, need, or appetite.") Rather than provide a rigorous and laborious demonstration of the connection between motivation and satisfaction, however, it is perhaps sufficient, after previous arguments, to make the point directly: An infinite number of factors can influence the degree of satisfaction that various people derive from their jobs, and even if some of these are important quite often, they are not likely always to have the same weight—the parameters of relationship are not constant. There is also a serious question here whether process-theory thinking is not once more expressing itself in variance-theory research, a point to which I will return before closing the discussion. For these reasons, then, one should expect the same sort of instability as one sees in research on participation and effectiveness.

But there is also an additional factor—a question of conceptualization and measurement that becomes important. The question is whether participation is conceptualized and measured as perceived by the very employee whose satisfaction is concerned—what Vroom (1960) called "psychological participation"—or as indicated by other observers or records. In thinking of employee performance as an outcome, both these renderings of participation could be important, and they should be expected to be involved in similarly unstable research results. With respect to employee satisfaction as the dependent variable, however, the same is not quite true, because psychological participation may easily introduce a complicating element of *spurious association* (Bachman and Tannenbaum, 1968, p. 240; Arvey and DeWhirst, 1976, p. 105).

The problem is that when one responds to questions about whether one gets to participate a lot in important decisions or whether one is frequently consulted by the boss or has some say in how things are done on the job (and the preponderance of the questions are indeed of this variety), one's responses are not in absolute terms, comparable across individuals, but are relative to one's unique experience and expectations. I found evidence of the differences that may exist between psychological and objective participation in my own research (Mohr, 1977, pp. 931–937) and have also noted what is perhaps even stronger evidence in a study by Vroom and Mann (1960). There, for members of small groups experiencing much interaction and interdependence, the correlation between the supervisor's authoritarianism (on the basis of personality measurement) and his participativeness as perceived by the employees was $r = -.58$ ($p < .05$). The more authoritarian he was, in other words, the less participation he was perceived by the employees to allow. For members of large groups, however, with little interdependence or interaction, the correlation was quite radically different, $r = .36$ ($p < .10$), so that the more authoritarian supervisors were perceived to be *more* participative (the difference between the two correlations was significant at the .01 level). Yet, other evidence indicated that the authoritarian supervisors in the large-group sample allowed about the same degree of participation as those in the small-group sample, and similarly for the more equalitarian supervisors. It only *seemed* different, depending on the subordinates and their context. What this means is that subordinates are likely, instead of reporting the objective fact of participation, to be expressing their *satisfaction* with, or sense of the adequacy of, the degree of participativeness—its conformance to their own private expectations. They are, in other words, expressing part of their job satisfaction itself in the measurement of participation, so that the correlation between the two variables will be inflated by an artifact of measurement. Superimposed on a basically unstable relationship, this spuriousness should give the appearance of greater stability when participation is measured by self-report than when it is not; it should yield stronger positive correlations and more statistically significant results in corroboration of the human relations hypothesis.

An additional test is possible for spuriousness of this type. Scholars have been interested in contextual, or moderating, variables (Lowin, 1968). Many suggest, for example, that the correlation between participation and satisfaction should be strongly positive only for those who desire participation or value it or have a strong need for independence, but it should be weak, nonexistent, or even negative for those in the opposite categories. But this prediction may easily be confounded by spuriousness. To the extent that satisfaction contaminates the measurement of participation, quite different subgroups become critically similar. The correlation between participation and satisfaction should be spurious for all. The coefficients in contrasting subgroups may not be precisely equal, but they should be quite close in magnitude, differing only because the artifact is only partial and the underlying instability suggested by these scholars may to a certain extent shine through.

All this is important because the body of research known to selected investigators can appear to provide stable support for the human relations hypothesis. It has been remarked that although the empirical research is equivocal with regard to many possible favorable outcomes of participation, it is firm at least on satisfaction (Blumberg, 1968, p. 123). In fact, it is not.

Let us approach the question whether there is a firm theoretical contribution regarding participation and satisfaction from the perspective of the complication injected by the possibility of spuriousness in the results. One would expect, first of all, that studies in which participation and satisfaction were measured by the report of the same subordinates would quite consistently show a positive relationship of at least moderate magnitude, statistically significant at least in samples above forty or so in size. The observed relationship should almost never be zero or negative.

Table 3 presents a summary of all the qualifying studies in what I have endeavored to make an exhaustive search.[2] In themselves, the results do not bear out an expectation of instability. The studies reveal remarkably consistent moderate associations between participation and satisfaction, clustering around the .35 level of Pearsonian correlation. Only three of the twenty-four relationships reported failed to attain statistical significance, and none was negative. Two of the nonsignificant results were variants of significant results in the same study and do not damage the pattern of stability.

There are, however, two possible interpretations of this degree of stability—that it reflects a truly stable underlying rela-

---

[2] Many studies that seemed to fit the analysis (including some of the best-known and most interesting ones) had to be eliminated on the basis of inconsistency of focus. It is important in a test of the stability of a certain relationship not to confuse and undermine the analysis by including results that cannot fairly confidently be considered to be on the same topic. The three factors that mandated exclusion of apparently similar research, in order of their frequency of application, were the following: (1) the variables used in the research were conceptually or operationally too distant either from participation or from satisfaction with job or supervisor, (2) participation was confounded with other human relations changes purposely made in the organization at the same time (this necessitated the elimination of several well-known field experiments), and (3) the subjects studied were not actual workers in organizations, responding to their own work situations (this excluded studies of laboratory work groups and other simulations). Some work that should have been included might have been overlooked in our search of past bibliographies and computer indexes, although the omissions would have to be numerous and consistent to dissolve the theoretical quandary illustrated by the examples in the text.

Table 3. Correlations between Psychological Participation
and Satisfaction with Job and with Supervisor

Source	Job	Supervisor
Vroom (1960)	$r = .36$**	
Smith and Tannenbaum (1968)	$r = .55$**	
Bowers (1968)	$r = .23$‡	
Hornstein and others (1968)		$r = .27$**
Tosi (1970)	$r = .44$**	
Ritchie and Miles (1970)		$F = 8.98$**
Patchen (1970)[a]	$r = .22$**	
	$r = .24$‡	
Obradovic, French, and Rodgers (1970)	$r = .172$**	
Lischeron and Wall (1974)	$r = .23$**	$r = .35$**
Falcione (1974)[b]		$r = .25$***
		$r = .32$***
		$r = .21$**
		$r = .14$‡
Mitchell, Smyser, and Weed (1975)	$F = 172.87$***	$F = 79.77$***
Arvey and DeWhirst (1976)	$F = 19.1$*	
Abdel-Halim and Rowland (1976)	$r = .32$**	$r = .54$**
Schuler (1976)	$F = 45.17$***	
Mohr[c]	$r = .52$***	$r = .70$***

[a]The first correlation is at the individual level ($N = 800$), and the second is at the group level ($N = 90$).

[b]The correlations are with four separate questionnaire items on participation. No correlation with a combined index is reported.

[c]Data not previously reported. The study is the same as that reported in Mohr (1971, 1977). The details of method and sample as well as the measurement of participation are presented there. The measures of satisfaction with job and supervisor were simple one-item indicators: "All in all, I am well satisfied with my present job," and "Our work group is not really satisfied with the way our supervisor is doing his job" (scoring reversed in the second item).

‡Not significant at the .05 level.
*$p < .05$.
**$p < .01$.
***$p < .001$.

tionship and that it derives from a measurement artifact and the spurious association that therefore results. If the first is valid, the results of these studies should be corroborated by research in which the measurement of participation is not by report of the subordinates concerned. If the second is valid, however, and these moderate positive associations are caused largely by spuriousness, then the associations should in general be weaker and perhaps sometimes even negative under more objective measurement of participation, and many of the positive associations that do then appear should be either nonsignificant or barely significant.

The evidence is summarized in Table 4, where the statistics that are reported qualify for inclusion because they derive from an objective measurement of participation. In some cases the degree of participation was determined by experimental manipulation, whereas in others it occurred naturally but was measured by some means other than report of the very subordinates whose satisfaction was surveyed. The table counts for each study all the groups and also the subgroups for which separate measures of the relationship in question were reported. There is therefore perhaps a bit of redundancy here,[3] but the proper way to investigate stability and instability is to seek out populations that differ in some ways[4] and observe then whether the results of concern are changeable across the various groups.

The last line of the table summarizes the evidence. Clearly, the picture presented is different from that depicted in Table 3. Of twenty-four relationships between participation and satisfaction found in twenty groups and subgroups, eight were positive but not statistically significant, eight were positive and significant, and eight were negative. The kinds of conclusions that must emerge

---

[3]In the studies by Obradovic, French, and Rodgers (1970), Berkowitz (1953), and Runyon (1973), the three groups indicated in the table are not three different sets of people but one parent group and two subgroups.

[4]They should not, however, be distinguished by virtue of their homogeneous scores on participation (as were some additional subgroups in the Berkowitz study) or satisfaction (as were subgroups purposely aggregated in the study by French, Israel, and Ås). In the former case the within-group variance would then be too constrained, and in the latter case too artificial, to provide meaningful correlations.

Table 4. Relationships Between Objective Participation and Satisfaction in Groups and Subgroups

Source	Number of Groups and Subgroups	Number of These That Are Subgroups	Number in Which Dependent Variable Is Satisfaction with			Number of Relationships That Are		
			Job	Supervisor	Job or supervisor	Positive, significant	Positive, not significant	Negative
Berkowitz (1953)	3	2	3		3			3
Morse and Reimer (1956)	1		1	1	2	1	1	
Baumgartel (1956)	1			1	1	1		
French, Israel, and Ås (1960)	1		1		1		1	
Obradovic (1970)	3	3	3		3	2	1	
Obradovic, French, and Rodgers (1970)	3	2	3		3	2	1	
Powell and Schlacter (1971)	1		1		1		1	
Runyon (1973)	3	2		3	3	2		
Lischeron and Wall (1975)	1		1	1	2		2	1
Latham and Yukl (1976)	1		1		1		1	
Ivancevich (1976)	1		1	1	2			2
Ivancevich (1977)	1		1	1	2			2
Summary	20	9	16	8	24	8	8	8

from this second survey are that satisfaction with job and supervisor are, on the whole, not related in an important way to participation but that there is variation such that sometimes there is a noteworthy correlation, sometimes not, and under some circumstances participation seems to produce quite the wrong effect. Taking Tables 3 and 4 together, it would appear that one must further conclude, at least tentatively, that the same unstable reality underlies the subjective studies as well. There, however, it is masked by a misleading measurement of participation, in which that variable veers toward the reflection of satisfaction itself and therefore results in partly spurious relationships.

This latter conclusion is susceptible of further test from the substantial array of existing research. To the extent that significant positive results are obtained because of spuriousness, subdividing the subjects in a given *subjective* study should, as noted earlier, yield quite similar correlations in the subgroups. Even though the subgroups differ from one another on an important dimension, still, there should be no significant interaction (difference in correlations). Approximately the same biasing effect of the subjective measurement should become manifest in each. The results cannot so conveniently be placed in a table but are summarized verbally as follows.[5]

Vroom and Mann (1960) studied both small groups with much interdependence and interpersonal interaction and large groups with little interdependence or interaction. The magnitude of the Pearsonian correlation between participation and job satisfaction was .54 for the former and .31 for the latter, a difference that is in the direction expected by Vroom and Mann but is not statistically significant.

Ritchie and Miles (1970) hypothesized that the main effect of participation on satisfaction with supervisor would be mediated by the supervisor's confidence in the subordinates. After subgrouping

[5] Two of the studies—Vroom and Mann (1960) and White and Ruh (1973)—were not reviewed in Table 3 only because they report subgroup correlations alone and none for the group as a whole. At this point, however, they may be seen as adding further support to the general message of that table.

on the basis of that variable, however, the test for interaction was nonsignificant (in fact, the reported F ratio was zero).

The study by White and Ruh (1973) was a well-planned, intensive effort to bear out the hypothesis that instability in former results has been due at least in part to the study of heterogeneous samples—samples that varied in the average desire of their members to participate. High correlations between participation and satisfaction should come from samples whose members want to participate; low correlations should come from samples whose members do not much care. However, the correlation between participation and job involvement (a scale that took in much of what others have measured as job satisfaction) for all managerial-level employees surveyed in the White and Ruh study was .53, while for workers it was .44, a difference that is not significant. The managers were further subdivided into groups high, medium, and low on desire to participate (as well as a number of other values), and the correlations for the high and low groups were .55 and .51, respectively—nearly identical. For workers, the comparable correlations were .44 and .42. Neither of the differences between the highs and lows was significant.[6] White and Ruh were clearly perplexed by their data, for it hardly seems possible that so reasonable a hypothesis would fail to be supported in so carefully designed a study. The results, however, do match quite exactly the predictions based on the spuriousness hypothesis, both in the size of the correlations and in the failure to find significant differences between subgroups.

In the study by Mitchell, Smyser, and Weed (1975), the important psychological scale of internal versus external control (the belief that one controls one's own fate rather than being controlled by outside forces) was investigated as a mediator of the relationship between participation and satisfaction with the supervisor. The interaction term was significant, contrary to the prediction from the

[6]White and Ruh divided both workers and managers into subgroups on the basis of nine other job-relevant values besides the value placed on participation. The results were the same on all these. I have mentioned only the one value in the text in order not to saturate the argument with data from one study, some of which could be redundant by virtue of correlation among the values.

spuriousness hypothesis. It was just barely significant at the .05 level, however, the F statistic being 3.87, compared with 79.77 ($p <$ .001) for the main, whole-group effect of participation on satisfaction. A fuller interpretation of the result is obtained by comparing it with a similar test in the study by Runyon (1973). The research of Mitchell, Smyser, and Weed replicates the earlier study by Runyon except that in the earlier study, being concerned about the very sort of spuriousness now under discussion, Runyon measured participation by the report of *other* subordinates than those whose satisfaction was measured. Mitchell and his coauthors, in contrast, used the same subordinates for both measures. There should therefore be a greater difference between subgroup correlations in the former study than in the latter. In Runyon's study, the interaction term for participation and internal/external control that reflects this difference was indeed highly significant ($p < .001$) and much stronger than the main effect of participation ($p < .01$). Furthermore, the relationship between participation and satisfaction was positive and significant for the internal-control group and *negative* and significant for the external-control group. With the more subjective measurement in the research by Mitchell, Smyser, and Weed, one must suspect that spuriousness altered the results. There, the relationship in both subgroups was positive and the magnitudes were quite close, although the difference did achieve statistical significance.

Arvey and DeWhirst (1976) explored whether the relationship between participation and job satisfaction might not be mediated by dimensions of the personalities of subordinates. They covered three dimensions—need for achievement, need for affiliation, and need for autonomy—but found none of the three interaction terms to be significant.

Obradovic, French, and Rodgers (1970) divided their sample into those high and low on desire to participate. One may judge from their wording that the difference in correlation of participation with job satisfaction between the two groups was not significant, although they do not report it explicitly. It is of interest here that in the same study, participation was also measured objectively. Again, the authors do not report a statistical test of the difference in the focal relationship when taken on the high-desire and low-desire subgroups, but given the values of the t statistics reported for

this analysis and others in the study, the difference is clearly significant. It happened also to be the wrong way around, so that participation was more strongly related to satisfaction among workers
with a *low* desire to participate than among those whose reported
desire was high. In any case, the difference in subgroup correlations was obscured when the measurement of participation was
subjective.

In 1960, Vroom divided his study population into subgroups
on the subordinates' authoritarianism, their need for independence, and a combination of the two. The results are quite important here, since they appeared to provide strong evidence for
statistical interaction. The difference in correlations between participation and job satisfaction for those high and low on need for
independence ($r = .55$ and $r = .13$, respectively)—leaving out a
middle third who were moderate on that need—was significant at
the .02 level. A similar difference subsetting on authoritarianism
($r = .53, r = .03$) was significant at the .01 level, and the difference
between the high and low fourths of the sample on a combination
of the two personality dimensions ($r = .73, r = .04$) was also significant at the .01 level. Those results are directly contrary to the
spuriousness hypothesis. However, Vroom's design has now been
closely replicated on four occasions with opposite results. The subgroup relationships in the replicating research are generally close
in magnitude, and the differences are never statistically significant.
This rather relentless failure to corroborate Vroom's findings is
consistent with the spuriousness explanation for moderate and
consistent correlations between participation and satisfaction, but
Vroom's original results remain unexplained. The four studies are
the following.

In Tosi's research (1970), the correlations for the subgroups
divided in the same way as above on need for independence were
$r = .46$ and $r = .39$; for authoritarianism, $r = .43, r = .45$; and for the
combination, $r = .47, r = .50$. None of these differences is statistically significant.

Abdel-Halim and Rowland (1976) used slightly different
measures and added satisfaction with supervisor as a new dependent variable. For job satisfaction, the subgroup correlations comparable to the foregoing were as follows: need for independence,

$r = .27$, $r = .47$; authoritarianism, $r = .45$, $r = .53$; and for the combination, $r = .05$, $r = .41$. Using satisfaction with supervisor as the dependent variable: on need for independence, $r = .53$, $r = .24$; on authoritarianism, $r = .41$, $r = .58$; and on the combination, $r = .65$, $r = .57$. None of the differences is significant although some are fairly large.

Schuler (1976) attempted to explain the discrepancy between the results of Vroom and Tosi. Statistically, he used the analysis of variance, so that he was looking for significant interaction terms rather than differences in correlations. Schuler dispensed with the need for independence as a mediating variable, but he added perceived repetitiveness of the job, which he hoped would go far toward explaining the prior instability. The results as reported are too involved for detailed critique here, although I will present the highlights. In sum, they are quite what one would expect on the basis of the spuriousness hypothesis. It must first be recognized that the perceived-repetitiveness variable is subject to precisely the same sort of measurement artifact and spurious outcome as perceived participation; one must suspect that the subordinates' subjective responses reflect their satisfaction with the degree of repetitiveness of the job rather than the degree of repetitiveness itself. One must therefore have four expectations regarding outcomes. First, both participation and repetitiveness are expected to be significantly related to job satisfaction, as in the other studies in Table 3. This expectation is borne out by the data, the respective statistics being $F = 45.17$ ($p < .001$) and $F = 48.10$ ($p < .001$). Second, authoritarianism should *not* interact either with participation or with repetitiveness, supporting Tosi (and Abdel-Halim and Rowland) rather than Vroom. This expectation is also borne out, the respective statistics being $F = 0.44$ ($p < .51$) and $F = 0.50$ ($p < .48$). Third, there may well be (although there need not be) a significant interaction between participation and repetitiveness, because the *mixed* subcategories defeat the normal effect of the spuriousness. That is, subordinates cannot express the same level of satisfaction on both the cause and effect sides of the equation if they are expressing two different levels on the causal side alone—for example, if they perceive the job to be at the same time both too repetitive and gratifyingly participative, or vice versa, as a great many did. There was indeed a small interaction: $F = 3.82$ ($p < .05$). Fourth, for those subordinates who report a *consistent* experience with respect to repetitiveness and participativeness, the spuriousness should be able to reassert itself, and there should then be no interaction between the two. One would eliminate the above-mentioned mixed categories for this analysis, in other words, leaving only those subordinates reporting either repetitiveness and nonparticipation or participation and nonrepetitiveness. Schuler did not report this analysis, but calculating from the cell means, it appears quite clear that the interaction disappears.[7]

Lastly, in my own study referred to in Table 3, I also measured authoritarianism, using almost the same questionnaire items as were used in the other studies just reviewed (Mohr, 1977, p. 942). Subsetting in the same fashion as did Vroom and the others, the correlations between participation and job satisfaction are as follows: low authoritarianism, $r = .63$, high authoritarianism, $r = .51$. For satisfaction with supervisor: $r = .73$, $r = .69$. Neither of the differences is significant. I also measured directly the subordinate's desire to be involved in supervisory decision making.[8] For job satisfaction, the correlation with participation in the high-desire group was .67 and in the low-desire group .43. For satisfaction with supervisor, the comparable statistics were $r = .74$, $r = .70$. Again, neither difference was significant.

In sum, the foregoing paragraphs have considered twenty-seven instances in which a dimension was explored, such as the desire to participate, that might cause the relationship between satisfaction and participation to fluctuate. These comprise the totality of instances in the literature that meet the qualifications for

---

[7]Schuler also reports a *three*-way interaction (authoritarianism, repetitiveness, and participation). There is no need to discuss it at length, because it again involves the mixed categories that defeat the spuriousness and thereby remove our simple basis for predicting whether an interaction should be found. Furthermore, to understand its true message from the standpoint either of Schuler's hypotheses or of my own, one must go beyond the analysis of variance to look at comparisons of within-group relationships.

[8]The item was "I have my own job to do; I would just as soon the supervisor did not try to involve me in making decisions." The same five-category response scale was used here as for authoritarianism.

inclusion in the analysis, to the best of my knowledge. In twenty-three of these twenty-seven instances, the dimension did not produce a statistically significant difference in relationship from one subgroup to the other, although in a few cases the magnitude of the difference was fairly large. Three of the four exceptions were in the study by Vroom, which appears to have been a low-frequency anomaly. The fourth, which used the dimension of internal/external control, was in fact not sharply different from some of the rest, since significance was narrowly achieved at the .05 level.

The evidence is fairly compelling, then, that spuriousness due to a commonly recognized measurement problem has inflated correlations between participation and satisfaction and has been responsible for a very large number of significant relationships, which, taken as a body, have been misleading.

It is quite clear from the evidence that the measurement problem has not been *consistently* serious in subjective studies, since individual correlations do differ quite noticeably in magnitude and some of them, perhaps 5 to 10 percent sprinkled throughout the various studies, do not reach statistical significance. This observation is useful in underscoring instability in connection with motivated behavior. In this case the behavior is questionnaire responses. There is no law of nature that compels respondents to answer questions on participation largely in terms of satisfaction, and many apparently do not, or they do so only in a very minor way. In the populations that have been studied, however, the tendency to do so has apparently been strong enough and widespread enough to be a factor that requires consideration in making research decisions.

The truth about the relationship between participation and satisfaction probably is that it, too, is unstable, as expected. This is indicated by the results in Table 4, which contains the only type of study that would appear eligible to be used in making such a determination. The pattern in Table 4 is, as observed earlier, a rather typical pattern of instability. It would be well to be able to complete the argument by providing a respectable proportion of instances in prior research in which subsetting with *objective* measurement of participation has produced differences in correlations, so that instability of statistics could be observed within studies and tested for significance. Unfortunately, however, the test population is extremely small: four cases, each of which appears as a set of subgroups in Table 4. Berkowitz (1953) obtained no significant difference when he divided the group according to how urgent the problems seemed to be that were dealt with by participation; the correlation between participation and satisfaction was negative in both subgroups. Obradovic (1970) reports a very weak (and nonsignificant) relationship among workers in automated technologies and a far stronger (and significant) one in both handicraft and mechanized technologies. He does not report whether 'iis difference is statistically significant, but it clearly is. Obradovic, French, and Rodgers (1970) subdivided their study group according to the desire to participate, and with participation measured objectively, the difference was clearly significant, although again the relevant statistic is not explicitly reported. As noted previously, instability is further highlighted in this case because it was among those with the *lower* desire to participate that participation had the stronger relationship with satisfaction. One can look at the details of the study population and the setting and find reasons that would explain this rather surprising turnaround as an "exception," but it is in one sense not an exception at all; such reasons, such differences in contextual detail, are the very foundation of the phenomenon of instability, and rather than erase the point, they serve to demonstrate it. Lastly, Runyon (1973) found a strong interaction ($p < .001$) with internal/external control as the mediator, the focal relationship being significantly positive in one group and significantly negative in the other. As far as this meager additional evidence goes, then, it supports the earlier conclusion that the effect of participation on satisfaction, just as on employee performance, is unstable (compare Perrow, 1979, p. 99).

This does not mean that there is no room in social science for study of the relationship between participation and satisfaction. The data indicate that at times there is indeed a favorable impact, and the only question is "Under what conditions?" From the standpoint of theory, that question will probably *never* receive a satisfactory answer, but from the standpoint of policy, of organizational practice, it could receive several. A different, but only slightly different, research orientation is required. One would accept the limits of theory in this area and seek instead a few conditions, if indeed there are such, under which there appears quite often to be a strong tendency for participation to lead (or not lead) to satisfaction, together with an understanding of why that is so. Such results—the discovery of a few strong and enlightening interacting conditions—would still be much more in the category of research than consultation, but many organizations would benefit. Toward this end, the end of improving levels of satisfaction in organizations, the traditional survey designs, which are a bit superficial, may have to be supplemented with more richly detailed contextual or intensive research (Brunner, 1977), the type designed to provide insight and heuristic guidance rather than general universals. Policy rather than theory would need to guide research, but with confidence that there do exist some conceptual connections between contexts, that each case is not totally uninformable by others. I suggest that powerful operating guidelines might emerge from such social science activity. The theoretical perspective tells one, of course, that policies derived in such fashion will probably not be infallible, but it would be foolish to expect infallibility no matter what the research orientation.

Furthermore, there may yet be something to Herzberg's (1966) suggestion that taking participation *away* may lead to *dis*satisfaction even though there is no variance-theoretic connection between participation and satisfaction as scaled, quantitative dimensions. Such a hypothesis cannot, however, be investigated satisfactorily by means of variance-oriented studies. What one has in mind in this case is a process theory. Something deep, concrete, and universal may happen to the emotions when a participatory say over one's affairs is withdrawn. Whether to call this something dissatisfaction and what is meant by a say are as yet unclear, but a beginning might certainly be made toward articulation of the theory through the study of participation in organizations.

Determinants of Leadership Style. Whereas most human relations research has been concerned with participation and allied variables as causes, or precursors, there has also been interest in these same kinds of factors as effects, or outcomes. The research is aimed at an empirical theory of leadership style—at uncovering the forces that determine whether supervisors and managers are democratic, considerate, highly task-oriented, and so forth. Is such a theory attainable? There is not nearly so much research to analyze in this category as in those of the previous section, and even what exists is somewhat fragmented by attention to dimensions of style other than participativeness. One may treat the broad question of leadership in rather undifferentiated fashion for the present purpose, however, since the arguments and evidence bearing on the frustration of theory in this case are essentially the same for one aspect of style as for another.

Research practice on this issue has not led to the particular problem of interaction stemming from a focus on the independent variable. On the contrary, a great many disparate factors have been considered, both separately and together, as possible determinants of leadership styles. Like innovation, however, leadership style is a clear and direct example of motivated behavior. Following the analysis in Chapter Three, therefore, its determinants could not be complete without including in the set the motivations for performing the behavior. But these are nonregular, nonuniversal. Instability in the parameters of predictors that might be investigated is, for these reasons, inevitable. The factors that are important (and their degree of importance) in determining levels of participativeness, consideration, and so on depend on the context in which the supervision occurs and the histories of the people who find themselves in that context. It is natural, then, that investigators should have entertained an impressive variety of predictors, but it is also to be expected that (1) a very large number of them—more than could be accommodated in a cogent theory—would have a weak or moderate relationship with aspects of leadership style, (2) few would have a strong relationship, (3) those that are examined in several contexts should vary in their explanatory power, and (4) if sensible statistical interactions are looked for, a great many should be successfully uncovered. These are the standard expectations for instability in efforts to explain with generality any complex motivated behavior. In this case, the results conform well to the expectations.

First consider the impressive array of independent variables that have been found to correlate with participativeness and similar supervisory behavior in just a few studies: In an elaborate laboratory experiment, well planned and theoretically sophisticated, Lowin and Craig (1968) found that closeness of supervision and consideration of subordinates were explained in part by how well subordinates performed their jobs. Blankenship and Miles (1968) found that the extent to which managers reported relying on subordinates in decision making (a form of participativeness) was positively related to independent variables such as hierarchal level, size of the organization, size of the group supervised, and autonomy and influence with respect to higher levels of management. The relationships were weak to moderately strong. Heller and Yukl (1969) found that decision centralization was weakly but significantly related to type of department (production, finance, or sales) and moderately related to hierarchal level. Moreover, decision making was less centralized when the decision outcomes affected the subordinates of the subordinates than when they affected the subordinates alone, and it was also less centralized when the decisions had to do with task functions than when they dealt with group maintenance functions. Both of the latter relationships were moderate in strength. Vroom and Yetton (1973) found weak to moderate, significant negative correlations between participativeness and whether the manager felt that he had sufficient information to make a high-quality decision unilaterally, whether he perceived the probability of acceptance of a unilateral decision to be high, and whether he found the decision situation to be well structured (that is, whether he knew exactly what information was needed, who had it, and how to get it). These authors found moderate and significant positive correlations with possession of important information by subordinates and with the manager's own general attitudinal inclination toward participative management. In my own research (Mohr, 1977), I found weak to moderate, significant negative correlations between participativeness and the supervisor's concern for status, the manageability or routineness of the subordinate's job, the bureaucratization of the organization as a whole, and the noise level on the job. Weak to moderate, significant positive correlations were found with the subordinates' professional level, the supervisor's own technological level, the supervisor's perception of the subordinates' decision-making potential, and the workers' interdependence on the job.

In short, numerous variables have been found to have a weak or moderate relationship with leadership style, and none has been found to have a strong one (although there is no reason that that should not occasionally occur; in particular settings there might well be an overriding determinant, but it would be unusual). The list highlights rationality. The majority of variables that have been sought and found to correlate with leadership style are simply plausible *reasons* the supervisor may have for adopting that style; that is, either they are or they clearly suggest possible motivations for performing a motivated behavior. Their prominence is not surprising, since without them, as argued in Chapter Three, variance in the behavior could not be accurately explained. The trouble is only that the number of possible reasons is great. Moreover, such reasons can coexist in a large variety of combinations, and their individual importance is unpredictable.

It follows from this perspective that many plausible reasons should *fail* to produce significant correlations in research, and most should have a mixed record if they have been investigated a number of times. This is indeed the case, and such results are interesting because as soon as the plausible relationships fail to materialize in empirical data, one can think of further plausible reasons that they did not materialize (and these are frequently given by the authors). Always, an unspecified multiplicity and complexity of plausible reasons lurks just below the surface of research.

Let us note a few instances in this category of nonsupportive results. Heller and Yukl (1969), for example, expected decision making to be significantly more centralized in line units than staff units, but it was not. Moreover, they did not find significant relationships between work-group size and joint decision making, whereas Blankenship and Miles (1968) did find a comparable relationship to be moderately strong and noteworthy in their data (no significance level reported). Note the ambiguity of rationality in connection with this factor: It is easy to see that one might cope well with the problem of large size either by centralizing or by delegating, depending on other active factors (see Child, 1972b—this simply illustrates what he calls the role of strategic choice). Rossel (1970) reasoned that the greater the needed commitment on the part of subordinates, the more the supervisor would be *expressive* (supportive, integrative) rather than *instrumental* (efficiency-oriented), but the relationship turned out to be weak and nonsignificant. He also reasoned that supervision would be more expressive the higher the hierarchal level of the supervisor, but this relationship was also weak and nonsignificant. The latter finding is of particular interest because hierarchal level was a successful predictor in other studies. It was found to be significantly related to similar dimensions of leadership style in the research of Blankenship and Miles (1968), Heller and Yukl (1969), and Mohr (1977). Pfeffer and Salancik (1975) found that leadership style sometimes conformed to the expectations of superiors, but sometimes it conformed instead to the expectations of subordinates. Vroom and Yetton (1973) reasoned that the shorter the time available in which to make the decision, the less likely would the supervisor be to involve subordinates, but the correlation was essentially zero. Furthermore, in carrying out similar studies on three different populations of managers, these investigators found that the extent to which the subordinates could be trusted to base solutions on organizational criteria, the importance for decision quality of choosing one alternative over another, and the importance attached to the subordinates' accepting the decision were all significantly correlated with participativeness in at least one population but not in all three. The extent to which there might be disagreement among the subordinates on what should be done, another plausible determinant, was a nonsignificant predictor consistently.

Thus, contrasting a priori plausibility with a posteriori results, as well as comparing results on the same variables explored in different studies, it begins to be clear that the importance of individual determinants of leadership style depends on context. Researchers in the area have expected this outcome and have purposely and successfully looked for statistical interactions in their data. The idea has been to clear up the instability by finding the contextual factors responsible for the bouncing around of parameters, but the search is inherently both quite successful and, for the same reasons, unending. It was noted earlier, for example, that Rossel (1970) found that neither required labor commitment nor hierarchal level of the supervisor was related to leadership style. His major finding, however, was that the two predictors interacted strongly, so that noteworthy relationships involving these variables did appear in particular contexts, but these offset each other and canceled to nonsignificance in the group as a whole. Among higher-level managers, being in an organization with a strong need for employee commitment seemed to produce expressive leadership, whereas for lower-level managers the opposite was true—the greater the need for commitment, the more instrumental or efficiency-oriented was the managerial style. Pfeffer and Salancik (1975) found the impact of others' role expectations on the supervisor's leadership style to be highly interactive. The greater the time spent in supervisory as opposed to routine work activity, for example, the more the supervisor's leadership style conformed to the boss's role expectations. In addition, the more demanding the boss was in terms of production, the more the supervisor conformed to the boss's expectations for type of leadership behavior. Male supervisors conformed more to the expectations of their bosses, females to the expectations of their subordinates (as clear an example as any of how "theoretical" results in an undifferentiated group may simply depend on the fortuitous proportions of types—in this case sexes—in the study population).

My own empirical work on participation (Mohr, 1977) also ended by highlighting interaction. Social-class differences, for example, interacted with status concerns. As long as supervisor and subordinates were class equals, attitudes toward status were a dormant force, but when the supervisor was of a higher social class, degree of concern about status seemed to become determinative of leadership behavior. Perhaps more important, the data suggested an interaction between job-relevant rationality and personal affect. When large status distances removed affect as a factor, predictions of participativeness on the basis of what would seem the rational thing to do were quite good, but in the groups in which positive or negative affect between supervisor and subordinates might more easily be the rule, predictions on rationality grounds were very poor indeed. Lowin and Craig (1968) noted a similar role for affect. Subjects who performed poorly on the job were disliked by the supervisors, and such affect appeared to color strongly a great deal of leadership behavior. With respect to rationality, it must be remembered that it is, even within itself, a highly interactive, complex force. One contextual variable may be positively related to an aspect of style, and that may appear rational, but change another ingredient of the context a bit, and the first variable can become negatively related and still appear rational. In Heller and Yukl's (1969) research, for example, *senior* managers tended to delegate rather fully when new on the job and to centralize heavily when they had accumulated much experience. For first-line supervisors, however, the opposite was true; they tended to decide unilaterally when new and to grant much autonomy to subordinates as their tenure in the position advanced.

Perhaps the most forceful demonstration that leadership style depends on context is found in the work of Vroom and Yetton (1973). These investigators explored whether the participativeness of a single person might not be capable of varying with circumstances (other research tends to assume a generalized behavioral style). The data showed this to be unquestionably true and, in fact, enabled the conclusion (pp. 105–106) that situational factors were far more important in determining behavior than the general style propensity of the person. And still, each situation that the person enters is itself complex; its characteristics do not relate in a constant way to his or her behavior. This is shown by interactions within the Vroom and Yetton data. For example, a manager might in general involve subordinates in a decision if the probability of their accepting an autocratic choice is low, but he might well not involve them even so if their acceptance is not very critical for effective implementation (p. 108). Increasing the picture of complexity by an exponential notch, the authors found a statistically significant interaction among three situational predictors, as well as two, and only seven predictors, not twenty or thirty, were included in the analysis out of which the interacting triplet emerged.

If any particular determinant does not have an impact in every supervisory relationship, or if the degree of its influence varies, there must be some special reason, but each such ad hoc reason is only a further nuance contributing to infinite variation of meaningful context. The picture is not so clear when a single study of motivated behavior is perused in isolation, but when six or seven similar studies in somewhat different settings are viewed together, one begins to develop a feeling for the fact that the meaningful variation is indeed infinite. One is incapable of putting together into a compelling whole what one already knows from research in this area, and one begins to see the certainty that there are unknown managers and supervisors out there who are doing what they are doing for still other combinations of reasons, combinations not yet contemplated by hard-pressed investigators.

In sum, to the question "Will there be a reliable explanatory theory of leadership style?" the answer must apparently be no, as must also be the case for all other motivated behaviors treated as objects of generalized explanation.

The Normative Theory of Participation. We have seen that there is little or no possibility of a theory of participation itself as an outcome, nor is there likely to be a theory relating participation to satisfaction with job or supervisor. The conclusion with respect to participation and effectiveness of performance will be developed in Chapter Six, but it is already clear that the prospects are not bright. The issue of participation in organizations, however, is an important one, and it is extremely unlikely that anyone will grapple with it at the level of ideas if social scientists do not. It is undoubtedly too important to be dropped altogether by social scientists on the ground that it is not vulnerable to domestication by explanatory theory.

It is abundantly clear from the history of research and consultation, however, that the interest of social scientists in this topic has been largely normative and not purely for the sake of explanatory social theory; the driving stimulus has been that autocratic rule anywhere in formal organizations appears contrary to the spirit and continued development of European-American democracy, Western civilization and thought, and similar cultural development in other parts of the world. The true issues are how, precisely, to justify something *better* than autocratic management in formal organizations and what, precisely, that something might be. It would seem to be ridiculous for social scientists to abandon these issues merely because of their failure to be absorbed into empirical theory—approximately as ridiculous as it would be to continue to pursue the empirical theory beyond the point at which its futility is long past denying.

European scholars have tended to have little compunction about advocating participation on the basis of values or political ideals such as socialism or democracy (see the excellent review and analysis by Dachler and Wilpert, 1978). In these views, organizations and work simply should be governed in a significant way by workers as well as managers. It appears, however, that the participation practiced under the basically simple impetus that workers *should* govern is frequently not as real a sharing of authority as its supporters would like it to be, and it can readily tend toward deleterious consequences, at least for some participants, when the sharing is made to be more real (Mulder, 1971; Adizes, 1971, pp. 159–164; Locke and Schweiger, 1979). With a few exceptions, American scholars have not found their way to advocacy on the basis of values alone (Dachler and Wilpert, 1978; Locke and Schweiger, 1979, pp. 266–267), perhaps because they view such advocacy as outside the boundaries of their role as scientists. But apparently a great many of the American scholars, too, have strong normative beliefs of some sort that support participation, strong enough that they persist in fairly frustrating and disappointing research and undertake consultation toward organizational change in the participative direction.

An alternative to untethered advocacy and empty theory is to engage frankly in the analysis of critical *descriptive* aspects of *normative*-theoretic questions with the conceptual and methodological rigor of empirical-scientific pursuit (not necessarily, it should be emphasized, to the exclusion of the traditional techniques of moral and political philosophy). Let us take a moment to examine participation in this perspective, since it is an important theme of the present volume that social scientists should do frankly (instead of in the name of theory) certain of the things that they are trying to do anyway and that pursuits such as the rigorous underpinning of policy by creative, sophisticated descriptive research should be accepted as a matter of course as mainstream social science.

To me, the defining characteristic of formal organization, which should be contrasted with spontaneous organization, is that it is composed of positions and roles that stand by themselves. When the people occupying them move out, the roles do not collapse, evaporate, or disintegrate; they remain in place. The activities and contributions of the roles are quite well understood, nearly in their entirety, without reference to the particular persons who might occupy them. Furthermore, large numbers of these self-contained roles carry authority over the occupants of other roles as part of their definition, and in that feature lies one of the most significant characteristics of formal organization for the scheme of social life. Formal organizations dole out by simple fiat astounding quantities of authority that in the spontaneous state would be acquired only by strength, intelligence, expertise, charisma, saintliness, and so forth, and then only temporarily. It is not that dominance relations were absent from the lives of primitive men and women or their hominid ancestors in the natural state; they apparently were present and important (Wilhoite, 1976), but they had no official status or permanence based solely on abstract principles or ideas. They depended on contemporaneous interaction and changed often. A free person steps into a formal organization, however, and suddenly is subject to a network of precast official authority that is spontaneous, dynamic, or flexible only around the edges. Both in the abstract and in the concrete, this throws up serious problems of relationship and behavior.

Of course, one may consider that people freely agree to be subject to authority when they enter an organization, and for this they are compensated. In a valuable article, Keeley (1980) argues most convincingly that persons and groups in formal organizations should not be considered as organs of an integral whole or system, which is the usual analogy, but as separate, mutually *contracting* individuals. There is a catch, however; the contract has not been *clear,* and that circumstance has been fertile soil for both tension and exploitation. Instead of vagueness and tension, it would seem to be time to work out for this setting a new social contract that recognizes both the anomaly and the necessity of the authority structure inherent in formal organization.

The contractual assumption suggests that democracy is not in itself good or right with respect to formal organizations, and neither is it bad or wrong, as some would argue (Locke and Schweiger, 1979). The proper locus of authority over a given question is not ideologically determined and cannot be taken for granted either way; it depends on the contract. What is needed, therefore, is one or more social science research approaches that will bring understanding and illumination to the evolving terms of the contract. One such approach was suggested to me by the analysis of data on participation (Mohr, 1977). I would not expect this approach to be popular among those with a strong ideological commitment to the generally accepted procedures, forms, and organs of democracy or socialism, such as representative boards or workers' councils, but it will perhaps not be offensive to those with a commitment more to some central idea or definition of democracy, dignity, and human development, particularly when the commitment is accompanied by a desire to reconcile these values with such others as property rights, expertise, organizational effectiveness, and the consistency of authority with responsibility.

The data drew attention to the interesting phenomenon of psychological participation and the distinction between that and objective participation. As noted in connection with the participation/satisfaction relationship, the suggestion was strong, although it surely needs further test, that psychological participation is scaled by the individual relative to some internal standard (not necessarily a static one). When asked in a number of ways the core question, "How much do you get to participate in shaping the outcome of decisions that concern you?," people appeared to respond on a scale anchored around their own expectations for participation. A moderate amount of objective participation and influence could therefore be recorded as very little for some and quite a lot for others. What is important about this in the present connection is the factual existence of the expectations, which are apparently usually neither for zero nor for unlimited participation. Subordinates (at all hierarchal levels) have, in other words, what Barnard (1938) called a *zone of indifference*—a collection of areas in which they do not care if authority is denied to them in favor of their supervisors (in fact, they frequently prefer it that way)—and a complementary collection of areas that I have labeled the subordinate's zone of retained authority, or simply *zone of authority*, in which the subordinate feels it is appropriate to retain some role in the determination of decision outcomes (Mohr, 1977). There exists in the organization, in other words, an empirical distribution of legitimate authority—that is, authority of supervisor over subordinate that is legitimated by the subordinates themselves. If true democracy were to be written into a contractual relationship in formal organizations, it would strive to follow the lines of that distribution, for then people would be deciding their own participation. Work groups would participate in some but, no doubt, not all decisions, nor would the structure of decision making be the same for all work groups or for all organizations or even for a single organization over time, so that one could not in this light impose universally some system of representation, for example, and correctly call it "democratic."

But formal organizations, although they could and might be conducted and regulated democratically, do not necessarily have to be. People in such roles as owner, mandator (see Abrahamsson, 1977), manager, and supervisor are also parties to the contract (many of them, interestingly enough in this context, being both supervisors and subordinates). They might well feel that they require more authority than democracy would leave them. In fact, given compensation, the best contract from all points of view might be one in which subordinates gave up some participation not only in the zone of indifference, which would still be eminently democratic, but in their zones of authority as well, which in a strong sense would not. It is difficult even to think about a large and complex idea such as the best contract, however, because one knows next to nothing at all at present about the zones of indifference and authority.

The issue for social science would be to conceptualize, produce, and analyze the empirical information necessary to reach more satisfying social decisions on the matter of this contract. One critical goal of such inquiry is whether, at any time, the contract can readily accommodate democracy, where *democracy* means not all-encompassing participation but following the lines demarcated by empirically determined zones of indifference and authority. In particular, studies are needed to show how much agreement there tends to be within work groups on zones of authority, how much agreement there tends to be between supervisors and subordinates, what mechanisms of reconciliation are available if needed, what variation exists among work groups of different types or of the same type in different organizations, what variation tends to take place over time, what some of the correlates of these differences may be (the conditions that seem to be associated with more and less inclusive zones), what impact management tends to have on the sizes of zones claimed by workers, what impact on one work group information about the zones that characterize others may have, what may be the best research techniques for determining empirical zones of authority with validity, how the concept of zone of authority should be quantitatively scaled (proposals can be found in Dachler and Wilpert, 1978, p. 14, and Mohr, 1977, p. 939), how organizations can monitor themselves for the evolution of zones of indifference and authority, what may be the roles for trade unions in the process of adjusting participation to empirical zones of authority, and so forth. The illumination of issues such as these with rigorous techniques and creative conceptualization is not theoretical in the sense in which that term has been defined and used in this volume, but it should surely be seen as belonging to the category of truly meaningful social science practice.

✳ 5 ✳

Decision Processes
in Organizations

Bounded-Rationality Models

There is no doubt that some of the most vital research in organization theory has been research on decision making, with bounded rationality at the core of its energizing assumptions. The seminal work was the first edition, in 1947, of Simon's *Administrative Behavior* (1976), with important elaboration of the fundamentals in March and Simon's *Organizations* (1958). The research in this tradition is surely regarded as being theoretical, but just why it may be theoretical, or indeed whether it is so, is an instructive issue that is rarely probed. In truth, bounded-rationality theory clearly says something powerful about human behavior. Not so clear, however, is just what it says about which behavior.

One conspicuous thrust of the approach has been negative. There have been repeated, persuasive demonstrations that deci-

154

sion making in certain salient areas is not made, in real life, on the model of pure rationality. That is important because rational decision making is rather casually taken for granted in a great deal of social science scholarship and is explicitly at the core of much economic theory, including the theory of the firm. Decision making is very frequently not rational in the classical sense because people lack the necessary information to operate in that mode, as well as the information-processing and computational capacity that would also be required. This is as true of groups as of individuals, and the shortfall in capabilities is so large that even computers are only of minor assistance. The object of the approach, therefore, is to replace classical, or pure, rationality in behavioral science thinking with the more accurate representational concept of bounded rationality. The latter may be roughly characterized by noting that it recognizes the constraints under which the decision maker operates, and it incorporates three critical compensatory components: a process of search for alternatives that is generally heuristic rather than algorithmic or exhaustive, a mechanism of choice that recognizes satisficing rather than optimizing goals (that is, aspiration levels that represent *good enough* rather than *best*), and mechanisms of learning and adaptation that dynamically affect both search processes and aspiration levels (Cyert and March, 1963; Simon, 1979, p. 510).

Decision Processes as Precursors. There has been a strong tendency in organizational behavior to look at bounded-rationality theories as *explanations* of certain recurring *outcomes,* including, for example, government budgets (Davis, Dempster, and Wildavsky, 1966; Crecine, 1969; Larkey, 1979; Padgett, 1980), pricing and output decisions (Cyert and March, 1963), and trust portfolio composition (Clarkson, 1963). In addition, very similar kinds of models, although more often verbal rather than mathematical models or computer simulations, have been applied to more general or miscellaneous policy-making outputs, particularly in the public sector (Lindblom, 1959; Wildavsky, 1964; Allison, 1971; Halperin and Kanter, 1973). Many of these latter are characterized as models of *incremental* policy making. There has been a focus, in other words, on certain kinds of problems and how they are solved or certain decisions and how they are made. A bounded-rationality process

with specific content becomes a precursor that explains an outcome. With this research orientation, for example, it occurs that
scholars will differ on the details of the particular bounded-
rationality process that produces a given outcome, as in Padgett's
(1980) amendment of the Davis-Dempster-Wildavsky model of
budgeting at the federal level.

This orientation is weak from the standpoint of explanatory
theory. These outcomes in themselves, such as budget allocations,
prices, and policies, are a distraction. They siphon energy into
directions that are unlikely to be theoretically productive beyond
the dramatic initial insights that have already been made. The burden of the point is realized when one considers whether such
theories, as modes of explanation, are variance models or process
models. In fact, they are neither; they seem to strive to be an
inherently infeasible and needless amalgam in which the precursor
is a process and the outcome is a variable.

These are not variance theories, because they contain no
true independent variables. There is clearly no set of quantitative
causes of budget allocations, prices, or policy outputs being proposed. It is most clearly seen in the several computer simulations,
perhaps, that the forces that do "cause" the outcomes are events in
an antecedent series rather than variables. The events include
heuristic search procedures and other behaviors of individuals and
groups that cannot possibly be construed as variables, as is pressure
or mass or even wealth or attitudes, and are not meant to be so
construed. The same is true even in those models having the external form of variance theories, such as regression models (Davis,
Dempster, and Wildavsky, 1966; Larkey, 1979) or more complex
formulations in equation format (Padgett, 1980). The apparent independent variables, such as revenues and prior budgets, are still
not proposed as true causes of the budget quantities observed.
That is not the spirit or thrust of any of these models. That it
cannot be their import is perhaps most easily seen by noting the
universal acceptance of the fact that the parameters on these factors are inherently short-term and contextual; that is, the relative
importance of the independent variables may well change from
sector to sector, war to war, president to president, decade to decade, year to year, or city to city, with no thought that some com-

plete set of interacting conditions may ever be imported into the models to make those parameters finally stable. There can be no true explanatory variance theory in the face of inherently unstable parameters; any variables in the world might be called a theoretical explanation or a law if their effects on the outcome were permitted to vary freely.

Rather, these factors such as prior budgets are simply some of the many important *considerations* that people involved in such decision making generally have to take into account; the case is a further example of the operation of the fundamental assumption on motivation and behavior as discussed in Chapter Three. Ultimately, neither ordinary citizens nor social scientists want to, or are ready to, believe in a variance theory of budgetary allocations, since these allocations will always result in part from people's interpretation of a fresh set of events and contexts. The same is true of prices of goods. It is true that the factors that appear on the causal side in these theories, such as last year's budget allocations, represent situational constraints that are often extremely powerful, but these do not explain the new budget figures as temperature and volume explain the pressure of a gas. In principle, last year's allocation can be ignored. Instead, the true import of these factors is to say something about the social configuration within which budgets are commonly produced and the process itself by which budgets frequently are made.

But neither are these models process theories, because the outcomes in the models, or the final causes, as I have called them, are uncertain. They are too much like variables to be proper process-theory outcomes, and as such they distract one's attention from concentration on the true recurring event as final cause. The outcomes cannot be precisely *municipal* budgets or *federal* budgets or *public* policy or *department-store* prices, although generally labeled in such terms. They seem to be something smaller and yet something bigger. They are smaller because they do not pretend to specify how budgets are made in every place that is municipal or how they have always been and always will be made at the federal level. They refer to certain more circumscribed conditions, but it would be impossible to say what those might be. And yet if one tried, and said, "This is a model that explains how budgets are made under the following precise conditions," that would not do justice to the research. Something bigger is involved. The true significance of the models lies in the clear and usually explicit claim that they are variants of a more general mode by which a very large class of collective decisions are made (but not all collective decisions—not, to take just one example, the mode in operation when sovereignty over a piece of territory is decided by a war). The general mode that characterizes the class is simply a translation to the collective level of Simon's bounded-rationality model of individual decision making or problem solving, summarized at the beginning of the chapter. But the question then must be "Precisely which outcomes are covered by this general precursor? What are the dimensions of this large class?"

The question has not been answered, and appropriately not, for I believe that the answer is "None"; the outcomes are almost beside the point, and the true focus and emphasis are instead on *how one gets to them*. Simon and his colleagues have established a *paradigm* in the true Kuhnian sense of the word (Kuhn, 1962, 1977)—that is, a conceptual framework for the guidance of attention in research and the research exemplars that clarify the framework as nothing else can. A paradigm, however, does not have to be an explanatory theory, and this one is not. If it approached such status at all as applied to organizations, the elements of the theory would be reversed. The more germane question is not one regarding how budget figures are determined, with the answer given in terms of a detailed process. Rather, the question concerns when decisions are made in a certain general manner, with the answer being "When budgeting, setting prices, and so forth." That is, the *process* is itself the outcome.

This is true of the so-called models of incrementalism, as well. The incrementalism is a characteristic of the result of the decision process and therefore is mostly beside the point. That is why the term *incremental* has been so hard to define for this purpose (Goodin and Waldner, 1979). In his seminal article, Lindblom (1959) justifiably concentrates not on demonstrating that new policies are only incrementally different from old ones but on characterizing a process, a bounded-rationality process of collective decision—the *branch* method—and distinguishing it from the perfect-rationality, or *root*, method. Lindblom probably over-stretched when he seemed to be claiming that nearly all policy is made by this method, but his critics, in jumping on the claim, have mainly disproved the universality not of the method but of incremental outcomes. It appears to me that Schulman (1975) and Lustick (1980), in excellent papers, have convincingly demonstrated that not all policy making is incremental, but it is quite another matter to show what is truly central—namely, that not all policy making is conducted by the branch method, what method does characterize it, and why it does (Lustick does go some distance in this direction, as well). The fact of the matter is that nonincremental policies as well as incremental ones can sometimes result from the branch method. In the U.S. space program during the 1960s, for example, which is the subject of Schulman's case study, decisions often resulted in large commitments of resources all at once rather than incrementally, but the study makes it plain that the decision processes themselves were of the bounded-rationality, branch-method variety, not the pure-rationality, synoptic variety. Whether branch-method decisions yield incremental or nonincremental results depends on the policy area and its history, on the actual aspiration levels in the active demand sets of participants, and, as Lustick cogently observes, on the relative power of the various participants.

The role of such concepts as budgeting, pricing, and policy making in this reverse perspective, in which process is outcome, is to allude suggestively, if imprecisely, to one or more precursors—sets of conditions under which bounded-rationality decision making will probably take place. The actual budget figures or policy outcomes themselves are in this view not final causes, which role is occupied by the mode of decision making itself, but implications or fallout of the operation of the model; they serve as data to test the validity of the model in some circumstances and provide a basis for improving it. To pursue the possible value of this reverse perspective, however, it will be well first to back away from the collective level and consider individual problem solving.

Decision Processes as Theoretical Descriptions. In the substrate, the work of Simon and his colleagues on human problem solving, almost no attention is given to explaining variation in the outcome of a problem-solving process (for example, why one sort of move in chess is made rather than another or why a person is able successfully to derive some theorems of symbolic logic but not others) and very little to explaining how certain decision-making or problem-solving strategies themselves come to be used. In other words, the decision processes are employed in this research neither as precursor nor as outcome in an explanatory theory. In fact, nothing at all is being explained by something else. When one applies the term *theory* to what this program of research has been trying to achieve, one uses it in a different sense from that of providing an explanation for the occurrence of phenomena, but a sense, nevertheless, that has been prominent in the history of other disciplines. Returning to the catalogue of functions of research offered in Chapter One, it is clear that the point of this program of study of problem solving is to describe. Description is often called theory in science not because it is an explanatory generalization or set of interrelated laws but because it is both important and conjectural. In order to develop explanatory theory or further description or significant applied programs, it is frequently important simply to describe the form, matter, or motion of something that cannot be directly observed, and this description is therefore conjectural. Thus, for example, we have a heliocentric theory, a theory of the structure of DNA molecules, a theory of the shape of planetary orbits, and so forth. These ideas do not in themselves explain anything at all—it is not a matter of one thing's being explained by others—but merely describe something. Almost the whole of the history of chemistry is punctuated by descriptions called theories that would not be such at all—that is, would not be conjectural—if people only had better eyes or better instruments, so that they could better observe what one is simply trying to describe: the phlogiston theory, the atomic theory, the theory of types or families of organic molecules, the various theories of the nature of ions, and so forth.

Describing the procedures people use to make decisions and solve problems is in the very same tradition, especially to the extent that these procedures and their underpinnings in brain physiology are universal and stable rather than intentional or motivated and thus capricious. And in fact, there is good reason to accept as a working hypothesis that the procedures are physiologically shaped and driven in significant part. Simon's perspective on the question, for example, is as follows: "The processes of human thinking, in fact, can be very effectively stated in the form of programs. We do not know what mechanisms store these programs in the brain and execute them; but we have as much reason to believe there are such mechanisms as earlier generations had to believe that there are mechanisms underlying the valences of atoms and the control of heredity by genes. A human being is able to think because, by biological inheritance and exposure to a stream of experience in the external world, he has acquired a program that is effective for guiding thought processes. If we wish to seek an efficient cause for his behavior, it lies in that program in its interaction with ongoing stimuli" (1977, p. 283).

One cannot know all the future applications of this descriptive work. There is surely the possibility that explanatory theories of decision making or indeed of quite different human behaviors will be developed whose formulation or testing depends critically on these results. For the moment, however, the uses appear to be not primarily explanatory but normative (in the sense of being guides to good or better ways of doing things) and applied. They feed into artificial intelligence research. They are used to build models by which machines can solve problems as well as or better than most humans and to suggest ways that some human beings might be able to upgrade their own abilities by taking better advantage of universal natural capacities. Apparently rejected or abandoned is the attempt to move deeply into explanatory theory—to conceptualize the distinctions between decision-making contexts in such a way as to be able to determine under what perceptual conditions a given sort of problem-solving strategy is likely to be spontaneously used. Instead, after discovering and describing the strategy, attention shifts—and productively so, it must be noted—to the conditions under which it can be *profitably* used.

But now return to organization theory and group decision making, to the study of social behavior rather than the analysis of cognitive processes. Beyond a surface affinity, the suitability of individual-level concepts and processes for duty at the collective level has perhaps been too casually accepted. There are two significant depressors of transferability.

One is that at the group level, description is in general less auspiciously normative, and design applications are not nearly so salient or relevant. Moreover, because explanation is not involved either, the function of the decision models thus becomes quite problematic. The normative weakness obtains because the decisions in which there has been greatest interest at the group level are different in kind from their counterparts at the individual level. The solutions achieved by problem-solving models of individual cognitive activity have essentially been capable of evaluation by a single criterion or set of consistent constraints. Sometimes the criterion is quite uncomplicated, such as whether a theorem in logic has been successfully and legitimately derived. In the collective case, in contrast, as in the problems of budgeting and general policy making, the solution must represent difficult choices among competing values, values that may well be incommensurable or even mutually inconsistent. As Lindblom (1959) points out, tests for the acceptability of policies in terms of whether they will satisfy goals are often inherently unavailable because the choice among both ends and means is made simultaneously, by the same act of decision. There are no validating end points comparable to "Checkmate" or "Q.E.D."

It is not, of course, that individual human beings do not have similarly complex problems to solve, but rather that the individual-level models have tended to deal with what Simon (1977, pp. 304–325) calls relatively *well-structured problems* rather than seriously *ill-structured problems*. The difference between these two can be based on several contributing criteria (Simon, 1977, pp. 305–306), but for the present purpose a single one will suffice: Let us think of ill-structured problems as those in which one or more choices must be made among incommensurable goals. It must be noted that Simon also argues convincingly that the mechanisms by which human beings solve problems in the two categories are perhaps not very different, but the question here, for the moment, is not how decisions may often be reached but the normative implications of models of such processes.

It is as though, on the individual level, one tried to use Simon's powerful general approach to construct a procedure for making the difficult and certainly ill-structured decision whether to accept a position as academic dean or continue in teaching and research, or whether to have a book published by a commercial press or a university press. Whereas one would be quite willing to give authority to a machine to derive theorems in symbolic logic, one would be much less enthusiastic about granting it the authority to reject deanships or select publishers, although the computer's solution would be of interest and no doubt taken under advisement. One would be lukewarm even if the program were built from research on the way many people actually do make such decisions. The distinguishing feature of ill-structured problems may well lie, at bottom, primarily in the amount and kind of information available from long-term memory (Simon, 1977, p. 324), so that the process itself may not differ basically from one or more of the methods already discovered for well-structured problems. However, the need for information from long-term memory presents a profound difficulty—that is, considering the aim of creating models that make our ill-structured decisions for us—not only because the task of supplying the information may be large but because the relevant store of information in long-term memory may in principle not be very accessible or specifiable and should properly vary radically from one person's application of a decision type (a deanship decision, for example) to another's.

In the same sense, then, one is not interested in collective decision-making models for the sake of their potential, even in artificial intelligence theory, for deciding the next year's municipal or federal budget allocations or producing incremental health, defense, or criminal justice policies. Solving such problems is not why one wants the models. However, since these are the kinds of problems to which group decision-making models have been applied (there are exceptions in the direction of group attack on relatively well-structured problems—see Cohen, 1980), understanding the role of such models becomes difficult. Being able to find solutions cannot have the same function and significance as in the individual-level, well-structured case. Thus, the main avenue of application of individual problem-solving models, the normative application oriented toward finding solutions, has little relevance for the kinds of group-level models that have primarily been considered in organizational research.

The second limitation on transferability to the group level concerns description itself rather than application. For two reasons, the descriptions that have been sought at the collective level are inherently less stable.

First, they have related primarily to processes for solving ill-structured problems, and such processes should be adjudged, for the present, to be less stable than their counterparts for solving well-structured problems. Consider the task of an architect in designing a house. Much of the overall problem can be divided into subtasks that are capable of being handled as well-structured problems, but there are still aspects that introduce a serious element of process instability, such as the organization of the overall design problem, the sequence in which well-structured subtasks are confronted, and particularly the recurring need to choose between conflicting and often incommensurable aspiration levels—size of rooms versus number, convenience versus esthetics, and so on (the example, but not the emphasis, is derived from Simon, 1977, pp. 310–316). These aspects are experientially conditioned, artistic, motivated, and therefore carried out in ways that appear mysterious and cannot as yet—perhaps never can—be stably described. Furthermore, in moving to the collective level, it is clear that the instability is increased. When the problem solver is a group, the subtasks may be factored among participants in many ways or perhaps not factored at all. Choices between inconsistent aspiration levels may be made by deference, bargaining, violence, and so on, among people who can vary in numberless ways in power, expertise, and other determiners of how such things are done. War, court cases, mediation, and intrafirm bargaining are some of the many processes, apparently fundamentally different from one another, by which collectivities reach solutions to ill-structured problems. There is no apparent stability of method for solving ill-structured problems, and the instability is more pronounced at the group level than the individual.

Second, there is at least a quantitative difference in stability between individual- and group-level processes because the stability of the former relies in important ways on brain physiology that is essentially uniform across individuals. Because there is no group brain, however, and unless genetic mechanisms are discovered that generally operate to mold individuals quite dependably into structures when they enter into collective decision processes, one must recognize that the mechanisms and characteristics of collective processes lie entirely within the troublesome category of motivated behavior. Under that heading, even for well-structured problems, instability interferes with description. A key factor to recognize in this connection is that whereas an individual is a serial processor, *parallel* processing becomes possible and indeed is common at the collective level. The group may readily divide up the task among participants, who may all work toward goals or subgoals on different channels at the same time. The difficulty is that this may be done in any number of ways. Or it may not be done at all; the group can work as one freely communicating, simultaneous unit. Cars may be assembled in predominantly serial fashion by the usual assembly-line method or, as in the well-known Swedish experiments, in parallel, by a small team of workers that has responsibility for, and works together on, a whole automobile. The question of a good theoretical description of how groups organize to solve well-structured problems is in fact very little different from the question of a good theoretical description of how formal organizations themselves are designed. Such description has floundered because the number of designs is fundamentally infinite.

This is not to suggest that it is impossible to impose useful description on infinite variety. It can be done, as witnessed by the classification scheme for biological species. Of course, it remains to be seen whether a good, *useful* classification scheme can be developed for the infinity of group decision modes, as it has been for the infinity of biological organisms. For the moment, being interested on a somewhat naive, incipient level in the modeling of group decision making, one notes that the task is imposing and perplexing, to say the least, in the face of the inherent instability.

Thus, descriptions of group problem solving cannot function theoretically like the double helix. The substantially increased instability means that they cannot even function like descriptions of individual problem solving. In part, the latter difference tends to blur into the consideration of well-structured versus ill-structured problems, for these have occupied relatively great attention in individual and group research, respectively. Ill-structured problems are significantly less susceptible to stable description even at the individual level than their well-structured counterparts. I suggest that an important point is missed—the fundamental nature of the distinction—in emphasizing their similarities while seeking to minimize their differences (Simon, 1977, pp. 320–324). Ill-structured problems demand that choices be made among incommensurable goals. How do people make these choices (see Simon, 1977, pp. 281–282, for some basic ideas)? Clearly, they are made as a matter of course in everyday life, but how? By what mechanisms? Not, it appears, by the same strategies and mechanisms as have been described for well-structured problem solving.

Lastly, even well-structured problem solving is unstable at the group level, as we have seen.

The possibility of valuable description of collective decision processes—important description of the type that could lay good claim to the label "theory"—would seem therefore to be reduced to two similar and rather modest types. Because of their modesty, I will refer to them as *descriptive quasi theory*.

One is creative description of ways that collective decisions are *sometimes* made, in which (1) the fit to reality, though not stable, is either quite common or otherwise intriguing, so that a justifiable claim to importance can be made, or (2) the potential for constructive normative application is auspicious. The normative applications are not likely to take the form of solution finding, but rather of process suggesting—of providing attractive and illuminating prototypes of organizational mechanisms for collective attack on problems. Where and when the mechanisms are to be utilized (or avoided) and with what payoff, however, would in principle be variable and indeterminate. Moreover, in the realm of the ill-structured problem, these must still be mechanisms for human beings to use, not for automata.

The second type of potentially valuable description would describe at so high a level of abstraction and simplification that—recognizing infinite variety at lower levels, as in the classification of species—a measure of stability might still be attained *within* a decision-making mode relative to the significant differences that are conceptualized to exist *between* modes. The work on budgeting, on the behavioral theory of the firm, and on branch-method policy making is valuable largely from this point of view. In very broad strokes of the conceptual brush, the research draws attention to an apparently important difference, that between decision making in which the orientation is toward mutual satisficing, on one hand, and, on the other hand, toward either goal maximization or domination of the goals of some by those of others, as in violence, war, voting, much political struggle, and jury trials (see Mohr, 1976).

The reception of previous work suggests that there is profit to be derived from the continued search for nonuniversal descriptions along these lines—descriptive quasi theory—with the caveat that disproportionate orientation to outcomes as opposed to the processes themselves can be a distraction, a source of the frustration of the kind of theoretical potential that does inhere in this kind of research.

Decision Processes as Outcomes. Group decision-making models are thus mainly descriptions rather than explanations, and because the ways of making group decisions are motivated behaviors, the scope of applicability of each descriptive model is inherently limited. The preceding paragraph, however, suggests a return to the question set aside earlier—namely, that of the decision process itself as an outcome in explanatory theory. Once it is recognized that there are several strikingly different modes in which collective decision problems are engaged, there can easily develop a social science curiosity to understand when or why one mode occurs rather than another. When or why, for example, do participants bargain toward satisficing rather than struggle toward domination? Answers such as "In budgeting situations" or "In policy making" or "In pricing and output decisions" are far too broad, undifferentiated, oversimplified, and basically noninformative, even if they do provide good predictions some portion of the time. To feel that one has an explanation, one needs something both more specific and more accurate.

Because arriving at a collective decision process involves motivated behavior and, moreover, that of two or more motivated persons simultaneously, it is bound to be, in general, complex.

Sometimes the mode of decision takes one track, sometimes another, and it is hard to say why. To take just one example, consider the celebrated case of the fountain manager in Dalton's *Men Who Manage* (1959, pp. 212–213).

She worked in one drugstore in a chain in which, typically, each store as a whole made a reasonable profit, but its soda fountain made little or none. The profit situation was strongly influenced by the quiet maintenance of what some might call institutionalized theft. The fountain heads gave food and confections free to relatives and close friends, gave drinks to fountain employees, and variously bartered with other employees. The fountain employees were not highly paid, and the heads would reward their good workers unofficially in the form of meals to hold them. The fountain managers discreetly helped themselves to canned foods, dairy products, and meats from the departmental stock, with the knowledge of the store manager, who received free meals and coffee at any time. The fountain head in question, however, behaved differently from the outset; she seemed to operate initially on the basis of different personal values and a different perception of what was best for the system as a whole, including customers, employees, store, and chain. She allowed no gratis consumption to employees, friends, relatives, or herself. She kept the refrigerators locked and closely supervised the handling of the stock. When emergencies prevented her from shopping for her family and she took a loaf of bread from the fountain stock, she deposited the price in the cash register. She consistently had the highest percentage of profits among the chain's soda fountains and was officially rewarded by the chain with a small share of those profits because they exceeded a certain threshold level. The management and employees of the store and the other fountain managers in the chain, however, felt that the system worked better the other way. They resented her behavior and took discreet steps at all levels to put pressure on her to conform. What will happen? What will be the mode of collective decision on these matters of pricing, revenue distribution, and other policy?

An exposure to Cyert and March's *Behavioral Theory of the Firm* (1963) indicates one prominent and highly probable manner of procedure: The participants will bargain and satisfice. In the choice of alternatives, actors must be sensitive to the need to maintain a viable coalition. In this complex situation, rational decision making is clearly bounded; it is impossible to know what all the choice alternatives are and what their consequences would be. One therefore casts about for merely workable alternatives, perhaps moving slowly, giving and taking a little here and there, and operating on the basis of reaction to feedback. In the end, a satisficing solution is found—no doubt some sort of compromise that minimally takes care of nearly all active goals, perhaps using a bit of organizational slack to make this possible.

But that is not what happened. Instead, the mode of collective process was political struggle in which each side sought to deny satisfaction to the other and in which one side eventually dominated and stripped the other of all system rewards. The outcome is perhaps better understood through a reading of another classic in organization theory, Selznick's *Leadership in Administration* (1957), than through *A Behavioral Theory of the Firm,* because management appeared to perceive in the situation the need to make a *critical decision* to create or preserve the character of the organization. In Dalton's words (1959, p. 213), "Her superior . . . was disturbed by her boasting of her standing in the chain, and by the innuendoes from other store managers about her 'pencil work.' . . . The resentment of other fountain managers—and of his own nonfountain employees against the woman's opposition to the perquisites usually allowed such personnel—forced him openly to check her records, to imply that she was making errors, and to withhold the praise she obviously craved. Higher chain officials also asked her to explain her unique performance and hinted that she could not be that much superior to other fountain managers. After two years of mounting resentments, she quit the firm."

This incident is not unique; Dalton's book, for example, which emphasizes the political aspects of organizational behavior, is full of similar ones. The question is why, in this and similar instances, a group gets caught up in one mode of problem solving or decision making rather than another, quite different one. Can a theoretical answer be given that relates some precursor to decision process as outcome? In an earlier article (Mohr, 1976), which examined plea bargaining in courts, I attempted to identify some elements of such a precursor. Chief among them is the compatibility of the goals of participants: If the goals are very highly compatible, especially if time and other resources are also ample, the group will be impelled toward a joint attempt to maximize; if they are utterly incompatible or contradictory, a political struggle is likely to ensue; if they are in between, and especially if system norms constrain against the utter domination of some by others, the tendency will be toward bargaining and satisficing. Another important factor, judging from the extensive research that has been carried out, is the consistency of participants: A strong tendency toward bargaining and satisficing inevitably develops when the same participants are institutionally constrained to meet over and over again, with somewhat divergent goals, to make choices of importance to all.

Viewed in this manner, the area would appear to lend itself to process theory in classic form, in which the probabilistic encounters of goals and constraints yield, or in essence define, various modes of collective procedure toward problem resolution. There is no dependent *variable* here; each type of decision making stands alone as an event and carries its own precursor. One might cast the model in Mendelian form such that the goals and constraints of each participant are analogous to gene loci, and the mating of the "chromosomes" of various participants with one another produces one of several decision modes just as one of several phenotypes—dominant, recessive, intermediate, codominant, and so forth—is produced by the mating of biological genes. Although one is dealing directly with the goals of individuals, it is not even necessarily true that the possibility of such models is frustrated logically by the fundamental assumption on motivation and behavior. The present application is one in which *specific* goals are not decisive, but rather a form of what in Chapter Three was called summary motivation. What matters is not the content of each goal chromosome but rather the relations among them, particularly their compatibility at a moment in time.

Nevertheless, and although further insights are no doubt to be gleaned, motives make extremely recalcitrant material to work with theoretically, and models with this purpose are likely to be frustrated. Measurement problems would always be severe, but there is a deeper and newer reason—newer, that is, in the sense of its recognition by social scientists, although it has always been lurking about to frustrate general explanations of motivated behavior. The problem is that in large measure the pertinent, critical goals do not exist or are not pursued if they do exist. But somehow, people act—and should act, must act—in spite of their detachment from, or at least quite mysterious relation to, goals. March (1978) has presented this position in an article that is undoubtedly a turning point in the study of the relation between goals and behavior. Goals change over time in unpredictable ways; people recognize this and therefore refrain from acting in accord with present aspirations. Preferences are endogenous; they are selected and created by the very behavior they are often supposed to determine. Preferences are ambiguous; they are frequently clarified only by acting in the face of the ambiguity. Goals are inconsistent; conflicting motivations for action arise from the existence of independent sources, such as self-interest, morality, tastes, and a variety of unblended social roles; the desire to both eat and have is ubiquitous. Goals are mistrusted; apparent or conscious motivations to spend, commit, sever, are beaten down internally because one is suspicious of their true depth or preference ranking. Clear specification and even recognition of goals are disadvantageous; clarity can lead to conflict, suboptimal performance, paralysis of choice, and the stifling of creativity, so that ambiguity is intelligently preferred. And finally, sin and hypocrisy—acting contrary to current preferences and values—are functional and perhaps indispensable; constructive behavior change would be stunted by the requirement that it be preceded rather than followed by corresponding changes in goals.

Imagine that one went back to the fountain manager, the store manager, and other participants and asked, "Why did you not compromise and satisfice in this situation?" And imagine further that each gave the highly plausible response "I always thought we probably would. The problem was that we apparently felt too strongly, all in all. But we didn't know that at the time—not until events had taken their course and we found that we had pushed to a winner-take-all solution." It is most problematic in this perspective, and risky, to bank on the understanding of collective behavior in terms of the *prior* goals of individuals. That, however, would seem to be a constant feature of the process-as-outcome approach. One recognizes that goals are on one side and behavior on another, but at the moment one can see only a black box in between. Choices among incommensurables are only the beginning. The goals in themselves are fetal, ambiguous, inconsistent, confused, and mistrusted, so that the black box connecting them with behavior cannot possibly contain a naive function. Yet behavior is somehow a result of motives. Conceptualizing the workings of the black box, the clever forms of the prominent mechanisms of transfer, is therefore a challenge to description or to process theory, with apparently handsome payoff.

Summary. For the present, it is clear that much of the theory of bounded-rationality decision making at the collective level is not theory in any well-worn scientific sense—it neither explains anything nor describes anything stable. The crux of its value, however, does lie in description—in creative conceptualization that uncovers processes that are *sometimes* the way human beings do things, conceptualization that simply reveals to us something about ourselves—something unstable, to be sure, but something that at best strikes one as being highly intriguing, important, useful, and nonobvious. This is one direction along which the future of good social science will undoubtedly lie, and since many alternative directions are not so hopeful, it clearly is important.

Postscript: The Garbage-Can Model of Organizational Choice

In Chapter Two the garbage-can model was raised as an example of process theory. It is true that the model is process-theoretic in form; in fact, it might be called classic or quintessential process theory, since it exhibits the characteristics of that form more straightforwardly, unambiguously, and graphically than almost any example one could adduce. Although it is process theory in form, however, an inherent ambiguity in scope robs it of full theoretical status.

In process theory, the precursor is necessary for the outcome, which in this case would translate into the proposition that the garbage-can process is a necessary precursor of the making of decisions. Yet it is not claimed that this process characterizes the way choices are made in all organizations; it is only proposed as a circumstantial phenomenon. When, then, is the precursor a necessary condition? That is, in which organizations or in what types of organizations is the decision-making pattern such that problems tend to be resolved indirectly (that is, by being inserted into the decision-making machinery for other problems) rather than directly, and choices are regularly delayed by the encumbrance of other, ambiguously relevant problems?

The response of the conceptualizers of the garbage-can process (Cohen, March, and Olsen, 1972) is that it characterizes decision making in *organized anarchies*—organizations in which goals are unclear, technology uncertain, and participation fluid. But organized anarchy is too sketchy and ambiguous to be a satisfactory response. To say that the model applies when participation is fluid is a bit unfair because fluid participation is a critical part of the model itself. To stipulate uncertain technology is to be quite vague; it is difficult to see whether, or by what standard criteria, the technology of teaching students and doing scientific research (universities are the prototypical organized anarchies) is more certain than that of caring for the sick in hospitals or developing advertising schemes or even selling home appliances. Chiefly, to say that an organized anarchy is identified by unclear goals is also to say very little that is definite, because, as the following chapter will elaborate in detail, the kinds of goals being referred to are always unclear—quite impossible to identify precisely. In short, like the bounded-rationality models at the group level considered in the previous section, and for the same reasons, it has not yet been said, and one probably cannot say, for which organizations—that is, for which collectivities of decisions—the garbage-can process is a necessary precursor.

It might be an advance to try to specify at least *one* set of conditions under which the garbage-can model would have an extremely high probability of prevailing. It seems uncertain what that might be. Looking about impressionistically as well as reviewing the relevant literature (March and Olsen, 1976), it appears that some governments and some colleges and universities are characterized in large measure by this decision-making pattern, but we are probably not so fortunate as to be able to say *all* governments and universities or even nearly all. Many American universities in the modern era would probably be found to qualify, but my information suggests that universities in developing countries are structured on much more authoritarian lines and thus would not qualify, although their goals and technology are much the same as in America. I doubt that many of the same American universities qualified in the nineteenth and early twentieth centuries, either. But the point of this difficulty of even minimal definiteness is not that the model has little value. On the contrary, it is that its value does not depend on definiteness. The value of the model lies not in understanding how decision making occurs in certain kinds of organizations but rather in eliciting and conceptualizing the heretofore hidden tendency for decision making to occur in this manner *sometimes,* even though precisely when is unclear, so that it no doubt characterizes some organizations largely and others only to a smaller extent. It is a good model not because it explains something definite (and there-fore qualifies well as explanatory theory) but because it explains something indefinite and is, nevertheless, intriguing, important, useful, and nonobvious. It is as though one had been able to say in the nineteenth century that *some* malaria was caused by mosquitoes, without being able to specify precisely which cases. The primary difference is that in the malaria example one might suppose that precision would eventually be possible, whereas in the present situation such a supposition would be naive.

It is significant that even though indefinite, such a model can indeed be useful as well as intriguing, important, and nonobvi-ous. It can be so both by enriching the process of further scientific, creative thought and by informing practitioners in organizations (Cohen and March, 1974, pp. 195–216), who do not require that the world be definite. In short, the analysis of the present section sug-gests, as did the previous discussion of bounded rationality, that good social science need not necessarily pursue explanatory theory.

If the subject were to be closed here, one would omit a large portion of the matter that has intrigued and preoccupied the audi-ence for the garbage-can model. Particularly with the publication of *Ambiguity and Choice in Organizations* (March and Olsen, 1976), a second kind of question has become important. It is a question of a different level of analysis—the individual *decision* level rather than the organizational decision-making system level. The earlier question was "What is the decision-making system of an organized anarchy?" The one treated now, however, becomes "When or why or how does an individual choice situation, in *any* organization, turn into a garbage can?" When, in other words, is a decision likely to become encumbered to the point of serious obstruction or diversion by ambiguously relevant problems, solutions, and participants? For many, this question may be the more interesting.

The idea of organized anarchy has considerably less relevance here both because the phenomenon apparently occurs in other types of organizations and because only some decisions in organized anarchies fall into this category. A great many decisions in universities, for example, are made on the basis of simple rational analysis or bargaining among directly interested parties or political domination, without becoming choked with extraneous matter or even becoming very public.

In the context of this volume, one should then ask whether there might be an explanatory theory at this level, if not at the former one. In answer, there is not one yet, nor is there likely ever to be one; the phenomenon is a clear example from the stubborn category of collective, motivated behavior. It is perhaps an instructive example to consider for a moment, however, because it illustrates some of the benefits and the limitations of the process-theory approach to outcomes in this category.

There has not really, to my knowledge, been a serious attempt to develop theory in this area at all—variance theory, process theory, or otherwise—apart from my own sketchy effort in an article cited earlier (Mohr, 1976). It lags behind the other decision-making models in this respect. I would suggest, however, that the process-theory *brand of thinking* suits the subject best, even though a true, explanatory process theory may be out of reach. What is indicated is a Darwinian kind of process, but in the world of decisions rather than organisms. Choice opportunities are born. The probabilistic question is then not whether they will survive in the environment but, almost the same thing, whether they will be consummated without the delay and obstruction that comes of being burdened with encumbrances in a jungle of problems and participants. Some have a higher probability than others of encumbrance—that is, of becoming garbage cans. But this model is different from the Darwinian one in two respects, resulting in large measure from their differing levels of generality. First, an aspect that is critical to the theory of natural selection is a minor matter here. Here, it is minor to look at the events as a probabilistic process. It is quite obvious that some choices will have rougher going than others, depending on many circumstances; there is not much gain in discovering that some choices have a higher and some a lower probability of consummation. Not so in Darwinism, where the whole idea of heritability and evolution, especially as opposed to Creation, makes this probabilistic mating of genotypes and environments the critical thrust of the theory. Second, the other way around—something with no direct role in the general theory of natural selection is critical here. In the case of the Darwinian statement, it is not suitable to ask, except in specified circumstances or detailed studies, what kinds of genotypes will survive. One knows that the answer depends on the characteristics of the environment, which could be anything, and that the surviving organisms will be molded accordingly. But in the present case, the whole point is to get insight into the question "Just what is it that gives one choice opportunity a higher probability of becoming a garbage can than another?" It is similar to a particularization of natural selection. It is as though one were studying, say, elephant seals and nothing else and were asking which kinds of elephant seals will become dominant in the population.

By way of precursor, some tentative answers to the question for individual choice processes have been suggested in the various writings on the garbage-can model. Chiefly, one would suspect, a choice has higher probability of becoming a garbage can, or (more correctly) a full garbage-can, if it arises in an organized anarchy rather than elsewhere—in a university rather than a highly routine bureaucratic organization, for example. Within the bounds of an organized anarchy, the probability of attracting problems is even greater when the choice is closer to solution (Cohen, March, and Olsen, 1972, p. 4). In all settings, the less segmented the organizational structure (that is, the less strict and confining the rules governing the access of participants and problems to choice processes), the more likely is any choice opportunity to become a garbage can

(Cohen, March, and Olsen, 1972). Another factor that matters is the extent to which the choice in question has a catch-all kind of character. For example, if the president tells the government that he is shaping a reindustrialization policy, then every group's need for a tax benefit, a subsidy, or a regulatory change is likely to jump into the fray for determined exercise. The visibility of the choice opportunity would also be important. Its relevance to the kinds of problems most abundant in its environment would be extremely important (for example, in the 1960s, the issue of grading was a frequent garbage can in universities largely because military service, therefore support for the Vietnam War, and so forth, depended partly on grade-point average). In this connection, one additional important characteristic should be noted—relevance of the decision to a value struggle when the organization's dominant or traditional value structure shows signs of weakening or is otherwise in doubt (Mohr, 1978). All organizations are susceptible to the generation of garbage cans of this nature. It is noteworthy that the group of case studies in *Ambiguity and Choice in Organizations* (March and Olsen, 1976) not only relates primarily to the level of the individual decision but is heavily oriented toward garbage cans of this latter type—struggles for the character of the organization—rather than the type, as exemplified by a reindustrialization policy, in which the value structure is only nibbled at and is otherwise accepted and stable.

Let us recognize that this group of factors—visibility, relevance, and so forth—will never make the precursor of a variance theory. These are not general efficient causes, but rather selected motivations and resources for the decision-making behavior of people. The coefficients will never be specified precisely, so that one might know that the more a choice opportunity is characterized by X, Y, and Z, the more problems it will attract. As in all other such examples considered in this volume, it is doubtful that one can even come close to such precision.

But by the same token, this collection of motives and resources is too loose and imprecise, too nonnecessary, to be the precursor of a true process theory. The idea in process-theoretic form is useful mainly because it provides a working image of an intriguing aspect of organizational decision making. It suggests that the potential for choice situations to become garbage-can processes always exists, but actualization becomes much more probable in some instances than others. Certain organizations can go for years without a single instance of garbage-can decision making if the necessary ingredients—the proper kinds of choices and the proper kinds of participant concerns—are sparse enough to yield a low probability of confluence. Even so, a garbage-can process might develop from time to time. For other organizations, particularly those with little segmentation and those in a time of value ambivalence, the probability of *escaping* periodic garbage-can processes may become extremely low.

The idea suggested in *Ambiguity and Choice in Organizations* (March and Olsen, 1976), that as choice opportunities rise and fall in the organizational world, a few do indeed become garbage cans, is not a theory. It is, in fact, a good example of nontheory. However, it encourages further work and thought. Although the blunt, direct explanatory approach is not likely to yield a theory, perhaps something else will, something that involves the central notion more obliquely. As it stands, the construction is a conceptual lever that will no doubt have a relatively long half-life in the world of ideas about organizational behavior.

✻ 6 ✻

The Elusive Theory of Organizational Effectiveness

The theory of effectiveness is the Holy Grail of organizational research. Such yearning is understandable in Western culture, first, because organizations, as primary instruments of goal attainment, must be made to work properly and, second, because a machine-oriented culture is almost bound to feel that a way can indeed be found to make instruments do what they are supposed to do, and do it well.

Whenever the possibility of a theory of effectiveness is not closely examined, it appears to be assumed, often casually, that the likelihood is there. The assumption permeates the entire body of literature on organizational behavior, from the classical period to the present day. It is assumed, that is, that there is some stable, reliable relation between effectiveness as an outcome, on one hand, and some particular precursor or partial precursor, on the other. All normative organization theory depends on this assumption, including the scientific management theory of Taylor ([1911], 1967), the classical management approach in the principles of Fayol (1949), the bureaucratic theory of Weber (1947), the public administration model assembled by Gulick and others (Gulick and Urwick, 1937), the consonance, or contingency, theory of the relation between structure and effectiveness (Woodward, 1965; Burns and Stalker, 1961), the human relations model (Likert, 1961), and a host of additional normative ideas about the proper way to run an organization. Implicit in each of these is the empirical hypothesis that an organization will be more effective if it practices the ideas offered than if it does not—at least a partial explanation, in other words, of effectiveness.

In much empirical research, the possibility of stable effectiveness hypotheses is often fairly explicit and frequently is indicated by the generalized term *organizational effectiveness* in the titles of articles and books—for example, "A Study of Organizational Effectiveness" (Georgopoulos and Tannenbaum, 1957), "Task Environment, Decentralization, and Organizational Effectiveness" (Neghandi and Reimann, 1973), "Predicting Organizational Effectiveness with a Four-Factor Theory of Leadership" (Bowers and Seashore, 1966), or simply *Organizational Effectiveness* (Price, 1968). More often, it is only implied. When Perrow (1977) discusses what he calls "gross malfunctioning analysis," for example, there is the suggestion that finding what leads to operational disaster in selected instances can help determine some of the requisites for doing things right in the more general case. The more usual example of the same sort of reasoning is typified by Hall's "System Pathology of an Organization: The Rise and Fall of The Old *Saturday Evening Post*" (1976). Over and over again in writings on organizations there is advice. It is usually subtle but sometimes can be rather straightforwardly proposed, as in Weick's (1977) admonition that the effective organization may need to be clumsy, superstitious, hypocritical, and wandering. Countless sentences begin with something like "But in order to achieve its goals, the unit must . . ." and continue with apparently sensible observations about how to achieve effectiveness. Organizational innovation is frequently presumed to be good in itself, betraying the assumption that innovativeness and effectiveness are positively correlated, as Rogers and Eveland point out (1973, pp. 18–19). Sometimes, statements framed as definitions of effectiveness are proposed, but it is difficult to distinguish them from hypotheses about effectiveness. For example: "From this perspective, effective organizations are those that accurately perceive patterns of resource interdependence, correctly perceive demands, and then respond to those demands made by those groups that control the most critical interdependencies. One can, of course, ask whether this definition of effectiveness is empirically correlated with other indicators. I suspect it is, particularly with the organization's long-term survival and growth" (Pfeffer, 1977, p. 145). In short, an overwhelming amount of scholarship on organizations cooperates with the notion that stable hypotheses about effectiveness can be discovered or developed.

When scholars address the question explicitly and directly, however, the tendency is quite the opposite. This is evident in the recent book by Steers (1977) and in the valuable collection of essays on the topic by Goodman, Pennings, and Associates (1977). The majority view is clearly that a theory of organizational effectiveness is not practical as a research goal. Still, the various contributors are not in agreement, particularly in the kinds of considerations they emphasize (see the summary by Kahn, 1977), and many of them, unable to renounce totally the pursuit of the Grail, gravitate perceptibly toward optimistic assumptions and orientations.

I suggest that it cannot be demonstrated logically that a valid theory of organizational effectiveness is impossible to attain. There are several perspectives on the idea of theory in this area, and each could possibly yield one or more strong generalizations. In spite of the unlikelihood of a categorically negative demonstration, however, when one specifies these perspectives and examines each in its most favorable light, one realizes that for a variety of reasons, all do appear to fall short of being able to accomplish what one requires from a theory of effectiveness.

The Current Case Against a Theory

Pulling the various bits and pieces of critique by different commentators together, it appears that the case for the impossibility of a theory of organizational effectiveness rests on three rather impressive grounds. Let me present first a summary of these ideas in the literature, then a rebuttal and a resolution of the issues raised during the course of the analysis.

First, it is pointed out that there cannot be a theory of effectiveness because the two terms *theory* and *effectiveness* are not pertinent to each other: "The very term *effectiveness* suggests an engineering focus. . . . It is enough to note that the two realms of activity are oriented differently. The pure scientist seeks to formulate abstract and timeless theories that explain properties of nature. The engineer seeks to use science to modify nature. . . .There is ample practical experience implying that both science and engineering benefit when the division of labor is explicit and different standards are used to evaluate the two kinds of work. . . .To introduce effectiveness considerations into attempts at formulating and testing general laws of organizational behavior confuses the two realms of activity to the detriment of both engineering and science" (Hannan and Freeman, 1977, p. 108). An organization or program, in other words, is viewed not as a descriptive system in the perspective of effectiveness but as a teleological system. The concept of theory as it functions in science is not applicable to such systems. The aim in constructing teleological systems is *design,* not theory.

The second important ground for denying the possibility of a theory of organizational effectiveness is that it must necessarily employ the concept of organizational goal in any test, and that concept is intractable. Since an untestable theory is not a valid theory in the canons of acceptable science, no theory of organizational effectiveness can be valid. The following sorts of reasoning are adduced to demonstrate that the goal concept is intractable:

1. *The organizational goal is not an objective concept.* This is a conclusion reached by many—for example, Scott (1977, p. 69): "Most important for present purposes is the recognition that assessments of organizational effectiveness are never purely descriptive or objective in character. The selection of properties, weights, and standards are decisions that always rest on more or less explicitly formulated normative statements or assumptions. To seek purely empirical methods for making these decisions is to pursue an illusion."

Scholars surely do not agree on the criteria to be used. One large difference in emphasis among them—the goal model versus the system model (Etzioni, 1960)—has persisted in a prominent and influential way for over twenty years; Goodman and Pennings (1977, p. 4) point out in the introduction to their volume that a reconciliation of these orientations would appear to be a prerequisite for progress on a theory of effectiveness. Aside from contending scholarly factions, there are also idiosyncratic views, such as that of Cummings (1977, p. 60): "From this perspective, an effective organization is one in which the *greatest percentage of participants* perceive themselves as free to use the organization and its subsystems as instruments for their own ends." Perhaps the most impressive demonstration of the nonobjective character of the goal in the work of researchers is provided by Campbell (1977). He shows that three prominent models of effectiveness, the operations research model, the organizational development model, and the Likert-ISR model, all have different ideas of the goal. He also lists thirty different goal-like criteria that have been used by a variety of scholars in effectiveness research, including productivity, efficiency, profit, quality, growth, morale, control, adaptation, readiness, and stability. It might be thought that a mathematical clustering technique would settle such differences in emphasis and orientation by reducing the various criteria to a well-behaved set of summary factors. Campbell reviews two well-known examples of this approach. In one (Mahoney and Weitzel, 1969), the summary factors that emerged from a factor analysis were development, democratic supervision, reliability, diversity, emphasis on results, understanding, planning, and productivity-support-utilization. In the other (Seashore and Yuchtman, 1967), they were business volume, production cost, new-member productivity, youthfulness of members, business mix, manpower growth, devotion to management, maintenance cost, member productivity, and market penetration. Clearly, what comes out of such clustering procedures depends on what goes in, and what goes in depends on who is doing the research and when and for what audience.

The only hope for objectivity, then, would seem to lie not in the findings of scholars but in the orientations of organizational members themselves. There is a deplorable lack of data on goal agreement within organizations, but the impressions and reports of scholars who have to some degree informed themselves indicate that different participants have different ideas about the goals of their organizations and that what cooperation takes place is made possible by mutual accommodation to the accepted fact of disagreement rather than by mutuality of purpose. This characterization is well illustrated by the case studies of Cyert and March (1963, pp. 47–66), for example, and forms the backbone of their influential view of organizational decision making. In one of the few studies to address the question directly, Gross (1968) found wide differences within universities concerning both what the goals of the organization should be and what they actually were—so wide in some instances that certain potential goal statements had to be dropped from the analysis. From his considerable research experience on hospitals and other organizations, Scott (1977, p. 74) concludes: "In sum, the search for universal criteria of organizational effectiveness would appear to be in difficulty because the many parties associated with the organization assess effectiveness by means of different and potentially conflicting criteria. . . . Add to these disagreements differences in time horizon and life cycle, stir, and we have a recipe for confusion and dissensus."

The goal concept is considered to be intractable, then, because its content is essentially arbitrary. Both scholars and participants disagree among themselves, and there is no objective basis for determining whose view to accept as *the* legitimate definition.

2. Even if the organizational goal could be determined objectively, *its content would in general be too difficult to specify.* The problem of the huge size of many organizational goal sets (see Simon, 1964) is just the beginning. To determine effectiveness, it is not enough simply to name all the different goals being pursued; one must match the level of performance with the level of goal attainment sought. It has long been recognized that this necessity presents essentially insurmountable difficulties. The nonlinearities involved are particularly damaging. *Good,* for example, is not always a linear function of attainment; that is, after a certain point, additional achievement may have zero or even negative value (Seashore, 1972). The precise functions, moreover, are almost ridiculous to try to specify. Time horizons complicate matters im-

mensely, because the trade-off between short-run and long-run accomplishment becomes bogged down in a plethora of unusual discount rates that are beyond the resources of most scholars and organization members to specify (Scott, 1977, p. 74; Hannan and Freeman, 1977, p. 115). The mode of aggregating divisible accomplishment on even one goal alone is generally unspecifiable. For example, shall the criterion be the average test score of the pupils, the percentage who score over a certain number of points, or the median as weighted by the inverse of the interquartile range (see Hannan and Freeman, 1977, pp. 123-124)? Shall it be the average delinquency score per subject treated, the average number of offenses per delinquent subject, the average seriousness of offenses per delinquent subject, or the percentage of delinquent subjects (Berleman and Steinburn, 1967)? Perhaps most overwhelming of all is the necessity of ordering goals by importance (see Edwards and Guttentag, 1975). It is virtually impossible to find or to manufacture common scales for the relative value of qualitatively different goals such as morale and productivity, race relations and urban esthetics (Banfield, 1962), or scholastic achievement and value socialization (Hannan and Freeman, 1977, pp. 124–125), in spite of the fact that the theoretical indifference curves of the economist give the task a deceptive appearance of manageability. The problem is exacerbated essentially to infinity by the notorious tendency of the combinations to be nonlinear; that is, certain combinations of levels of goal attainment are to be valued, either positively or negatively, beyond any prediction possible from their individual utility functions taken separately. All these difficulties are, of course, complicated further by the necessity to weight differentially the preferences of different organizational participants (Edwards and Guttentag, 1975). And lastly, nearly all organizations are to some extent organized anarchies (Cohen, March, and Olsen, 1972), and to that extent their goals are simply unclear.

3. Even if the content of the organizational goal were not too difficult to specify, *it is so intricately complicated and so dependent on persons and situations that there is probability zero that two organizations have the same goal.* Moreover, it must be assumed that in principle a different program is required to achieve a different goal; therefore, *a particular theory of organizational effectiveness can have no gener-*

ality (Campbell, 1977, pp. 47–49; Hannan and Freeman, 1977, pp. 111–115, 126–128).

4. Even if many organizations had the same goal, *the efforts that go into achieving it are so complex that it is impossible to discern which activities contribute how much to what aspect of the outcome.* So many dovetailing activities are carried out—with day-to-day variation in the kind and level of effort—that precise or even rough impacts cannot be pinned down (Hannan and Freeman, 1977, pp. 117–118). This is essentially a degrees-of-freedom problem; nearly infinitely many organizations with the same goal would be necessary to provide the controls or the variance required to discern the true causes of goal attainment.

Beyond the issues of theory versus design and the intractability of the concept of organizational goal, the third ground in the case is that things *besides* the organizational program have an impact on effectiveness. There would be no problem if these factors were well behaved—that is, additive with respect to the organizational program—but they are not. They form a context whose elements interact with the program, so that the theory of effectiveness would be more valid or less—or not valid at all—depending on conditions outside the boundaries of the theory itself (Scott, 1977, pp. 79–80; Hannan and Freeman, 1977, pp. 116–117, 119, 121). These factors are numerous and powerful, including the status and drift of general economic, political, and social conditions, the mood of customers and clients, the activities and strategies of other organizations in the environment, the quality of personnel available to the organization, the quality of the raw materials, the value structure of the community, the degree of support from higher levels of government or industry, stipulations of pertinent tax law, and so forth. It is doubtful that these factors can be tamed by bringing them explicitly into the theory as interacting variables. In short, this is another in the series of instances noted in the present volume in which theory is frustrated by complexity.

The three grounds just elaborated would seem to constitute a final case against the possibility of a theory of organizational effectiveness. The argument does indeed contain many telling points, but it is not as strong as it might seem, and the issue deserves closer attention. In fact, two of the three grounds are not in themselves very damaging when one considers the true basis of interest in a theory of effectiveness. The third is another matter. It is neither logically nor empirically devastating, but in it lies a truly serious obstacle.

It is first essential to note that theories of effectiveness may be and in fact are sought in two forms. One may be called the goal-specific form (Scott, 1977, p. 89) and the other the goal-free form. The first is a theory of the attainment of a certain objective or group of objectives that is specified as the goal of organizational effort; the second is a single theory of the attainment of organizational goals, no matter what they may be. The objections just elaborated are heavily oriented toward the goal-specific form, in which the difficulty of specifying the goal is a significant obstacle to the existence of a theory. The following discussion is accordingly directed first toward that form, but we will then turn to goal-free theories, for it is clear, utopian though it may seem at first glance, that the main orientation is in that direction.

Goal-Specific Theories

Consider the first objection that programs to achieve goals are designs, and designs are not theories. One can make that distinction, and its application to the present issue is incontrovertibly valid. Furthermore, there is utility in maintaining the distinction in general. It is true that an organizational program or any other human artifact is in a sense a part of the natural world because all human activities exist in nature. Scientific theory, however, is rightfully reserved to explanation of that part of the natural world which excludes intentional human meddling. One knows that humans can meddle and in so doing can infinitely complicate the natural world, but one would like to understand regularities in the way the world operates when it goes without intentional human interference. One reason, as Chapter Three was designed to show, is that the powerful regularities tend to disappear once motivated human behavior is included in the target of explanation. Thus, it is important to keep human artifacts, social or mechanical, separate from theoretical explanation. That requirement understood, however, one may also recognize that the logic of theory and of design are in many ways not so very far apart; moreover, maintaining simply that one category is irrelevant for the other does not adequately address the issue of effectiveness theory and the concerns that generate it.

Let us consider in what sense, and in how strong a sense, an organizational program, being a design, is not also a theory. Theory as treated in the present volume presumes a precursor that is either necessary or necessary and sufficient for the outcome to be explained. Applied to the issue of organizational effectiveness, this would signify that some program, some way of doing things, was either necessary or necessary and sufficient for achievement of a specified goal. But the program clearly is not necessary. Drawing again as an axiom on the proverb that there is more than one way to skin a cat, it is plain that no particular manner already devised is the only manner in which an objective can be achieved. One can never accept in principle that *this* is the only way to accomplish something in the same sense as one can accept the descriptive hypothesis that in the natural world, X is the only way in which Y happens to occur. One must accept, on the contrary, that another successful program departing more or less radically from the first can be found, whether people are able to divine it at the moment or not. An organizational program is a process and so might be taken, in conjunction with the goal, to be a process theory, which rests on the necessary-but-not-sufficient condition. But processes should not automatically be presumed to be theories. In the present case, not only is the precursor not necessary for the outcome, but there is substantial additional departure from the idea of process theory both in letter and in spirit. The organizational goal is a target, and the program is steered by feedback so as to home in on the target as narrowly as possible. A process theory, in contrast, requires objects that, under the influence of external directional forces, proceed on natural courses *independently* of one another and are combined or otherwise relationally rearranged only through the unaided and unhampered operation of the laws of chance. A process theory therefore necessarily precludes outside steering or other human interference in the probability of the outcome, whereas such interference is the very essense of an effective design.

Although specific programs are not necessary conditions of goal attainment, there is, paradoxically, a narrow usage in which they might be considered necessary and sufficient and therefore variance theories of goal attainment. This is in the sense of experimental design or program evaluation, which is variance theory in microcosm (see Chapter Two). Microcosm, however, means that the program has been found to be necessary and sufficient for the outcome only with respect to the given set of applications and nonapplications (controls) purposely examined in the experiment, in a time period that is already past. The soul of effectiveness *theory*, however, is that it be generalizable; it is well known and not an advance to learn that some programs have indeed been effective at some times and in particular organizations. As soon as generalizability is required, the sufficiency of the program is cast into doubt, and its necessity must be denied in principle, as noted earlier. Furthermore, most organizational programs become ridiculous as variance-theory precursors because of their *degeneracy*. If they are considered as a complex series of actions and behaviors, then the variance-theory logic means that the series must occur in one precisely prescribed way or ineffectiveness must be predicted (see Chapter Two), but that is rarely the manner in which an organizational program can either operate or be described.

Perhaps the program, as precursor, is merely sufficient to attain the desired outcome. In that case, degeneracy, at least, would not be a problem; it may be freely admitted that one particular series of behaviors is not required absolutely, that it may be varied a good deal in application—that other programs, in a word, may also be sufficient. Here is where design approaches theory even if the two do not technically become one. The position was adopted in Chapter Two that the merely sufficient precursor is inadequate as a theoretical explanation of Y because the latter would occur frequently and enigmatically without the former. That position must be maintained, but the standards for design are a bit different. True, a particular organizational program is no more a theory of organizational goal attainment than an airplane is a theory of flying. But an airplane *is* in a sense a theory of flying—in the sufficient-condition sense, and in a realm in which the gulf between the merely sufficient and the necessary and sufficient does not appear to be so critical. The requirements for theory are not technically met, but to drop the subject, having demonstrated logically that they are not, would be to fail to address adequately the real issue concerning a theory of effectiveness. If not a theory of effectiveness, is there in any case a design for effectiveness? Is it possible to arrive at an organizational program that is as good a theory of profit or growth or morale or the prevention of criminal recidivism as an airplane is a theory of flying? If so, then many of those seeking a theory of effectiveness may be well satisfied. Honoring the spirit of the inquiry, one must have other grounds if one is to reject the possibility of a theory of effectiveness out of hand.

Consider next the objection that the concept of organizational goal is intractable. Elsewhere (Mohr, 1973) I have set out a conceptualization of the organizational goal that attempts to render it rigorously operationalizable, small in content, and generally manageable as a criterion of effectiveness. I do not believe, in other words, that the goal concept must necessarily be as intractable as it may sometimes seem. But it is not necessary to decide here the issue of the proper conceptualization of the organizational goal. Aspects of the intractability of the goal concept are important—mainly in connection with the complexity objection, which will be considered next—but the issue as presented earlier is perhaps a matter of raising some of the right concerns at the wrong time. The truth is that few would feel the inclination to confine a theory of effectiveness to attainment of the *organization's* goal in any case; it is, after all, just one of the many possible criteria. Theoretical interest would seem to lie, rather than in a monstrously huge, uncertain, nebulous, and idiosyncratic standard, in means by which an organization may reliably be expected to achieve *certain* goals, such as profit, growth, morale, stability, population control, prevention of recidivism, prevention of mortality from certain diseases, or, in fact, any particular goal in which there is substantial interest among scholars or participants (Kahn, 1977, pp. 237–238). Even if one works within the *system model* (Etzioni, 1960; Katz and Kahn, 1966), in which organizational effectiveness must be rendered in terms of doing well as a sociological unit, it is highly desirable to have a concrete criterion rather than a potpourri of anything that anybody cares about (for excellent examples of such a criterion, see Yuchtman and Seashore, 1967, and Keeley, 1978). A theory of design for the attainment of a multipartite, multifaceted, complex situation-bound goal is hardly worth the effort required to think about it. Effectiveness is almost invariably considered in connection with simpler and more circumscribed criteria. If an organization's complete goal set happens to be one that is commonly encountered, compact, and straightforward, then that is one thing, but if it is unique and complex, it would seem to be rather a useless commodity from the standpoint of goal-specific theory.

Thus, intractability itself is not a problem. It does not matter that the criterion is not objective, nor even, as suggested in the previous chapter, that the goals of participants may be ambiguous. Any and all criteria in which there is substantial interest, whether labeled the organizational goal or not, are possible and worthy targets. Nor does the difficulty of specification become an obstacle, because one naturally confines one's interest to targets that are manageably specifiable. Whether the effort that achieves this simpler sort of goal is too complicated to specify is an empirical question. Perhaps in some cases it may be, but the existence of programs that do reliably achieve even certain difficult goals, such as sanitation programs in public health, shows that the problem is at least not universal. And lastly, it is no objection that each organizational goal set, being so vast and intricate, is unique to one organization; in reality one may simply select as outcome—in fact, one *insists* on selecting as outcome—simpler, less encyclopedic criteria that are more broadly applicable.

The one objection that in context is truly a serious one is the third, the objection that any design for effectiveness in achieving a specified goal must struggle for validity against a host of environmental forces and conditions that militate against theoretical stability. A theory of goal attainment—profitability, for example—that is successful under one set of conditions may well perform poorly under others. One encounters yet again, in other words, the problem of complexity or interaction or, in terminology appropriate to program evaluation, to which this entire issue is closely related, the problem of *external validity* (Campbell and Stanley, 1963). It must be emphasized, however, that complexity is not a logical obstacle to theories of effectiveness but only an empirical one. It is plain that this objection does not categorically negate all possibility of broadly workable organizational programs, since many effective programs do exist. Population immunization, for example, is effective enough in the control of enough communicable diseases in enough settings to meet almost anyone's standards for stability, robustness, or universality, as applied either to theory or to design. We will return to this example.

It is even more plain, however, that complexity does defeat many designs. It undermines their standing, that is, in the perspective of theory. Certain kinds of factors have been found to be common sources of severe interaction, and there are many other factors that are less common—they are more a matter of individualized context—but no less severe. Some of the factors were noted earlier: general economic and political conditions, the kinds of interests that happen to be salient to customers, clients, and other potential supporters, the quality of personnel and raw materials available, and the strategies used by competing or otherwise interacting organizations. To these must now be added an important additional disturbance. Now that a limited, circumscribed goal is the focus of attention, the *other* goals of organizational members become relevant as elements of context. It is here that the intractability of the concept of organizational goal makes its weight felt. Whether these other elements should properly be considered organizational, how they should be aggregated, or what may be their preference ordering and utility functions matters little. What matters is that people in the organization are concerned with attaining them, and because of what these other goals may be and how people may have to behave in pursuing them, the parameters of the design for the particular ends in question become unstable. In plainer terms, what it takes to get a job done may depend on what else the people concerned are trying to accomplish at the same time. The seriousness of the problem is self-evident, but a conspicuous recent example in the criminal justice field that may be cited is the police diversion program, as analyzed insightfully by Klein and others (1977, p. 551). There are ten or more fairly major possible purposes or functions of the program, some of them mutually inconsistent, and communities have experienced small success in achieving some simply because they have harbored considerable interest in others.

Complexity is able to frustrate theories of organizational effectiveness because environments or contexts do tend to vary and because this variation presents obstacles that are difficult for the theory to circumvent or overcome. This suggests two directions along which broadly generalizable theories of effectiveness might lie: insulating the program from the perturbing effects of its environment and building into it self-adaptive mechanisms that will cause it, by changing itself, to respond successfully to environmental variation. Simon (1969) has written at length about the possibilities of producing such designs, and we will return to his analysis in the next section. One may report for the moment, however, his dominant theme that for tasks of any significant complexity, the challenge of design can be formidable indeed. He recalls, for example, how difficult it was, because of the uncertainties of the outer environment, to design time-sharing systems for computer facilities, and this task was rather tame compared with many (1969, pp. 20–21). Stable goal-specific designs are indeed possible, but in many cases, particularly in the nontrivial, interesting kinds of cases that would make one long for a theory of organizational effectiveness, the complexity of organizational environments, both inner and outer (Simon, 1969; Duncan, 1966), becomes a formidable obstacle. Imagine trying to do for profit or organizational prestige or rehabilitation of delinquents what has been done for time-sharing systems!

There is one apparent way out that is of great interest. For many tasks, the complexity could possibly dissipate quite readily and thoroughly in the wake of a good theory (a true variance or process theory, not a design) of how the outcome of interest occurs naturally. Or, perhaps even more relevant, the complexity may be subdued by a technological breakthrough that makes achievement of the goal in question almost certain. Communicable disease presents a good example. There, the organizational task of prevention was staggering in its complexity before the germ theory was accepted and before the technologies of sanitation and immunization were developed. Once this theory and technology were in place, however, especially immunization technology, complexity was defeated and a stable design achieved. But in form, something else of importance also occurred. Not only did the prevention goal become broadly achievable, but it suddenly was viewed in a different light. We would now be strongly disinclined to consider the means of achieving that goal to be a theory of organizational effectiveness. It is a technological triumph, not a theory of effectiveness. Precisely the same shift would occur if technology were developed for the prevention of juvenile delinquency as it has been for communicable diseases or if break-even-or-better technology were developed for making a profit or winning an election as it has been for tic-tac-toe. It therefore seems that interest in a theory of effectiveness lies in what the organization should *be* rather than in what it should *do*. That is, interest lies not so much in the technology as in the *organization* of the organization—in what many would loosely call its structure or its plan for coordination. There is much that is compelling in this emphasis, and it will be well to take the step of confining the issue of *organizational* effectiveness to structural and managerial kinds of contributions, to the exclusion of the contribution of technological mastery in a given substantive area.

But the same kind of analysis must now be carried a step further. Even if complexity were overcome by organization rather than by goal-specific technology, the design still could not possibly satisfy scholars that a theory of organizational effectiveness had been found. It could not because, by that logic, time-sharing systems would also be theories of organizational effectiveness, as would the assembly-line theory of mass production, and so forth, and in fact one would clearly already be in possession of a very large number of theories of organizational effectiveness. The possibility of such theories would never have been in doubt. At the time when one is floundering along without a systematic design to attain a particular goal—when the goal is not being achieved at an adequate level—it tends to appear to all that what is lacking is a theory of organizational effectiveness that would let one know how to proceed successfully. Once the goal-specific organizational design is in place, however, and efficient attainment is guaranteed, it becomes clear that what one has is still not a theory of *organizational* effectiveness, but rather merely a theory of mass production or traffic-jam prevention, energy resource allocation, and so on. What was wanted all along for the goal-specific case—in terms, that is, of assistance from a theory of organizational effectiveness—was not a solution only to the problem at hand but rather a *general* solution that could be *applied* to the problem at hand. Complexity, therefore, is even more formidable an obstacle to a theory of organizational effectiveness than it seemed, because it must somehow be neutralized not in an ad hoc, individually tailored fashion for each challenging goal but in a sweeping, inclusive fashion for all challenging goals.

In sum, the true obstacle to theories of organizational effectiveness is neither the distinction between design and theory nor the intractability of the goal concept but complexity. Although organizational designs that overcome complexity in the goal-specific case are possible, it is clear that these are not general enough to satisfy the question behind the issue. The question remains, then, whether goal-free theories are possible; there, generality is certainly satisfactory, but complexity is essentially infinite.

Goal-Free Theories

Although the kind of theory that we would now consider is not exclusively tailored to the attainment of a particular kind of goal, it would be incorrect to assume that the goal concept is therefore irrelevant, that it can present no difficulty. Any theory of goal attainment that is proposed would have to be tested, and its validity can, of course, be established only by way of the measurement of goal attainment. Still, the intractability of the global concept of *organizational* goal need not be a problem. There would instead be interest in applying potential goal-free theories to the attainment of certain major objectives that have been singled out, whatever they may be, while considering all other simultaneous goals to be part of the complexity that bedevils the task. (The obvious model is the objective function and the constraint inequalities in linear programming.) In this way, those simultaneous goals that are felt not to have a significant impact on the parameters of the basic program need never be considered; there is no need to systematize and measure every single ingredient of the entire set of goals of organizational members. Still, one might well wonder what sorts of designs there could possibly be that would achieve goals universally under the diverse and no doubt adverse conditions introduced by the endless complexity of outer and inner environments, including the kinds of constraints imposed by varying sets of intrusive, simultaneous organizational goals. There are two kinds of approach: One would specify the content of a particular theory that would apply to all goals; the other would specify a universal basis for finding the different content that would hold for each different goal. We will consider them in reverse order.

The Science of Design. Frederick W. Taylor had a system, only roughly specified, to be sure, for calculating the best way to perform a number of tasks. These were perhaps not in themselves organizational goals, and they were confined mainly to manual labor, but if the theory were put into practice for a number of major tasks in a single organization, the relevance to the organizational goal would be real indeed (see Taylor, [1911], 1967; March and Simon, 1958). Taylor's Scientific Management was not just a method for shoveling ore, handling pig iron, working sheet metal, and laying bricks but a procedure for determining *how* to do these things and a great many more besides. It is of more than passing interest to note that Scientific Management failed because of complexity—that is, because the outer environment in which the design had to be applied contained people with other values and goals, humanistic goals, that made such persons resist Taylorism vigorously and successfully (Aitken, 1960; Nadworney, 1955). Scientific Management as conceived by Taylor is now dead, but a potentially viable contender in the same genre, although not yet well developed, is the science of design as envisioned by Simon (1969).

Simon sees the problem of producing complex, highly organized designs as a great challenge. Each task may be difficult and limited, perhaps, in application, but rewarding. He visualizes academic curricula in which the elements of the science of design would be taught and extensively researched on a continuing basis. It is not pertinent to elaborate Simon's ideas in detail, but his own summary of the elements of this science—the topics that need purposeful research, both in themselves and in their inter-relatedness—may be scanned to give the flavor of his thought (Simon, 1969, pp. 79–80):

The Evaluation of Designs

1. Theory of Evaluation:
   Utility Theory, Statistical Decision Theory
2. Computational Methods
   a. Algorithms for choosing *optimal* alternatives, such as linear programming computations, control theory, dynamic programming
   b. Algorithms and heuristics for choosing *satisfactory* alternatives
3. The Formal Logic of Design:
   Imperative and Declarative Logics

The Search for Alternatives

4. Heuristic Search: Factorization and Means-end Analysis
5. Allocation of Resources for Search
6. Theory of Structure and Design Organization:
   Hierarchic Systems
7. Representation of Design Problems

It is clear that this ambitious program, to the extent carried out, would not be a theory or design in the same goal-specific sense that was considered in the previous section. It would be a more general theory in the sense that it is a design for finding designs, an organizational program for producing organizational programs, a metadesign.

The question here is whether such a concept can stand as a theory of organizational effectiveness. Since it is far from being maturely developed, one might take the conservative position and doubt that its practical potential is very high, but let us recognize and file that reservation and assume that the science might become sufficiently well developed for fairly broad application as an integrated, purposeful approach. What then might be the objections?

It might first be objected that as a theory of effectiveness, the science of design would appear to have critical limitations of scope. It cannot produce an effective design to accomplish a task unless key aspects of technology are already available. This objection is not necessarily always valid, but it is an important point. For example, as a society we have a large, complex, and expensive organization in place to treat psychosis and minimize its ill effects on all concerned. Few, however, would consider this program to be highly effective in combating psychosis. There appear to be some key things we do not yet know. Until those puzzles are solved (a pill for schizophrenia would help), psychosis is not likely to be managed in a way that would be considered generally effective, and nothing on Simon's list is likely to be of telling assistance. How can a science of design be considered valid or powerful, then, if it can produce solutions only when the solutions are already there? But this is not a true objection. The fact is that a pill or its equivalent must be sought outside the science of design; if a cure for schizophrenia were developed, the problem as a whole would probably no longer be a significant target for that science. As noted earlier, the theory of effectiveness has little to do with such technological advances as pills but much to do, rather, with areas in which the true challenge lies in the organization, coordination, and management of relations among people and things. If it can nail down goal attainment by these means, as in the assembly line and the time-sharing system, then it is achieving within its proper realm. The science of design is not limited in scope by ignorance of theory or technology in the substantive domains appropriate to particular organizational goals; it is limited only by the technology of design—that is, by ineptness in the kinds of domains noted in the list by Simon just quoted. The science of design cannot solve all problems; one must first determine whether the problem at hand is truly an organizational one.

It might also be noted that the science of design is not a true science and is not a true theory, in spite of the fact that Simon uses that terminology contagiously. It is not a descriptive theory of how designs naturally occur in the world or come to be created, but is rather a design itself—an elaborate goal-specific design whose outcome is other designs. This is merely to say, however, that the metadesign is not different from other possible theories of effectiveness considered in the present chapter; being a design, it does not rise above others by being twice removed from organizational goals instead of once. True, it was recognized earlier that theories of effectiveness are intrinsically different because of their teleological nature, but it was recognized as well that they may have many similarities to true theory in form. Teleology happens to place them inevitably in the category of the merely sufficient, but the teleological criterion also makes that category less inadequate. Here, one seeks powerful instrumental generalizations rather than powerful explanatory generalizations, and in that case, as reviewed earlier, the merely sufficient is quite acceptable.

A third possible limitation of the science of design construed as theory would be complexity. In this case, however, the potential theory is virtually made to deal with complexity; that is its essence, its reason for being. Quoting Simon (1969, p. xi): "The reader will discover, in the course of discussion, that artificiality is interesting principally when it concerns complex systems that live in complex environments. The topics of artificiality and complexity are inextricably interwoven." The science of design explicitly singles out for treatment the obstacles placed in the path of valid goal-specific theory by complexity. It is not limited by complexity, but rather feeds on it. It is no more proper in this sense to see the science of design as being limited by complexity than to see astronomy as being limited by the stars. Only if complexity were inherently and totally unmanageable, which it clearly is not, would it defeat the possibility of a science of design.

But there is one important reservation. To a substantial extent, human beings, particularly their emotions, are part of both the inner and the outer environments of systems whose creation would be enhanced by the science of design, and that factor can be a formidable source of complexity. It was the human element in the environment, for example, not organizational problems, that defeated Taylor's grand design. It is striking that Simon's list of topics contains no research area dealing with recalcitrance on the part of some human beings at some times in the face of what designers consider rational. Perhaps there is the feeling that this human aspect of environmental complexity for artifactual systems will inevitably become a factor from time to time, but that dealing with it is art rather than science, insight rather than design. (The human relations theorists, of course, would not agree and would have this subject matter added to the laboratories and curricula of the sciences of the artificial.)

It is also true, however, that sometimes a good algorithm, either organizational or technological, may itself be the very medicine to drive out resistance and cross-purposes. Polio prevention, for example, is much more harmonious both in delivery and in acceptance than juvenile delinquency prevention; because it works smoothly, effectively, and dependably, there is not so much room for the intrusion of extraneous concerns. Unfortunately, a good algorithm only sometimes drives out resistance and cross-purposes, not always. The fluoridation controversy is one of many counterexamples, as was resistance to Taylorism itself, since Scientific Management, as far as I have been able to discover, worked beautifully as an algorithm in every application that followed Taylor's prescription.

To summarize complexity as a possible problem, if the potential science of design were to become more and more mature, the complexity of environments would presumably become more and more manageable, either through insulation or by means of adaptive subroutines. The one exception at this point would seem to be human reaction. If it can be at all systematically understood, it should be part of the science; if it is simply omitted from consideration, it will without any doubt be a source of instability.

A science of design, with one possible inherent limitation, should therefore be seen as one realistic and serious kind of response to the quest for a theory of effectiveness. I say "realistic and serious" in order to contrast the science of design with the numerous exhortations to be adaptive, to build adaptibility into structure (as exemplified within the Goodman and Pennings volume, 1977, by the ideas of Weick and of Pfeffer cited earlier), which are in the same genre but more simplistic. Instead of recognizing and dealing with the fact that the complexity of environments is likely to be reliably overcome only by detailed planning and design, they offer primarily the idea that adaptiveness to changes in context is one of the critical determinants of effectiveness. That is true as far as it goes, but it does not, in the present perspective, go very far.

Although the science of design is realistic and serious, one does not have the feeling that it is precisely the kind of solution that people have had in mind under the heading of "theory of effectiveness." It would appear that people have sought a *way*, not a way to find a way. The type of solution suggested by Simon is not only indirect but vast, protracted, and progressively evolving. It is best viewed as a serious approach to design and complexity that assumes that a simple general theory does not exist and proceeds on a level of substantially greater detail and specificity. It is best viewed, perhaps, as the kind of approach in which scholars should be interested *instead* of seeking a theory of effectiveness. Let us not prejudge such as issue, however, but rather first explore briefly the most prominent type of standardized, universally applicable response to the quest for a theory.

Structural Theories of Effectiveness. Aside from the advice to be adaptive, the most prominent single-solution approaches have been structural: Weberian bureaucratic theory, classical management and public administration theory, human relations theory, and the structural consonance hypothesis. Each of these proposes a method of attaining organizational effectiveness in all or nearly all settings by structuring the organization in a certain way, the first advocating hierarchal authority, clear rules and procedures, and so on, the second relying on the principles of management (unity of command, span of control, and so forth), the third advocating participative management, supportiveness, and other exercise of person-oriented leadership, and the fourth proposing that the organization can and should bring its internal structure into harmony with the requirements of its environment, technology, and size. In view of the monumental difficulty and detail recognized by the science of design, one might say that such unitary nostrums can hardly be considered serious. In what way are they indeed serious?

First, these solutions clearly do not constitute quantitative theory with parameters of specified magnitude. They would be related to effectiveness not in some specific degree but only in direction, or sign. That is, the theoretical statement has the form "The use of this approach will lead to greater effectiveness than its nonuse, other things being equal." Precisely how much greater effectiveness should result is unspecified and presumably varies from one context to another. This fact immediately suggests a possible weakness: If dimensions of context affect the amount of benefits to be derived, they might well be able to bring that amount to zero and even cause it to be negative. It also raises the question that the attempt to apply the technique may not be worth the cost in instances in which the benefits are small.

Even as theories of sign only, rather than quantitative relations, can one claim that any of the existing single-solution remedies is valid? Are these designs for effectiveness stable in the face of contextual variation? It is well recognized that a substantial amount of research convincingly answers these questions in the negative (see, for example, Burns and Stalker, 1961; White and Ruh, 1973; Mohr, 1971; Dewar and Werbel, 1979). At the simple level, in other words, these designs appear to be defeated by complexity; they may work well at times, but in some cases they appear to have no significant effect or even a negative effect. A search continues for additional variables that will explain the discrepancies, in the hope that the variables can then be brought into the models as interacting forces, thus producing stability of parameters (or at least of sign) and predictability of results in management practice. However, there is as yet no good basis for hope that the search will be successful. One wonders whether the hope of success is inherently vain.

It will be well to approach the issue by asking just how such simple and general remedies might be expected to work. Consider, as examples of problematic goals, time sharing in connection with computer facilities, the control of endemic communicable diseases such as malaria or schistosomiasis, the provision of medical services in hospitals, the large-scale manufacture of products such as automobiles or wearing apparel, and the conduct of a military campaign. All these programs would appear to have severe and unique problems of organization and management. It is unclear what the single-purpose approaches would have to say about the specifics of any one of these cases, and because the problems appear to have little in common, it is particularly unclear why the remedies might be expected to be relevant to all of them.

I suggest in response that, viewing from the perspective of this kind of design, a great many organizations do indeed share a critical, common problem, although it may not always be a sharply conspicuous one, and that the claim to validity would rest on the ability to do effective battle against this particular widespread concern. That problem is the inconsistency of goals among people (Barnard, 1938, pp. 244–257; Ouchi, 1980); the true aim of the well-known structural theories of organizational effectiveness is to minimize the damaging effects of cross-purposes. Although this problem may not be seriously relevant to all organizational design challenges—for example, time-sharing systems and disease control—it is a formidable concern in others, such as hospital services, manufacturing, and war.

Consider a single person with a single goal. Human relations and the other approaches considered here are clearly not valid designs to assure achievement in such a case; that is, they are not applicable to the attainment of any possible goal by any given person working alone. Next, consider a single person with many goals and constraints. It is still clear that such designs as bureaucracies and human relations programs are irrelevant. A one-person organization does not need them. Notice in passing, however, that effectiveness theory itself is not irrelevant to this case, as multiple-goal problems, even if only one individual is concerned, can be quite germane and important subject matter for the science of design. An example is a time-sharing system in which the "individual" with many goals and constraints is a machine.

Next consider an entire organizationful of persons, all with precisely the same goals, preference orderings, indifference relations, and utility functions. The situation in its pure form is hypothetical, of course, especially if one accepts that to a great extent, people do not know what their goals are and do not follow them when they do. It is approximated in significant ways, however, in groups working together under certain crisis conditions, in the example of communicable disease control, and in many other circumstances, stable or transitory, in which the bulk of inconsistent self-interest goals, subunit goals, inappropriate subgoals, and similar extraneous intentions is subordinated or simply excluded by the particular characteristics of the program and context. I have spoken to health workers on their return from smallpox control duty in Third World countries, for example. Because of the desperate need for program success, the dramatic effect of vaccination on disease incidence, the simplicity of the core procedure (vaccination), and the obviousness to every worker of the main thing that must be done—vaccinate as close to 100 percent of a target population as possible—the group approached in orientation the hypothetical unitary goal set described. This kind of organization would not be very different in nature from a single person, and what is important is that the structural mechanisms under consideration are likely to be of no greater assistance in this instance than in the previous two. It might be thought that they would apply in spite of common goals because different people working together might still need to be organized and coordinated. That is true enough, but the kind of organizational information needed is the kind that would be specific to the task, such as would be supplied by the science of design, and clearly not a single, universal structural formula. When such methods as participative decision making, hierarchal authority, or standardized procedures are truly needed, they are obvious enough that people of one mind can be expected with substantial confidence to figure it out and adopt them. To advocate those techniques for all such occasions, however, is grotesque. They can clearly be quite irrelevant and even counterproductive. For example, consider insisting on hierarchal control or even participative management in connection with a football or basketball team or, perhaps, a group of experienced hands working hurriedly together to prepare a Florida resort against an onrushing hurricane.

Thus, to the extent that there is a clear, shared preference ordering of goals, the common single-solution design for effectiveness is inapplicable. It is only for that universe of cases in which there are or might at any moment be cross-purposes (for example, a hospital, manufacturing, the military) that such a design is relevant as general theory, and it is functional there expressly to mitigate such inconsistency.

With respect to bureaucratic theory, for example, the structure has been found to be, in essence, a *strategy of control* (Child, 1972a)—that is, a means by which management assures that *its* purposes are carried out by the organization, regardless of whether those at lower levels know their goals, like their goals, have consistent goals, or, especially, have goals that are similar to or different from those of management. Similarly, in Weber himself (1947), the several characteristics, or dimensions, of bureaucratic structure are repeatedly and explicitly connected with *predictability of performance* from the perspective of those responsible for carrying out the overall mission of the organization. The once-celebrated *dysfunctions* of bureaucracy (March and Simon, 1958, pp. 34–47) are ways in which bureaucratic structure itself works to manufacture cross-purposes—a classic example of the ironic: Selznick's paradox of delegation results in the subordinating of organization-level goals to subunit goals; Merton's displacement of goals means the counterproductive abandonment of true purpose in favor of safety in the rigid adherence to rules and procedures; and Gouldner was concerned about minimum standards because although they make good, clear bureaucratic rules, they subvert the true goals of management by allowing worker inclinations to take precedence once the minimum standards are attained.

In connection with bureaucratic structure, goal consistency, and effectiveness, note that the bureaucratic principles of management have never been thought applicable to certain kinds of organizations. The reason for the lack of fit is that bureaucratic structure is a strategy for effectiveness through goal coordination and the mitigation of cross-purposes, and some organizations need only the barest minimum dose of such tonic. Hierarchies play only a small role in academic departments, Congress, and the courts, for example, because the channeling of preferences in a common direction is largely irrelevant—they are not the sort of organization in which cross-purposes can be much of a problem.

In human relations theory, the need to bring goals into harmony receives considerable attention and was recognized as long ago as the Bank Wiring Observation Room (Roethlisberger and Dickson, 1939) and Argyris's *Personality and Organization* (1957). I am going a bit further here, advancing the need to mitigate cross-purposes as the essence of the theory's orientation toward effectiveness. Sensitivity, supportiveness, listening, participation—these are all mechanisms to promote awareness of the goals and interests of others, mutual understanding, compromise, adjustment, and a sense of common purpose. Effectiveness in human relations theory is clearly pursued by means of the overcoming of centrifugal forces.

The consonance hypothesis would support the importance of bureaucratic structure for some settings but would introduce more decentralization of true authority (see Chapter Four) as the means to effectiveness in others. The essence of the change is the recognition that in some environments the locus of the most effective decisions does not necessarily lie in hierarchal position but in expertise. The primary thrust of the structure is then to facilitate a communication system in which the proper people can be readily in contact with the proper experts at the proper time. This prevents the scattering of energy in the direction of diverse inefficient subgoals and, more important, subordinates the strong, traditional, but in this case debilitating orientation toward hierarchal orderliness to the clear and direct pursuit of recognized and shared organizational goals. As Burns and Stalker (1961) have shown, hierarchal control in the wrong environments would, for its own sake, simply misdirect organizational effort into unproductive channels while heightening frustration in the experts and raising the level of exactly those preoccupations with personal needs that human relations mechanisms are designed to avoid. Decentralized structure is an alternative basis of coordination that, like most coordination, keeps effort focused on one set of goals, subgoals, and constraints in preference to others.

In all these designs, there is a tacit but critical assumption that some participants know or can readily find a program that will result in adequate performance on a given set of ordered goals; the only problem is whether the efforts of people in the organization can be kept channeled in the proper direction. The structural designs clearly do not supply required task-specific organizational ideas in the fashion of the science of design; they assume them and focus instead on clearing the organizational air of distractions. But note that as such, in the strict sense, and in the most productive sense, this particular variety of goal-free theory is not goal-free at all. The theories apply to organizations performing a wide variety of tasks, it is true, but the immediate aims of these prominent responses to the search for effectiveness are rather well defined and specific: to keep people from working at cross-purposes; to mitigate the undesirable effects of inconsistencies in goals. This delimitation makes the function of the theories much more modest, because it may be recognized that other factors are also at work and that overall effectiveness may therefore still be problematic even if substantial goal unity is achieved.

But one must ask, still, whether it is modest enough. Can one technique eliminate deleterious cross-purposes in all settings? A positive answer is hardly credible. The complexity—the variety and even the perverseness of contexts in which work-relevant goals occur—is still formidable, and furthermore, it would not seem more likely, in natural settings, to be able to *control* motivated behavior reliably through the motivations than to explain it, at least not without resort to coercion or excessive psychological manipulation. This is to suggest that even recognizing the confined and rather precise pathway by which the structural "goal-free" designs are supposed to work, it is doubtful that they can ever answer the need for a theory of organizational effectiveness; control over goal consistency could be accepted as an adequate response, but whether a design can be developed to achieve it reliably is another matter. It will be recalled that goal-specific designs that are focused directly on organizational objectives fail the test of theory in this area because they are not general enough. That is not a problem here, where generality is achieved by a focus on the broadly relevant subgoal of unification of effort. The single obstacle to theory is complexity; it is highly doubtful at this point that even a moderately reliable design to achieve such an aim is possible of construction.

Research has made this conclusion abundantly clear in the case of bureaucratic theory and the structural consonance hypothesis. The latter hypothesis is, in fact, essentially an admission of the failure of the former one, together with an injection into it of certain interacting variables representing context: Bureaucratic structure is effective in some settings, but only decentralization of true authority leads to effectiveness under certain conditions of environment, technology, and size. But the consonance hypothesis also fails. Apparently insurmountable difficulty has been encountered in specifying just what structure must be adopted for which environment, and beyond that, research shows that Child (1972b) was correct in his article on strategic choice: Managers can ignore the constraints of technology, environment, and size to a large degree without damage to effectiveness. There are other concerns, probably infinite other contextual concerns, that are at times more important.

Human relations theory remains as a possibility, and this was the main reason for my opinion, expressed at the beginning of the chapter, that a categorical demonstration of the impossibility of a theory of effectiveness is not available. It cannot be logically proved that no definitions of dignity, humanity, and participation, qualified by the proper interacting contextual variables, will yield a design for the mitigation of cross-purposes that is sufficiently powerful to satisfy the label "theory." One can only say that in recognition of the relentlessness of counterexamples in empirical research and the fact that such a theory must struggle for stability against the complexity of infinitely varied patterns of motivations both within and among human beings, the possibility is remote. This does not mean that one should not treat employees at all levels with dignity and humanity. It means only that such treatment is not necessarily going to result in higher yields on management goals that would be effected by other styles of leadership that might be exercised in the same context and time period. Of course, many believe that humanity and dignity in supervision are fundamentally valuable in themselves and do not need management goals for their justification (see Dachler and Wilpert, 1978), but that is another matter—perhaps a more important one.

All this is not to say that there is no value in recognizing the nature of the primary intervening variable between the structural designs and effectiveness. Clinically, heuristically, in one setting at a time, it may well help to know that goal consistency is what is needed, that the mitigation of cross-purposes is what one is apparently striving for with these techniques. I suggest that what to do may in this fashion be clearer to those well acquainted with an individual situation, although which technique or variant should best be applied will surely vary from one context to another, and in some contexts there is no guarantee that an efficacious mechanism can be found at all. People may simply have to struggle with their cross-purposes and either find solutions in political contention or palliate the differences through the quasi resolution of conflict (Cyert and March, 1963, pp. 117–118).

In conclusion, we have found no hope of a theory of organizational effectiveness within the goal-specific category and essentially none in the goal-free category. What we have found under the latter heading is an odd complementarity. The science of design is concerned with the simultaneous satisfaction of multiple goals and constraints but assumes a consistent preference ordering; the structural approaches assume an adequate solution given a single preference ordering but are concerned instead with the channeling of effort in mutually consistent directions. In spirit, the structural approaches represent the kind of solution that has apparently been wished for, suggesting that the feeling of need for a theory of effectiveness grows not so much out of such situations as the time-sharing problem, in which one does not know what, organizationally, should be done, but out of situations in which one is at a loss to know how to ensure that the organization will do it, or at least do it properly. The problem of effectiveness is therefore a problem of control, but it is doubtful that the problem of control can be solved in any robustly general way, no matter how many contextual variables are added to models. Leaving aside the requirement for robust generality—that is, for theory—there is no doubt that improvements in goal consistency can be brought about by one means or another in a great many individual situations and that such increased harmonization of purpose is almost bound to enhance performance on the goal set that predominates, other things being equal.

There has not, apparently, been significant progress toward the realization of Simon's goal of an integrated science or discipline of design since he suggested the program in a series of lectures in 1968 (Simon, 1969). If there were, one cannot help thinking that organizational effectiveness would have been enhanced. People would probably not point to the activity taking place in science-of-design programs on campuses throughout the world and say, "This is our long-sought theory of organizational effectiveness," but the benefits would be just as palpable. Still, the benefits would be intermittent. Not only are there technical limitations, but it is of interest to note that in some degree the science of design is confined by the lack of a reliable *structural* approach to organizational effectiveness. Rational designs may be devised, but given that there is no design to ensure people's acceptance of rational designs, the historic failure of Taylorism is certain to be frequently repeated.

❋ 7 ❋

Conclusions
and Projections

The Possibilities for
Productive Theory and Research

The primary organizing device for all the preceding has been a definition of the term *theory*. The confession was made early that the definition is arbitrary; the analyses that followed showed frequently both that theory as defined has fuzzy edges, so that it is sometimes difficult to distinguish from nontheory, and that the definition can appear to be too restrictive. Precisely what shall be called theory is not important. What is important is to observe that organization theorists and other social scientists have been trying to do a number of theorylike things, some of which have received much attention and resources and others relatively little. Moreover, some of these efforts are apparently frustrated while others are not. In this perspective, the definition has been used throughout as a basis for asking and answering the question "What is this or that sort of work trying to do? Where does it fit?"

The definition has also served to highlight and distinguish a major research category, one which is awarded a lion's share of the effort but which is experiencing heavy frustration. Social scientists have been trying hard to provide general, stable explanations of recurrent phenomena, a feat which has been accomplished in other disciplines, physical and biological, and which forms the scientific backbone of many of them. This attempt exudes from the pores of modern social research in the form of models, regression equations, preoccupation with validity and reliability of measurement, case-study aggregation, repetitive study of the same concept, causal analysis, and the value placed on generalizing and on being theoretical and no doubt in many other ways. The discussion has therefore asked where this effort at stable explanation stands both philosophically and empirically, at least in organization theory, and how it compares with and relates to other things that are being done by contemporary scholars. The answer that emerges is that in its main lines the effort has been stymied and is probably futile. There are, however, some hopeful rays of light both within it and surrounding it.

Some initial negative conclusions are these: (1) Parameter instability is built into many current research pursuits and will still be there fifty years from now, embarrassingly enough—only doubled in accumulated bulk—if the same sorts of questions continue to be addressed in the same sorts of ways. (2) One is unlikely to achieve theory in the face of complexity by the method of piling-on. Complexity in social science cannot be beaten into submission by a barrage of new studies featuring fresh independent variables; it needs to be gamed, sidestepped. (3) The variance-theory approach does not deserve its preeminent status in theoretic social research.

Organization theory as a discipline grew out of the old public administration and classical management schools of thought with the rise of behavioralism in social psychology, sociology, and political science—behavioralism being the movement to base ideas on adequate, systematic, and generally quantitative empirical research. It is now evident that this movement is not as sure a route to theory as was once hoped; there are other obstacles to stable explanation besides the once-prevalent scarcity of systematic empirical observation. Behavioralism, however, is not about to be abandoned. On the contrary, it seems to me to have left a strong and constructive legacy in the widely shared conviction of the importance, even in nontheoretical research, of explicit, clear conceptualization and of rigor and discipline in marshaling evidence and arriving at conclusions. Lack of progress, of cumulativeness, is beginning to be broad enough and deep enough, however, to cause one to back away from some aspects of current practice and expectations in the pursuit of behavioral theory. Reappraisal and perhaps redirection appear to be the orders of the day.

I do not wish in this final chapter to amend the basic thrust of the critique in the previous six. Recognizing that the thrust is in some ways a bit negative, however, it will be well at this point to summarize some of the positive implications that have bubbled to the surface in the course of the analysis. Still, prescriptions will be avoided; academic research has a life of its own that is quite independent of prescriptions, and the collectively generated momentum appears to be infinitely more creative than the pet ideas of any one prescriber. I would like, rather, to point out some of the categories that seem to be possible and impossible, encouraging and discouraging, and occasionally from these observations to hazard a few predictions.

Variance Theory and Process Theory as Styles of Research

A first projection is that the process-theoretic approach to problems will gain substantially relative to variance theory as a research orientation (see Weick, 1974). In this connection, the two critical aspects of process theory are that it focuses on a recurrent flow of events and that it explains existence as the result of encounters or recombinations. The second is the more critical, because in that aspect lies the philosophical essence of the process-theoretic mode of explanation. In the causal mode, some new characteristic or changed state of the world comes about as the result of a force impinging on an entity and pushing it, as it were, from here to there on some scale of measurement; in the probabilistic mode, change and existence result from the uniting of entities that previously were separate.

A second projection is that of the two aspects, the first will get more exercise, in spite of its being the less critical from the standpoint of theory. I base this prediction on the observation that a well-demonstrated tendency already exists among organization theorists and other social scientists to illuminate a problem by elaborating a flow of events, telling how something happens. There are good reasons for this tendency, particularly when one considers that the alternative is some sort of variance-theoretic rendering of the phenomena in question.

The basic reason for the ease and naturalness with which one gravitates toward process elaborations may be that the human brain is itself a serial rather than a parallel processor. It appears to be physiologically easy and natural to think in terms of flows of events. Social behavior is multicausal, but the mind does not readily grasp, all at once, the nuances and implications of six or eight parallel causal factors, each going up or down by several units, perhaps independently and perhaps not, while the outcome variable reacts accordingly. This configuration is difficult to memorize, master, retain, and feel comfortable with. Give the mind a good story, however, and it thrives; the entire flow often seems capable of being stored and recalled instantaneously, almost as one "chunk," to use the information-processing terminology. Regardless of how the world actually is, we are preequipped to interpret it with process-theoretic machinery. Furthermore, the creatures whose behavior one is trying to capture and explain are themselves acting on their problems and environments like good serial information processors. It will not be surprising, for example, if process theories of learning and decision making turn out to be compelling while variance theories experience frustration, since the learners and decision makers are cognitively preequipped to proceed in the one manner rather than the other. The conjecture, also, is not confined to internal cognitive processes themselves but necessarily extends to the external ordering of one's affairs. If executives do indeed prefer to handle the separate but related goals of subordinates sequentially rather than simultaneously (Cyert and March, 1963), the reason may lie not only in the need to contain conflict, which is the most common explanation, but as well in intelligent deference to the difficulty of managing on-line, real-time calculations involving the interaction of multiple goals.

A final and closely related consideration regarding the flow-of-events property of the process-theory style is its attractiveness as an object of descriptive quasi theory. Description as theory in the more mature sciences has targeted the form, matter, and motion of phenomena, but the kind of description that would seem to have the greatest potential in social science is description of processes—how things are done by people and groups. To the extent that the pursuit of description increases in prevalence as a research goal, social science will take on an increasingly process-theoretic flavor, at the expense of variance theory.

The world of social research practice will probably be slower to exploit the advantages of probabilistic-encounter thinking than flow-of-events thinking. Nevertheless, there are some important advantages. It is difficult to claim that the social world is better conceptualized in terms of recombination than causality, but the latter has such problems that the other is likely to begin to crop up with greater regularity. Explanation by probabilistic encounter offers a richness of fresh opportunities. Straight prediction is de-emphasized in favor of ramifying insight, based on a host of research operations such as the manipulation of probability distributions to observe the consequences for outcomes and the creative conceptualization of just what is being combined.

Furthermore, a persistent, strong, and troublesome inclination to express ideas in dichotomies—happening/not happening, existence/nonexistence—is manifest in social research. The tendency is too frequent and widespread to be written off as lack of sophistication or as a phenomenon of early stages of theoretical development in an area, to be replaced in due course by the stage of continuous dimensions. Although one can use log-linear models and other tricks to deal with the basically incongruous explanation of dichotomies by multiple causes, the fact remains that the dichotomous outcome is awkward, both conceptually and analytically, in a framework best suited to expression in the medium of continuous mathematical functions. Rearrangement of single-valued objects, however, is what process theory does best, so that it accommodates well this conceptual inclination toward dichotomies on the part of investigators by being happy to dichotomize everything it can into yes or no, present or absent.

The variance-theory style will tend to persist in part for substantive reasons but in part also for comfort—not only the comfort of statistics as an analytical tool but the comfortably ingrained notion, a handicap by now, that theory is used first and foremost to predict, to show that one side of an equation can be matched with the other. This pull toward comfort and convenience may, however, be offset by another. The essence of variance theory, especially in the development stage, lies in the matching up of different pockets of variety, which always means looking at a broad array of instances. Variance parameters can be established only by examining variance. That is generally expensive of money, time, and energy, and it also means that the investigator must frequently make the bulk of his or her observations by proxy when the preference might very well be to make them first-hand, to allow one's own senses and one's finely tuned conceptual perspective the potential of drawing profit from this most basic of all scientific operations. The process-theory style is radically different in this regard. Although a backdrop of variety and some amount of contrast may be helpful or even necessary, the systematic collection of comparative observations is quite distant from the essence of the approach. What it often takes to develop a process theory is to begin to see the phenomenon just one time in the proper conceptual clothes. True, ordinary variance is often handy at some stages, as in Mendel's experiments or in the testing of the implications of a subtheory (for example, the greater the variance in reproduction among males of a species, the greater the size difference and other dimorphisms between males and females—see Alexander and others, 1979). But since the process is in some sense universal, even testing and refinement often proceed by the carefully instrumented observation of just one unfolding of the events in question, at least just one at a time. Further observations are primarily for corroboration and new ideas, not for establishing parameters. This can be important in many disciplines and particularly so in organization theory, in which the variance approach can mean and often has meant surveying hundreds of organizations across a nation or the world, while the process approach can mean studying one or a few organizations close at hand. As the comforts of statistics and the predictive mode slip their hold in the culture, or if they do, the comforts of convenient first-hand observation must begin to appear more and more attractive.

Theory and Nearly Theory

What looks impossible and discouraging is to fly in the face of infinite complexity, to flout the fundamental assumption—to try, in short, to develop stable, general explanations of motivated behavior. What looks possible and encouraging is somehow to avoid the head-on explanation of motivated behavior while still remaining substantially within the spirit of the theoretical. To avoid does not mean to disguise, as in the substitution of variables not overtly motivational while truly so at bottom, but to accept certain limitations and track the powerful and universal within them. The avoid mechanism can successfully take a vast variety of forms, I am sure, but I will note only the few that surfaced in the course of the previous analyses.

First, social science and organization theory can concern themselves with tractable outcomes that are not behaviors at all. Although the number of such is no doubt very large, it is not so easy as it might seem to identify or manufacture them. Organizational structure, for example, seems on the surface not to be a behavior and therefore to belong in this category, yet it assuredly is tantamount to a behavior—a structure may be called centralized, for example, purely in virtue of the fact that participants behave in accord with some definition of the term *centralized*. Nor does satisfaction appear on the surface to be a behavior, yet it is apparently subject to the fundamental assumption just exactly as though it were. Nevertheless, this category of characteristics of groups and individuals, although its precise description may be complicated and subtle, is certainly not empty. Consider, for example, the hypothesis, inchoately formed at this point, that certain types of interaction among persons, as between mother and child or members of an organizational work group, produces an exceptionally strong bonding between them that can arise in few, if any, other ways (Homans, 1950, pp. 110–117, 181–187, 241–265; Selznick, 1966, pp. 257–258; Simon, 1969, pp. 105–106; Alexander, 1979, pp. 108–112). To take a somewhat simpler example, consider the development of a function that would relate intelligence to both heredity and environment, as is suggested in the recent work of Axelrod and Scarr (in press). The outcomes in these two cases, strong bonding and intelligence, are durables but are not behaviors. They may be suitable subjects for ordinary explanatory theory.

Although not all examples in that category necessarily have a biological flavor, the two that were provided do have. Another category, then, is the identification of the nature and extent of the biological component of organizational, political, or other motivated social behaviors. This effect lies at the core of what has come to be called *sociobiology*. Although it may in many respects be of little interest to social scientists outside anthropology, some questions of this nature have already begun to attract organization theorists, political scientists, and others, and the trend has the earmarks of one that is likely to grow. Consider, for example, the early work by Wilhoite (1976), which stimulates further inquiry into the biological connection between dominance hierarchies observed in primates and the similar-appearing relations that exist in formal and informal human groups. More recently, the work of Hamilton and Axelrod (1981), an interdisciplinary team of evolutionary biologist and political scientist, presents promising possibilities for insight into the evolution or development of cooperative relations in animals, including humans in groups. (One might note parenthetically that their method is based on the prisoner's dilemma, a game-theory setting that is usually normative in genre; that is, it addresses questions such as "Is there a best strategy? What might that be?" In the Axelrod/Hamilton application, however, the gaming is descriptive rather than normative, asking "What happens when players who are using the following strategies are mixed together in a population?" Although not presented so as to emphasize the form, their answer to this question is immediately recognizable as classic process theory. Moreover, the format is *ceteris quietis:* The active motive is to maximize payoff—raw personal advantage—as defined in the game; all other motives, especially altruistic ones, are inactive.)

These kinds of studies, designed to tap biological and evolutionary underpinnings, deal in simplified or abstracted representations of individual and group interactions. One has the intuition, however, that the descriptive quasi theories and process theories that one can sense developing have the potential for generating large increments in the understanding of human social behavior.

Descriptive quasi theory is itself an important category. There appear to be a large number of social and psychological mechanisms that strongly attract inquiry and are amenable to illumination in this mode. Some phenomena repel explanation but invite description. Consider socialization as a possible example (including the socialization of new participants in organizations). There will probably never be an explanatory theory of socialization, because the concept as it stands is quite irrelevant to explanation. It is not a proper outcome. There is little interesting variance (some people more socialized than others) and few interesting avenues of probabilistic combination (some turning out socialized and others not). What one might be able to do, however, is conceptualize and describe only the process of socialization itself—how it always unfolds (or nearly always, or sometimes)—without reference to any outcomes at all. If such description can be intriguing and nonobvious, and I strongly suspect that it can, it surely has the potential for being important and useful. Thus, in all, it would closely approach the domain of good theory.

It is worth repeating in this connection that there may well be payoff in basic research that would seek to produce descriptive quasi theories of how choices are made not only among behaviors or solutions but among *goals*. How, for example, do people decide that it is not so important after all to have two and a half bathrooms and that it is more important to live within walking distance of the school and not lack for closet space? It was observed in Chapter One that there appear to be few, if any, bottlenecks in organization theory that could potentially be cleared by a descriptive breakthrough. Here may be one exception, not just for organization theory but for general social science. Considerable progress has been made in understanding the human approach to well-structured problems, but ill-structured problems, making preferential choices among incommensurable goals, are critical because they are both so common and so important for behavior. Simon's work, as interpreted in Chapter Five, shows that one's understanding of problem solving for the well-structured case may be viewed in addition as an understanding of the well-structured component of problem solving for the ill-structured case. The primary component that is missing, then, the piece that could reasonably be expected to set the stage for dramatic advances, is the manner or manners in which choices are made among goals.

In direct connection with motivation, the other theoretical forms that seemed to arise as examples of the possible in discussion of the impossible are *ceteris quietis* models and summary-motivation models. The former assume that behavior is controlled by one or a few explicit motives and that all other motives are inactive; the latter either assume or measure the existence of motivation to perform some act, but without naming or distinguishing among the aims that compose the general motivation. The explicit content of theory in both these forms is primarily nonmotivational. For example, neither the status drive itself nor any other motive appears explicitly in the status model of decentralization of authority (Chapter Four), nor do the goals of solving problems and making choices, or any other goals, appear explicitly in the garbage-can model. One potential significance of these forms, and the reason they seemed to be strongly suggested during the analyses, lies in their being only slight, though critical, modifications of kinds of research that are currently common but stuck. This current research appears to pursue social theory in a plausible, informed, almost inevitable way, but it is stymied nevertheless. The *ceteris quietis* and summary-motivation modifications yield a different kind of product, it is true, but dodge some of the important sources of instability and potentially clear the road to progress.

The place in theory occupied by these two motivation-restricted forms may perhaps be best appreciated by returning for a moment to a basic sort of paradigm for approaching the study of human behavior, the motivation-resources paradigm. My own early formulation of this approach was worked out in connection with the study of innovation (Mohr, 1969), but Atkinson (1957) had worked out a closely similar formulation even earlier in connection with motivated behavior in general, and indeed it would seem to apply well to the larger class. The two motivation-restricted theoretical forms, then, either omit or de-emphasize about half of the total explanation—the motivations—and work more intensively with the other half—the resources. The general paradigm can provide clues to the more specific nature of the intensively treated part—namely, that it must consist of certain resources and their opposite, certain *constraints*.

In the shortened form of the paradigm, constraints were omitted and simply relegated to the position of conceptual negatives, or inverses of resources. This was convenient because it permitted a heuristically illuminating model (which also fit the data of the innovation study quite well) in which behavior followed multiplicatively from motivation and resources, or $M \times R = B$. This formulation indicates not only that the precursor is necessary and sufficient but that both parts of the precursor are necessary. The behavior cannot take place without the motivation, but neither can it occur without the resources. An alternative is also of interest— namely, to omit resources, considering them to be the inverse of constraints (see Down's treatment of the *resource constraint* in this regard, in Downs, 1976, pp. 53–54). Using C for constraints, one then has the formulation $M/C = B$. Motivation is still seen as a necessary condition. For constraints, assuming a nonzero level of motivation, as C goes to zero, one would expect to observe a surfeit of the behavior in question, or pell-mell or frenzied behavior, and as C goes to infinity, the behavior becomes almost nonexistent but is never completely extinguished. And finally, rather than consider resources to be merely the inverses of constraints or vice versa, one can consider both of them explicitly, yielding $M/C \times R = B$ (see Downs and Mohr, 1979, pp. 401–404).

Taking the last formulation for the sake of completeness, and noting that it is a variance-theoretic function, one recognizes that the resources and constraints are causes of behavior, but if and only if there is nonzero motivation. Centralization, formalization, and other dimensions of organizational structure might be causes of innovation, for example (Hage and Aiken, 1967; Zaltman, Duncan, and Holbek, 1973), but only if a given level and perhaps source of *motivation to innovate* have been theoretically assumed and operationally documented. In that case, but only then, it is the variation in R and C that pushes the behavior up and down the scale on which it is measured. Since motivations, though causes, do not make good *theoretical* causes, the imagery suggests taking a nonzero level as given and concentrating on the resources and constraints. That is exactly the role of *ceteris quietis* and summary-motivation models. Even if the summary motivation or specifically included motivation were measured, and variation in M thereby utilized in the equation, still these motivation-restricted forms highlight a simplification of M, either by summarization or by exclusion, and a shift of emphasis to R and C. This M-C-R paradigm, in sum, provides a template for the visualizing and perhaps the working out of motivation-restricted theoretical forms.

This discussion has been couched almost completely in variance-theory terms, perhaps giving the impression that process theory is inapplicable to the motivation-restricted forms. This is not the case, as the status model and the garbage-can model plainly indicate. A precursor composed of motivations, constraints, and resources may surely be conceptualized so as to be only necessary, rather than necessary and sufficient, with outcomes that are probabilistic rather than functionally scaled. The discussion does, however, highlight a possible continued and constructive avenue for development of variance theories of motivated behavior, and that is perhaps worth pointing out.

It remains to be seen whether resources and constraints have their own fundamental assumption, restricting their use as well, but I suspect not. I suspect that resources and constraints can and will be conceptualized so as to function theoretically as specific, universal causes of certain behaviors, taking as given the motivation-restricted conditions and other conditions that may be specified with a theory to establish boundaries of valid scope. It is true enough that the givens or assumptions are restrictive, but that does not necessarily render such theories unrealistic.

It is true enough, also, that excluded motivations can destroy the accuracy of prediction from a *ceteris quietis* model. The desire for organizational effectiveness, for example, or simply the desire to thwart the pretensions of social scientists might destroy predictions of nondecentralization from the status model. But as

Chomsky once pointed out (1975, p. 83), these same kinds of motivations can destroy the accuracy of prediction from physical laws as well. Humans can always intervene. The prediction that an object will have a certain trajectory and will fall to the ground in a specified length of time can be thwarted by blowing on the object or by knocking it into the left-field bleachers. Selective breeding destroys the accuracy of what would otherwise be the predictions from the theory of natural selection, but this did not bother Darwin. Far from it; he repeatedly cites selective breeding as an analogue of natural selection in *The Origin of Species* ([1859], 1962), and he clearly learned much about natural selection from such intervention. Interfering with predictions from a theory, in short, does not invalidate the theory; the latter may be an excellent representation of the underlying reality in spite of the contrary force imposed by specific, nonregular human motivations. That is as true in principle of behavioral theories as it is of physical ones.

Looking at the same objection from another angle, one might feel that motivation-restricted theories are questionably genuine because they cannot be proved wrong; if projections or implications of the model are not vindicated empirically, one may always invoke as an excuse that an excluded motivation interfered or that the level of summary motivation assumed must simply have been in error. The theory may not be proved wrong, to be sure, but it still may well be shown to be rather useless. By the same token, it may also be shown to be useful and probably right, by some nonabsolute definition of that term, by drawing out its implications and repeatedly validating them against observed reality. Furthermore, the motivational "excuse" can be turned in this way to serious social science profit: When one has developed confidence in a motivation-restricted theory, one can use it to learn something about applications in which the operative motivations are otherwise difficult to measure. If goal compatibility plus all resource and constraint factors indicate that a decision will be made by bargaining and satisficing, for example, but it is made instead by political struggle and domination, and if one has justifiable confidence in the theory on the basis of tests and other experience, then one has learned something about the true goal compatibility that operated in that decision: Unsuspected motivations figured into it, perhaps, or in some other way it was simply lower than it was assumed to be. This is precisely consonant with Brunner's (1977) recommended use for the practical syllogism and other intentional analysis in public opinion research.

It is true, also, that not only are motivation-restricted theories incomplete, in that they do not contain the conditions under which they do precisely describe observable behavior, but they can never aspire to such completeness. That is an important logical constraint, and it will, I would guess, eventually restrain scholars from trying to add ever more motivations into a general explanation of some behavior. Motivation-restricted theory need not be dismissed categorically on that account, however, but should cause one, rather, to reappraise the nature and function of social science.

The saving consideration for explanatory social theory, such as it may be, is that completeness and predictive accuracy are by no means the only or even the most important criteria of theoretical quality; they may just be the most readily measurable. The fact that all *ceteris quietis* models will be incomplete does not put all in the same theoretical class. Some will not only be technically incomplete but will truly be descriptions of mere happenstance at best. Some will be boring. Like descriptive quasi theories, however, some motivation-restricted models can be *good*. Simon's models of human problem solving and Crecine's characterization of the budget process teach a great deal. In spite of serious incompleteness and although many will not be powerful, I suspect that motivation-restricted theories can be powerful because they can climb well up into the range of the intriguing, important, useful, and nonobvious. These are criteria that will perhaps be accepted as more germane in social science than the size of one particular error term.

There is a noteworthy difference in power between restricted theoretical statements and associational statements. The former capture basic underlying tendencies, universally operating even when not discernible in behavior. The latter are limited to association within a restricted setting or population, without pretension of saying how people are in general.

A critical implication is that associational statements are, of course, free to employ prominently and without feelings of guilt the specific motivations that appear to be operative and important in the target population. In practice, the statements or models are usually in the variance-theory mode and make up a very large proportion of the research reported in journals. There is no issue here at all of discouraging such research, but one may note that it could be more self-conscious and that it could be improved. By *more self-conscious* I mean that it might examine itself to find and communicate the kinds of purposes to which it relates—whether to feed eventually into theoretical work on specified questions, so that one might critique it on the basis of its theoretical potential, or to serve some of the more applied aims listed in Chapter One.

By *could be improved* I do not refer to ordinary methods and analysis, but rather to an apparent disinclination to honor interaction. If associational research is accepted as such—that is, as having no claim to being theory at present but rather to being relevant, perhaps in an extremely important way, to a certain subpopulation at a certain time (for example, voting behavior in U.S. presidential elections in the sixties)—then one will naturally begin to wonder what some of the limiting conditions may be. Why is the association merely associational? For some of the main ideas or findings, when will the associations be strong and when weak? There is no thought of answering such questions with completeness, but only of adding some *thickness* to bivariate and multivariate associations. Cronbach (1975) has pointed out that interactions are rarely looked for or reported and that when they are reported, there is a tendency to forget them immediately thereafter. They often do not figure prominently in the investigator's conclusions, nor do the same or other investigators tend to use them as a foundation on which to build when further work is actually done. Let us say that an investigator is able to report a fairly strong and noteworthy association. If he or she could add to that but one nearly equally noteworthy statement about when the first association is strong and when weak, a very substantial advance would have been made, especially for practitioners whose operations are assisted by information on the topic (Pillemer and Light, 1979, p. 725). This extra step has been missed in innovation research, for example, where it is rarely taken, and in human relations research, where it has been taken from time to time but then not taken seriously. I suggest that investigators will be freer to work with interaction when the goals are less theoretical—finding the interacting variables or conditions that will eventually complete the theory—and instead more applied: finding the interacting variables or conditions that provide a bit more help.

Social Theory and Social Science

The theoretical aspect of the science of human behavior cannot, apparently, occupy the same position as it does in the physical and biological sciences. Because of differences in the targets of explanation, chiefly the need to understand motivated behavior, social theory, in the main, cannot be as strong. This means that theory must function differently and that the science must go its own unique and independent way. There is nothing to copy from. That way will include prominently an inclination toward the expression of observable regularities of powerful but undefined scope and near-universal undercurrents that are sometimes detectable, sometimes not.

Theory thus occupies an odd position in social science, the management of which will no doubt be worked out only by evolution over time. It is important and can aspire to an illustrious future, but one implication for the near term is that it would probably not be amiss if the odd and rather humble position of theory were to impart to it a certain modesty relative to other pursuits. Consider associational research as applied in such areas as forecasting, the informational function, and the undergirding of important decisions. Consider, also, systematic normative research, organizational design, program evaluation, social experimentation, policy analysis, information systems, and public opinion research. All these should in substantial degree be held to the same methodological standards as theoretical development, including prominently the canons and rigors of evidence and inference. Moreover, although the products of these pursuits are not readily comparable in terms of some common denominator of overall benefit, it is not at all clear that the theoretical function would emerge at the top in such a comparison if it could be made. In particular, looking carefully at the list, it is difficult at this writing to have faith that social theory will be as vital to the other pursuits as the older theoretical sciences are to engineering, medicine, and chemical manufacturing. It does not seem appropriate, therefore, to make invidious status distinctions between theory and nontheory in social science.

But finally, it does appear appropriate at this stage for the two branches, theory and nontheory, to remain distinct as they proceed side by side in equal partnership. It goes without saying that theoretical development and nontheoretical research can inform each other and that the relationship can afford to be close. But to the detriment of all, they are too easily blended into an ill-defined mush. For the benefit of all, it is important that each be guided by its own goals and its own criteria of excellence.

References

Abdel-Halim, A. A., and Rowland, K. M. "Some Personality Determinants of the Effects of Participation: A Further Investigation." *Personnel Psychology,* 1976, *29,* 41–55.

Abrahamsson, B. *Bureaucracy or Participation.* Beverly Hills, Calif.: Sage, 1977.

Adizes, I. *Industrial Democracy: Yugoslav Style.* New York: Free Press, 1971.

Aitken, H. G. J., *Taylorism at Watertown Arsenal.* Cambridge, Mass.: Harvard University Press, 1960.

Alexander, R. D. *Darwinism and Human Affairs.* Seattle: University of Washington Press, 1979.

Alexander R. D., and others. "Sexual Dimorphisms and Breeding Systems in Pinnipeds, Ungulates, Primates, and Humans." In N. A. Chagnon and W. Irons (Eds.), *Evolutionary Biology and Human Social Behavior: An Anthropological Perspective.* North Scituate, Mass.: Duxbury Press, 1979.

Allison, G. T. *Essence of Decision: Explaining the Cuban Missile Crisis.* Boston: Little, Brown, 1971.

Argyris, C. *Personality and Organization.* New York: Harper & Row, 1957.

Aristotle, "Physica [Physics]." In R. McKeon (Ed.), *The Basic Works of Aristotle.* New York: Random House, 1941.

Arvey, R. D., and DeWhirst, H. D. "Relationships Between Goal Clarity, Participation in Goal Setting, and Personality Characteristics on Job Satisfaction in a Scientific Organization." *Journal of Applied Psychology,* 1976, *61* (1), 103–105.

Atkinson, J. W. "Motivational Determinants of Risk-Taking Behavior." *Psychological Review,* 1957, *64,* 359–372.

Axelrod, R., and Scarr, S. "Human Intelligence and Public Policy." *Scientific American,* in press.

Bachman, J. G., and Tannenbaum, A. S. "The Control-Satisfaction Relationship Across Varied Areas of Experience." In A. S. Tannenbaum (Ed.), *Control in Organizations.* New York: McGraw-Hill, 1968.

Banfield, E. D. "Ends and Means in Planning." In S. Mailick and E. H. Van Ness (Eds.), *Concepts and Issues in Administrative Behavior.* Englewood Cliffs, N.J.: Prentice-Hall, 1962.

Barnard, C. I. *The Functions of the Executive.* Cambridge, Mass.: Harvard University Press, 1938.

Baumgartel, H. "Leadership, Motivations, and Attitudes in Research Laboratories." *Journal of Social Issues,* 1956, *12,* 24–31.

Berkowitz, L. "Sharing Leadership in Small, Decision-Making Groups." *Journal of Abnormal and Social Psychology,* 1953, *48,* 231–238.

Berleman, W. C., and Steinburn, T. W. "The Execution and Evaluation of a Delinquency Prevention Program." *Social Problems,* 1967, *1* (4), 413–423.

Billings, R. S., Klimoski, R. J., and Breaugh, J. A. "The Impact of a Change in Technology on Job Characteristics: A Quasi-Experiment." *Administrative Science Quarterly,* 1977, *22* (2), 318–339.

Bingham, R. D., Freeman, P. K., and Martin, C. F. "Toward an Understanding of Innovation Adoption: An Empirical Application of the Theoretical Contributions of Downs and Mohr—A Preliminary Analysis." Paper presented at annual meeting of the Southern Political Science Association, Atlanta, November 1980.

Bingham, R. D., and others. *Professional Associations and Municipal Innovation.* Madison: University of Wisconsin Press, 1980.

Blankenship, L. V., and Miles, R. E. "Organizational Structure and Managerial Decision Behavior." *Administrative Science Quarterly,* 1968, *13,* 106–120.

Blau, P. M., and Schoenherr, R. *The Structure of Organizations.* New York: Basic Books, 1971.

Blauner, R. "Work Satisfaction and Industrial Trends in Modern Society." In W. Galenson and S. M. Lipset (Eds.), *Labor and Trade Unionism.* New York: Wiley, 1970.

Blumberg, P. *Industrial Democracy: The Sociology of Participation.* New York: Schocken Books, 1968.

Bowers, D. G. "Organizational Control in an Insurance Company." In A. S. Tannenbaum (Ed.), *Control in Organizations.* New York: McGraw-Hill, 1968.

Bowers, D. G., and Seashore, S. E. "Predicting Organizational Effectiveness with a Four-Factor Theory of Leadership." *Administrative Science Quarterly,* 1966, *11* (2), 238–263.

Brown, L. A. "Diffusion Research in Geography: A Thematic Account." Discussion Paper No. 53. Columbus: Department of Geography, Ohio State University, 1977.

Brown, R. "The Accessibility of Genuine Social Laws and Theories." In L. I. Krimerman (Ed.), *The Nature and Scope of Social Science.* New York: Appleton-Century-Crofts, 1969.

Brunner, R. D. "An 'Intentional' Alternative to Public Opinion Research." *American Journal of Political Science,* 1977, *21* (3), 435–464.

Brunner, R. D., and Brewer, G. D. *Organized Complexity.* New York: Free Press, 1971.

Burns, T., and Stalker, G. M. *The Management of Innovation.* London: Tavistock, 1961.

Campbell, D. T. "The Social Scientist as Methodological Servant of the Experimenting Society." *Policy Studies Journal,* 1973, *2* (1), 72–75.

Campbell, D. T., and Fiske, D. W. "Convergent and Discriminant Validity by the Multitrait-Multimethod Matrix." *Psychological Bulletin,* 1959, *56* (1), 18–106.

Campbell, D. T., and Stanley, J. C. *Experimental and Quasi-Experimental Designs for Research.* Chicago: Rand McNally, 1963.

Campbell, J. P. "On the Nature of Organizational Effectiveness." In P. S. Goodman, J. M. Pennings, and Associates, *New Perspectives on Organizational Effectiveness.* San Francisco: Jossey-Bass, 1977.

Charters, W. W., Jr., and Pellegrin, R. J. "Barriers to the Innovation Process: Four Case Studies of Differential Staffing." *Education Administration Quarterly,* 1972, *9* (1), 3–14.

Child, J. "Organizational Structure and Strategies of Control: A Replication of the Aston Study." *Administrative Science Quarterly,* 1972a, *17* (2), 163–177.

Child, J. "Organizational Structure, Environment, and Performance: The Role of Strategic Choice." *Sociology,* 1972b, *6* (1), 1–22.

Child, J., and Mansfield, R. "Technology, Size, and Organizational Structure." *Sociology,* 1972, *6* (3), 369–393.

Chomsky, N. *Reflections on Language.* New York: Random House, 1975.

Clarkson, G. P. E. "A Model of Trust Investment Behavior." In R. M. Cyert and J. G. March, *A Behavioral Theory of the Firm.* Englewood Cliffs, N.J.: Prentice-Hall, 1963.

Cohen, M. D. "Conflict and Complexity: Goal Diversity and Organizational Search Effectiveness." Discussion Paper No. 153. Institute of Public Policy Studies, University of Michigan, Ann Arbor, 1980.

Cohen, M. D., and March, J. G. *Leadership and Ambiguity: The American College President.* New York: McGraw-Hill, 1974.

Cohen, M. D., March, J. G., and Olsen, J. P. "A Garbage Can Model of Organizational Choice." *Administrative Science Quarterly,* 1972, *17* (1), 1–25.

Coleman, J. S. *Policy Research in the Social Sciences.* Morristown, N.J.: General Learning Press, 1972.

Coleman, J. S., Katz, E., and Menzel, H. "The Diffusion of an Innovation Among Physicians." *Sociometry,* 1957, *20,* 253–270.

Collingwood, R. G. *An Essay on Metaphysics.* Oxford: Clarendon Press, 1940.

Comstock, D. E., and Scott, W. R. "Technology and the Structure of Subunits: Distinguishing Individual and Workgroup Effects." *Administrative Science Quarterly,* 1977, *22* (2), 177–202.

Cornfield, J. E., and others. "Smoking and Lung Cancer: Recent Evidence and a Discussion of Some Questions." In E. Tufte (Ed.), *The Quantitative Analysis of Social Problems.* Reading, Mass.: Addison-Wesley, 1970.

Crecine, J. P. *Government Problem Solving: A Computer Simulation of Municipal Budgeting.* Chicago: Rand McNally, 1969.

Cronbach, L. J. "Beyond the Two Disciplines of Scientific Psychology." *American Psychologist,* 1975, *30* (2), 116–127.

Cummings, L. L. "Emergence of the Instrumental Organization." In P. S. Goodman, J. M. Pennings, and Associates, *New Perspectives on Organizational Effectiveness.* San Francisco: Jossey-Bass, 1977.

Cyert, R. M., and March, J. G. *A Behavioral Theory of the Firm.* Englewood Cliffs, N.J.: Prentice-Hall, 1963.

Dachler, H. P., and Wilpert, B. "Conceptual Dimensions and Boundaries of Participation in Organizations: A Critical Evaluation." *Administrative Science Quarterly,* 1978, *23* (1), 1–39.

Dalton, M. *Men Who Manage.* New York: Wiley, 1959.

Darwin, C. *The Origin of Species.* New York: Macmillan, 1962. (Originally published, 1859.)

Davis, O. A., Dempster, M. A. H., and Wildavsky, A. "A Theory of the Budgetary Process." *American Political Science Review,* 1966, *60,* 529–547.

Dewar, R., and Werbel, J. "Universalistic and Contingency Predictions of Employee Satisfaction and Conflict." *Administrative Science Quarterly,* 1979, *24* (3), 426–448.

Downs, G. W., Jr. *Bureaucracy, Innovation, and Public Policy.* Lexington, Mass.: Heath, 1976.

Downs, G. W., Jr., and Mohr, L. B. "Conceptual Issues in the Study of Innovation." *Administrative Science Quarterly,* 1976, *21* (4), 700–714.

Downs, G. W., Jr., and Mohr, L. B. "Toward a Theory of Innovation." *Administration and Society,* 1979, *10* (4), 379–408.

Downs, G. W., Jr., and Rocke, D. "Complexity, Interaction, and Policy Research." *Policy Sciences,* 1981, *13* (3), 281–295.

Dray, W. "The Historical Explanation of Actions Reconsidered." In S. Hook (Ed.), *Philosophy and History.* New York: New York University Press, 1963.

Duncan, O. D. "Path Analysis: Sociological Examples." *American Journal of Sociology,* 1966, *72* (1), 1–16.

Duncan, O. D., Featherman, D. L., and Duncan, B. *Socioeconomic Background and Achievement.* New York: Seminar Press, 1972.

Duncan, O. D., Haller, A. O., and Portes, A. "Peer Influences on Aspirations: A Reinterpretation." In H. M. Blalock, Jr. (Ed.), *Causal Models in the Social Sciences.* Chicago: Aldine-Atherton, 1971.

Edwards, W., and Guttentag, M. "Experiments and Evaluation: A Reexamination." In C. A. Bennett and A. A. Lumsdaine (Eds.), *Evaluation and Experiment.* New York: Academic Press, 1975.

Emery, F. E., and Trist, E. L. "The Causal Texture of Organizational Environments." *Human Relations,* 1965, *18* (1), 21–31.

Etzioni, A. "Two Approaches to Organizational Analysis: A Critique and a Suggestion." *Administrative Science Quarterly,* 1960, *5,* 257–278.

Evan, W. M. "The Organization-Set: Toward a Theory of Interorganizational Relations." In J. D. Thompson (Ed.), *Approaches to Organizational Design.* Pittsburgh: University of Pittsburgh Press, 1966.

Eveland, J. D., Rogers, E. M., and Klepper, C. *The Innovation Process in Public Organizations.* Final Report, NSF Grant RDA75-17952. Ann Arbor: Department of Journalism, University of Michigan, 1977.

"Exercise and Your Heart." *Consumer Reports,* 1977, *42* (5), 254–258.

Falcione, R. L. "Credibility: Qualifier of Subordinate Participation." *Journal of Business Communication,* 1974, *11,* 43–54.

Fayol, H. *General and Industrial Management.* London: Pitman, 1949.

Festinger, L. *A Theory of Cognitive Dissonance.* New York: Harper & Row, 1957.

Filley, A. C., House, R. J., and Kerr, S. *Managerial Process and Organizational Behavior.* Glenview, Ill.: Scott, Foresman, 1976.

Fox, S. M., III, and Haskell, W. L. "Physical Activity in the Prevention of Coronary Heart Disease." *Bulletin of the New York Academy of Medicine,* Series II, 1968, *44,* 950–967.

Freeman, J. H. "Environment, Technology, and the Administrative Intensity of Manufacturing Organizations." *American Sociological Review,* 1973, *38* (6), 750–763.

Freeman, J. H., and Hannan, M. T. "Growth and Decline Processes in Organizations." *American Sociological Review,* 1975, *40,* 215–228.

French, J. R. P., Israel, J., and Ås, D. "An Experiment in a Norwegian Factory: Interpersonal Dimensions in Decision Making." *Human Relations,* 1960, *13* (1), 3–19.

Galbraith, J. *Designing Complex Organizations.* Reading, Mass.: Addison-Wesley, 1973.

Georgopoulos, B. S., and Tannenbaum, A. S. "A Study of Organizational Effectiveness." *American Sociological Review,* 1957, *22,* 534–540.

Goldberger, A. S. "Structural Equation Models: An Overview." In A. S. Goldberger and O. D. Duncan (Eds.), *Structural Equation Models in the Social Sciences.* New York: Seminar Press, 1973.

Goodin, R., and Waldner, I. "Thinking Big, Thinking Small, and Not Thinking at All." *Public Policy,* 1979, *27* (1), 1–24.

Goodman, P. S., Pennings, J. M., and Associates. *New Perspectives on Organizational Effectiveness.* San Francisco: Jossey-Bass, 1977.

Gouldner, A. W. *Patterns of Industrial Bureaucracy: A Case Study of Modern Factory Administration.* New York: Free Press, 1954.

Gross, E. "Universities as Organizations: A Research Approach." *American Sociological Review,* 1968, *33,* 518–544.

Gulick, L., and Urwick, L. (Eds.). *Papers on the Science of Administration.* New York: Institute of Public Administration, Columbia University, 1937.

Haefner, D. P. "Arousing Fear in Dental Health Education." *Journal of Public Health Dentistry,* 1965, *25* (4), 140–146.

Hage, J., and Aiken, M. "Program Change and Organizational Properties." *American Journal of Sociology,* 1967, *72* (5), 503–519.

Hagerstrand, T. *Innovation Diffusion as a Spatial Process.* Chicago: University of Chicago Press, 1968.

Hall, R. I. "A System Pathology of an Organization: The Rise and

Fall of the Old *Saturday Evening Post*." *Administrative Science Quarterly,* 1976, *21,* 185–211.

Halperin, M., and Kanter, A. (Eds.). *Readings in American Foreign Policy: A Bureaucratic Perspective.* Boston: Little, Brown, 1973.

Hamilton, W. D. "The Genetical Evolution of Social Behavior." *Journal of Theoretical Biology,* 1964, *7,* 1–52.

Hamilton, W. D., and Axelrod, R. "The Evolution of Cooperation." *Science,* 1981, *211,* 1390–1396.

Hannan, M. T., and Freeman, J. "Obstacles to Comparative Studies." In P. S. Goodman, J. M. Pennings, and Associates, *New Perspectives on Organizational Effectiveness.* San Francisco: Jossey-Bass, 1977.

Hasenfeld, Y. "People Processing Organizations: An Exchange Approach." *American Sociological Review,* 1972, *37* (3), 256–263.

Heller, F. A., and Yukl, G. "Participation, Managerial Decision Making, and Situational Variables." *Organizational Behavior and Human Performance,* 1969, *4,* 277–241.

Hempel, C. G., "Covering Laws Are Presupposed by Any Adequate Rational Explanation." In L. I. Krimerman (Ed.), *The Nature and Scope of Social Science.* New York: Appleton-Century-Crofts, 1969.

Hempel, C. G., and Oppenheim, P. "The Covering Law Analysis of Scientific Explanation." *Philosophy of Science,* 1948, *15* (2), 135–174.

Herzberg, F. *Work and the Nature of Man.* New York: World, 1966.

Hickson, D. J., Pugh, D. S., and Pheysey, D. C. "Operations Technology and Organization Structure: A Reappraisal." *Administrative Science Quarterly,* 1969, *14* (3), 378–397.

Hickson, D. J., and others. "A Strategic Contingencies Theory of Intraorganizational Power." *Administrative Science Quarterly,* 1971, *16* (2), 216–229.

Hirschman, A. O. *Exit, Voice, and Loyalty: Responses to Decline in Firms, Organizations, and States.* Cambridge, Mass.: Harvard University Press, 1970.

Holland, J. *Adaptation in Natural and Artificial Systems.* Ann Arbor: University of Michigan Press, 1975.

Homans, G. C. *The Human Group.* New York: Harcourt Brace Jovanovich, 1950.

Hornstein, H. A., and others. "Influence and Satisfaction in Organizations: A Replication." *Sociology of Education,* 1968, *41* (4), 380–389.

Hull, C. L. *Principles of Behavior.* New York: Appleton-Century-Crofts, 1943.

Ivancevich, J. M. "Effects of Goal Setting on Performance and Job Satisfaction." *Journal of Applied Psychology,* 1976, *61,* 605–612.

Ivancevich, J. M. "Different Goal Setting Treatments and Their Effects on Performance and Job Satisfaction." *Academy of Management Journal,* 1977, *20,* 406–419.

Jacobs, D. "Dependency and Vulnerability: An Exchange Approach to the Control of Organizations." *Administrative Science Quarterly,* 1974, *19* (1), 45–59.

Johnston, J. *Econometric Methods.* (2nd ed.) New York: McGraw-Hill, 1972.

Kahn, R. L. "Organizational Effectiveness: An Overview." In P. S. Goodman, J. M. Pennings, and Associates, *New Perspectives on Organizational Effectiveness.* San Francisco: Jossey-Bass, 1977.

Kaplan, A. *The Conduct of Inquiry.* San Francisco: Chandler, 1964.

Katz, D., and Kahn, R. L. *The Social Psychology of Organizations.* New York: Wiley, 1966.

Keeley, M. "A Social Justice Approach to Organizational Evaluation." *Administrative Science Quarterly,* 1978, *23* (2), 272–292.

Keeley, M. "Organizational Analogy: A Comparison of Organismic and Social Contract Models." *Administrative Science Quarterly,* 1980, *25* (2), 337–362.

Kelly, P., and Kranzberg, M. *Technological Innovation: A Critical Review of Current Knowledge.* Atlanta: Advanced Technology and Science Studies Group, Georgia Institute of Technology, 1975.

Kimberly, J. R. "Organizational Size and the Structuralist Perspective: A Review, Critique, and Proposal." *Administrative Science Quarterly,* 1976, *21* (4), 571–597.

Klein, M. W., and others. "The Explosion in Police Diversion Programs: Evaluating the Structural Dimensions of a Social Fad." In M. Guttentag (Ed.), *Evaluation Studies Review Annual.* Vol. 2. Beverly Hills, Calif.: Sage, 1977.

Krimerman, L. I. (Ed.). *The Nature and Scope of Social Science: A*

Critical Anthology. New York: Appleton-Century-Crofts, 1969.

Kuhn, T. S. *The Structure of Scientific Revolutions.* Chicago: University of Chicago Press, 1962.

Kuhn, T. S. "Second Thoughts on Paradigms." In F. Suppe (Ed.), *The Structure of Scientific Theories.* (2nd ed.) Urbana: University of Illinois Press, 1977.

Lammers, C. J. Letter to the editor. *Administrative Science Quarterly,* 1974, *19* (3), 422–430.

Larkey, P. D. *Evaluating Public Programs: The Impact of General Revenue Sharing on Municipal Governments.* Princeton, N.J.: Princeton University Press, 1979.

Lasswell, H. D., and Kaplan, A. *Power and Society.* New Haven, Conn.: Yale University Press, 1950.

Latham, G. P., and Yukl, G. A. "Effects of Assigned and Participative Goal Setting on Performance and Job Satisfaction." *Journal of Applied Psychology,* 1976, *61,* 166–171.

Lave, C. A., and March, J. G. *An Introduction to Models in the Social Sciences.* New York: Harper & Row, 1975.

Lawrence, P. R., and Lorsch, J. W. *Organization and Environment.* Homewood, Ill.: Irwin, 1967.

Leavitt, H. J. "Applied Organizational Change in Industry: Structural, Technological, and Humanistic Approaches." In J. G. March (Ed.), *Handbook of Organizations.* Chicago: Rand McNally, 1965.

Leifer, R., and Huber, G. P. "Relations Among Perceived Environmental Uncertainty, Organization Structure, and Boundary-Spanning Behavior." *Administrative Science Quarterly,* 1977, *22* (2), 235–247.

Levine, S., and White, P. E. "Exchange as a Conceptual Framework for the Study of Interorganizational Relationships." *Administrative Science Quarterly,* 1961, *5* (4), 583–601.

Lewis-Beck, M. S., and Mohr, L. B. "Evaluating Effects of Independent Variables." *Political Methology,* 1976, *3* (1), 27–48.

Likert, R. *New Patterns of Management.* New York: McGraw-Hill, 1961.

Lindblom, C. "The Science of Muddling Through." *Public Administration Review,* 1959, *19,* 79–88.

Lischeron, J., and Wall, T. D. "Attitudes Toward Participation Among Local Authority Employees." *Human Relations,* 1974, *28,* 499–517.

Lischeron, J., and Wall, T. D. "Employee Participation: An Experimental Field Study." *Human Relations,* 1975, *28,* 873–884.

Litwak, E., and Hylton, L. F. "Interorganizational Analysis: A Hypothesis on Coordinating Agencies." *Administrative Science Quarterly,* 1962, *6* (4), 395–420.

Locke, E. A., and Schweiger, D. M. "Participation in Decision Making: One More Look." In B. Staw and L. Cummings (Eds.), *Research in Organizational Behavior.* Greenwich, Conn.: JAI Press, 1979.

Lowin, A. "Participative Decision Making: A Model, Literature Critique, and Prescriptions for Research." *Organizational Behavior and Human Performance,* 1968, *3,* 68–106.

Lowin, A., and Craig, J. R. "The Influence of Level of Performance on Managerial Style: An Experimental Object-Lesson in the Ambiguity of Correlational Data." *Organizational Behavior and Human Performance,* 1968, *3,* 440–458.

Lustick, I. "Explaining the Variable Utility of Disjointed Incrementalism: Four Propositions." *American Political Science Review,* 1980, *74* (2), 342–353.

Mahoney, T., and Weitzel, W. "Managerial Models of Organizational Effectiveness." *Administrative Science Quarterly,* 1969, *14,* 357–365.

Malcolm, N. "Intentional Activity Cannot Be Explained by Contingent Causal Laws." In L. I. Krimerman (Ed.), *The Nature and Scope of Social Science.* New York: Appleton-Century-Crofts, 1969.

Mansfield, E. *Industrial Research and Technological Innovation: An Econometric Analysis.* New York: Norton, 1968.

March, J. G. "The Technology of Foolishness." In J. G. March and J. P. Olsen (Eds.), *Ambiguity and Choice in Organizations.* Bergen: Universitetsforlaget, 1976.

March, J. G. "Bounded Rationality, Ambiguity, and the Engineering of Choice." *Bell Journal of Economics,* 1978, *9* (2), 587–608.

March, J. G., and Olsen, J. P. (Eds.). *Ambiguity and Choice in Organizations.* Bergen: Universitetsforlaget, 1976.

March, J. G., and Simon, H. A. *Organizations.* New York: Wiley, 1958.

Mayhew, D. R. *Congress: The Electoral Connection.* New Haven, Conn.: Yale University Press, 1974.

Medawar, P. B. "Unnatural Science." *New York Review of Books,* February 3, 1977, pp. 13ff.

Michels, R. *Political Parties.* New York: Dover, 1959. (Originally published, 1915.)

Mill, J. S. "Man: The Subject of an Exact Science?" In L. I. Krimerman (Ed.), *The Nature and Scope of Social Science.* New York: Appleton-Century-Crofts, 1969.

Miller, R. G. "The Probability of Rain." In J. Tanur and others (Eds.), *Statistics: A Guide to the Unknown.* San Francisco: Holden-Day, 1972.

Mitchell, T. R., Smyser, C. M., and Weed, S. E. "Locus of Control: Supervision and Work Satisfaction." *Academy of Management Journal,* 1975, *18* (3), 623–631.

Mohr, L. B. "Determinants of Innovation in Organizations." *American Political Science Review,* 1969, *63* (1), 111–126.

Mohr, L. B. "Organizational Technology and Organizational Structure." *Administrative Science Quarterly,* 1971, *16* (4), 444–459.

Mohr, L. B. "The Concept of Organizational Goal." *American Political Science Review,* 1973, *67,* 470–481.

Mohr, L. B. "Organizations, Decisions, and Courts." *Law and Society Review,* 1976, *10* (4), 621–642.

Mohr, L. B. "Authority and Democracy in Organizations." *Human Relations,* 1977, *30* (10), 919–947.

Mohr, L. B. "Review of J. G. March and J. P. Olsen (Eds.), *Ambiguity and Choice in Organizations." American Political Science Review,* 1978, *72* (3), 1033–1035.

Morris, W. (Ed.) *The American Heritage Dictionary of the English Language.* New York: Houghton Mifflin, 1969.

Morse, C., and Reimer, E. "The Experimental Change of a Major Organizational Variable." *Journal of Abnormal and Social Psychology,* 1956, *52,* 120–129.

Mulder, M. "Power Equalization Through Participation?" *Administrative Science Quarterly,* 1971, *16* (1), 31–39.

Nachmias, D., and Nachmias, C. *Research Methods in the Social Sciences.* New York: St. Martin's Press, 1976.

Nadworney, M. J. *Scientific Management and the Unions, 1900–1930: A Historical Analysis.* Cambridge, Mass.: Harvard University Press, 1955.

Nagel, E. *The Structure of Science: Problems in the Logic of Scientific Explanation.* New York: Harcourt Brace Jovanovich, 1961.

Neghandi, A. R., and Reimann, B. C. "Task Environment, Decentralization, and Organizational Effectiveness." *Human Relations,* 1973, *26,* 203–214.

Obradovic, J. "Participation and Work Attitudes in Yugoslavia." *Industrial Relations,* 1970, *9,* 161–169.

Obradovic, J., French, J. R. P., and Rodgers, W. "Workers' Councils in Yugoslavia." *Human Relations,* 1970, *23,* 459–479.

Osborn, R. N., and Hunt, J. G., "Environment and Organizational Effectiveness." *Administrative Science Quarterly,* 1974, *19* (2), 231–246.

Ouchi, W. G. "Markets, Bureaucracies, and Clans." *Administrative Science Quarterly,* 1980, *25* (1), 129–141.

Padgett, J. F. "Bounded Rationality in Budgetary Research." *American Political Science Review,* 1980, *74* (2), 354–372.

Patchen, M. *Participation, Achievement, and Involvement on the Job.* Englewood Cliffs, N.J.: Prentice-Hall, 1970.

Patton, M. Q., and others. "In Search of Impact: An Analysis of the Utilization of Federal Health Evaluation Research." In C. H. Weiss (Ed.), *Using Social Research in Public Policy Making.* Lexington, Mass.: Heath, 1977.

Pennings, J. M. "Measures of Organizational Structure: A Methodological Note." *American Journal of Sociology,* 1973, *79* (3), 686–704.

Pennings, J. M. "The Relevance of the Structural Contingency Model for Organizational Effectiveness." *Administrative Science Quarterly,* 1975, *20* (3), 393–407.

Perrow, C. "A Framework for the Comparative Analysis of Organizations." *American Sociological Review,* 1967, *32* (2), 194–208.

Perrow, C. "Three Types of Effectiveness Studies." In P. S. Goodman, J. M. Pennings, and Associates, *New Perspectives on Organizational Effectiveness.* San Francisco: Jossey-Bass, 1977.

Perrow, C. *Complex Organizations: A Critical Essay.* (2nd ed.) Glenview, Ill.: Scott, Foresman, 1979.

Peters, R. S. *The Concept of Motivation.* (2nd ed.) London: Routledge & Kegan Paul, 1960.

Peters, R. S., and Tajfel, H. "That Behaviorism Cannot Account for Human Thinking." In L. I. Krimerman (Ed.), *The Nature and Scope of Social Science.* New York: Appleton-Century-Crofts, 1969.

Pfeffer, J. "Usefulness of the Concept." In P. S. Goodman, J. M. Pennings, and Associates, *New Perspectives on Organizational Effectiveness.* San Francisco: Jossey-Bass, 1977.

Pfeffer, J., and Salancik, G. R. "Determinants of Supervisory Behavior: A Role Set Analysis." *Human Relations,* 1975, *28* (2), 139–154.

Pillemer, D. B., and Light, R. J. "Using the Results of Randomized Experiments to Construct Social Programs: Three Caveats." In L. Sechrest and others (Eds.), *Evaluation Studies Review Annual.* Vol. 4. Beverly Hills, Calif.: Sage, 1979.

Popper, K. R. *Conjectures and Refutations: The Growth of Scientific Knowledge.* New York: Harper & Row, 1963.

Popper, K. R. "The Hypothetical-Deductive Method and the Unity of Social and Natural Science." In L. I. Krimerman (Ed.), *The Nature and Scope of Social Science.* New York: Appleton-Century-Crofts, 1969.

Powell, R. M., and Schlacter, J. L. "Participative Management: A Panacea?" *Academy of Management Journal,* 1971, *14,* 165–173.

Price, J. L. *Organizational Effectiveness.* Homewood, Ill.: Irwin, 1968.

Pugh, D. S., and others. "Dimensions of Organizational Structure." *Administrative Science Quarterly,* 1968, *13* (1), 65–105.

Putnam, H. "The Analytic and the Synthetic." In H. Feigl and G. Maxwell (Eds.), *Minnesota Studies in the Philosophy of Science.* Minneapolis: University of Minnesota Press, 1962.

Rapoport, A. "Various Meanings of 'Theory.'" *American Political Science Review,* 1958, *52,* 927–988.

Reimann, B. C. "On the Dimensions of Bureaucratic Structure: An Empirical Reappraisal." *Administrative Science Quarterly,* 1973, *18* (4), 462–476.

Ritchie, J. B., and Miles, R. E. "An Analysis of Quantity and Quality of Participation as Mediating Variables in the Participative Decision-Making Process." *Personnel Psychology,* 1970, *23,* 347–359.

Roethlisberger, F. J., and Dickson, W. J. *Management and the Worker.* Cambridge, Mass.: Harvard University Press, 1939.

Rogers, E. M. "Reinvention During the Innovation Process." In M. Radnor, I. Feller, and E. Rogers (Eds.), *The Diffusion of Innovations: An Assessment.* Evanston, Ill.: Center for the Interdisciplinary Study of Science and Technology, Northwestern University, 1978.

Rogers, E. M., and Eveland, J. D. "Diffusion of Innovations Perspectives on National R&D Assessment: Communication and Innovation in Organizations." Paper prepared for the National Science Foundation, Washington, D.C., 1973.

Rogers, E. M., and Shoemaker, F. F. *Communication of Innovations.* New York: Free Press, 1971.

Rossel, R. D. "Institutional and Expressive Leadership in Complex Organizations." *Administrative Science Quarterly,* 1970, *15,* 306–317.

Runyon, K. E. "Some Interactions Between Personality Variables and Management Styles." *Journal of Applied Psychology,* 1973, *57,* 288–294.

Schuler, R. S. "Participation with Supervisor and Subordinate Authoritarianism: A Path-Goal Theory Reconciliation." *Administrative Science Quarterly,* 1976, *21* (2), 320–325.

Schulman, P. R. "Nonincremental Policy Making: Notes Toward an Alternative Paradigm." *American Political Science Review,* 1975, *69* (4), 1354–1370.

Scott, W. R. "Effectiveness of Organizational Effectiveness Studies." In P. S. Goodman, J. M. Pennings, and Associates, *New Perspectives on Organizational Effectiveness.* San Francisco: Jossey-Bass, 1977.

Scriven, M. "The Covering Law Position: A Critique and an Alternative Analysis." In L. I. Krimerman (Ed.), *The Nature and Scope of Social Science.* New York: Appleton-Century-Crofts, 1969a.

Scriven, M. "A Critique of Skinner's Operational Reduction of Mental Concepts." In L. I. Krimerman (Ed.), *The Nature and Scope of Social Science.* New York: Appleton-Century-Crofts, 1969b.

Seashore, S. E. "The Measurement of Organizational Effectiveness." Paper presented at the University of Minnesota, Minneapolis, 1972.

Seashore, S. E., and Yuchtman, E. "Factorial Analysis of Organizational Performance." *Administrative Science Quarterly,* 1967, *12,* 377–395.

Selznick, P. *Leadership in Administration.* New York: Harper & Row, 1957.

Selznick, P. *TVA and the Grass Roots.* New York: Harper & Row, 1966.

Shapere, D. "Scientific Theories and Their Domains." In F. Suppe (Ed.), *The Structure of Scientific Theories.* (2nd ed.) Urbana: University of Illinois Press, 1977.

Simon, H. A. *The New Science of Management Decision.* New York: Harper & Row, 1960.

Simon, H. A. "On the Concept of Organizational Goal." *Administrative Science Quarterly,* 1964, *9,* 1–22.

Simon, H. A. *The Sciences of the Artificial.* Cambridge, Mass.: M.I.T. Press, 1969.

Simon, H. A. *Administrative Behavior.* (3rd ed.) New York: Free Press, 1976.

Simon, H. A. *Models of Discovery.* Dordrecht: D. Reidel, 1977.

Simon, H. A. *Models of Thought.* New Haven, Conn.: Yale University Press, 1979.

Skinner, B. F. *Science and Human Behavior.* New York: Macmillan, 1953.

Smith, C. G., and Tannenbaum, A. S. "Organizational Control Structure: A Comparative Analysis." In A. S. Tannenbaum (Ed.), *Control in Organizations.* New York: McGraw-Hill, 1968.

Steers, R. M. *Organizational Effectiveness: A Behavioral View.* Pacific Palisades, Calif.: Goodyear, 1977.

Stogdill, R. M. *Handbook of Leadership. A Survey of Theory and Research.* New York: Free Press, 1974.

Suppe, F. (Ed.). *The Structure of Scientific Theories.* (2nd ed.) Urbana: University of Illinois Press, 1977.

Suppes, P. "The Structure of Theories and the Analysis of Data." In F. Suppe (Ed.), *The Structure of Scientific Theories.* (2nd ed.) Urbana: University of Illinois Press, 1977.

Tashman, L. J., and Lamborn, K. R. *The Ways and Means of Statistics*. New York: Harcourt Brace Jovanovich, 1979.

Taylor, F. W. *The Principles of Scientific Management*. New York: Norton, 1967. (Originally published, 1911).

Thompson, J. D. *Organizations in Action*. New York: McGraw-Hill, 1967.

Thompson, V. "Bureaucracy and Innovation." *Administrative Science Quarterly*, 1965, *10*, 1–20.

Tosi, H. "A Reexamination of Personality as a Determinant of the Effects of Participation." *Personnel Psychology*, 1970, *23*, 91–99.

Turk, H. "Interorganizational Networks in Urban Society: Initial Perspectives and Comparative Research." *American Sociological Review*, 1970, *35* (1), 1–18.

Urwick, L. "Foreword." In H. Fayol, *General and Industrial Management*. London: Pitman, 1949.

Van de Ven, A. H., Emmett, D. C., and Koenig, R., Jr. "Frameworks for Interorganizational Analysis." *Organization and Administrative Sciences*, 1974, *5* (1), 113–130.

von Wright, G. H. *Explanation and Understanding*. Ithaca, N.Y.: Cornell University Press, 1971.

Vroom, V. H. *Some Personality Determinants of the Effects of Participation*. Englewood Cliffs, N.J.: Prentice-Hall, 1960.

Vroom, V. H., and Mann, F. "Leader Authoritarianism and Employee Attitudes." *Personnel Psychology*, 1960, *13*, 125–140.

Vroom, V. H., and Yetton, P. W. *Leadership and Decision Making*. Pittsburgh: University of Pittsburgh Press, 1973.

Warren, R. L. "The InterorganizationaI Field as a Focus for Investigation." *Administrative Science Quarterly*, 1967, *12* (3), 396–419.

Weber, M. *The Theory of Social and Economic Organization*. New York: Oxford University Press, 1947.

Weick, K. E. "Middle-Range Theories of Social Systems." *Behavioral Science*, 1974, *19*, 357–367.

Weick, K. E. "Educational Organizations as Loosely Coupled Systems." *Administrative Science Quarterly*, 1976, *21* (1), 1–19.

Weick, K. E. "Repunctuating the Problem." In P. S. Goodman, J. M. Pennings, and Associates, *New Perspectives on Organizational Effectiveness*. San Francisco: Jossey-Bass, 1977.

White, J. K., and Ruh, R. A. "Effects of Personal Values on the Relationship Between Participation and Job Attitudes." *Administrative Science Quarterly*, 1973, *18* (4), 506–514.

Wildavsky, A. *The Politics of the Budgetary Process*. Boston: Little, Brown, 1964.

Wilhoite, F. H., Jr. "Primates and Political Authority: A Biobehavioral Perspective." *American Political Science Review*, 1976, *70* (4), 1110–1126.

Willer, D., and Webster, M., Jr. "Theoretical Concepts and Observables." *American Sociological Review*, 1970, *35* (4), 748–757.

Winch, P. "Sociological Understanding and the Impossibility of Nomothetic Social Science." In L. I. Krimerman (Ed.), *The Nature and Scope of Social Science*. New York: Appleton-Century-Crofts, 1969.

Woodward, J. *Industrial Organization: Theory and Practice*. London: Oxford University Press, 1965.

Wyszewianski, L. "Determinants and Effects of Organizational Strategies of Control Directed at Quality of Care in Organized Ambulatory Care Settings." Unpublished doctoral dissertation, Department of Medical Care Organization, University of Michigan, 1980.

Yin, R. K. *Changing Urban Bureaucracies: How New Practices Become Routinized*. Publication No. R-2277-NSF. Santa Monica, Calif.: Rand Corporation, 1977.

Yuchtman, E., and Seashore, S. E. "A System Resource Approach to Organizational Effectiveness." *American Sociological Review*, 1967, *32*, 891–903.

Zaltman, G., Duncan, R., and Holbek, J. *Innovations and Organizations*. New York: Wiley, 1973.

Zand, D. E., and Sorensen, R. E. "Theory of Change and the Effective Use of Management Science." *Administrative Science Quarterly*, 1975, *20* (4), 532–545.

Name Index

Subject Index

253

tives related to, 24; and participation, 146–147; ugliness related to, 23–24

Interorganizational analysis, and labeling tide, 12

Interorganizational interaction, as not durable, 17

Intervening variable, physiology as, 95

Investigator's interest: as durable, 16; and research functions, 32

Israel, Workers' Council in, 124

L

Labeling tide, and inconsistency, 12–13

Law-cluster concept, 78–79

Leadership style: and context, 145–147; determinants of, 141–148; as motivated behavior, 142

Loose coupling, as concept, 20

M

Malaria, contraction of, process theory of, 45, 47, 48, 57, 58, 60

Management theory: and forecasting, 26; and intuitive validity, 3; as normative, 2

Mendelian segregation: and goals of individuals, 170; process theory of, 47, 48, 50, 54, 55

Meteorology: and causal connection, 82; and forecasting, 26; regression model in, 42

Modeling, and ugliness, 23

Models, and forecasting, 26–27

Motivation: analysis of, 71–101; assumption fundamental to, 80; behavior distinct from, 78; *ceteris quietis* models of, 88–90; circumstantial associational or theoretical statements on, 82–84; and completeness, 93–94; conclusions on, 72; and covering-law status, 81*n;* as dependent variables, 100; and instability and

interaction, 85; limited generality models of, 90–91; obstacles to theory on, 86–87; practical syllogism and causal law and, 72–80; resources related to, 14, 17–18, 77–78, 220–222; satisfaction related to, 126–127; and social science, 75, 98–101; status as, 111–122; weakness of, as theory, 80–85. *See also* Specified motivation; Summary motivation

Motives: defined, 73; interaction related to, 24; roles for, 85–91

Multitrait-multimethod matrix, and confidence by convergence, 11

N

Nonapplicability, as interaction, 20

Normative theory: analysis of, 2–4; and empirical hypotheses, 3; intuitive validity of, 3; and participation, 148–153

O

Ohm's law, 41, 78

Oligarchy, iron law of, 120

Organizational effectiveness, and science of design, 197–199

Organizational environment, and independent variables, 12

Organizational program, as design, not theory, 188–190

Organizational structure: and aggregation, 105; analysis of, 102–153; as artifact, 102–103, 111; centralization and decentralization in, 102–123; and complexity, 194; contractual relationships in, 150–152; inconsistency in, 11; inertia in, 108–109; as not durable, 16; as outcome, 103, 117; and participation, 123–153; research on, 107–110; roles in, 149–150; technology, environment, and size related to, 103, 104, 105, 106, 107–110, 114, 119–120; un-